BY THE SAME AUTHORS... THE DEFINITIVE BOOK

"ON HUNTING"

COMING SOON...

IN THIS BOOK WE EXPLORE:

- The deep roots of hunting, how it is woven into our being;
- The ethics of hunting, from ancient to modern times;
- The underlying skills of the hunter;
- Hunting to live, for police, military and self-defense; and
- Living to hunt, the politics and economics of hunting... and the love of the hunt that ties back into the deep roots of hunting.

WHY WE WROTE THIS BOOK

The basic premise of this book is that we are what we were when[1] we were formed. And we (Homo sapiens) were formed in our modern configuration sometime during the Pleistocene epoch[2], when we were all hunters. No matter how we socialize ourselves, 'under the covers' we are all wired the same way. We were all hunters then, and we are still, whether we see wild animals as our prey or we have other urban-appropriate targets. You can see it in sport, in business and in sexual behavior.

[1] Paraphrasing the value analysis pioneered and popularized by Dr. Morris Massey "What you are is where you were when."
[2] The Pleistocene era started about two million years ago and ended about 10,000 years ago, characterized by widespread glacial ice and the advent of modern humans.

SECRETS OF MENTAL MARKSMANSHIP

Dedication

To all of our teachers
and
To all of our students

POLICE

MILITARY

COMPETITION

HUNTING

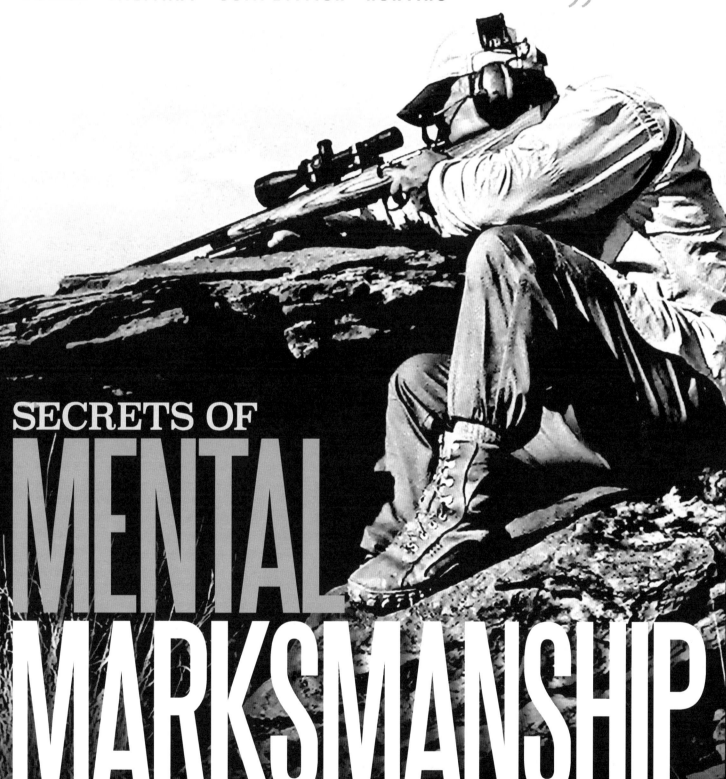

SECRETS OF
MENTAL
MARKSMANSHIP

HOW TO FIRE PERFECT SHOTS

By Linda K. Miller and Keith A. Cunningham | *With a foreword by Lt. Col. Dave Grossman*

Secrets of Mental Marksmanship: How to Fire Perfect Shots
by Linda K. Miller and Keith A. Cunningham

Copyright © 2010 by Linda K. Miller and Keith A. Cunningham

Second Edition

— Acknowledgments —

"I learned wisdom from all my teachers and teaching from all my students."
– Abraham ben Meir ibn Ezra (c. 1089–1164)

We are indebted to the thoughtful writers and coaches whose ideas started us on the path that provided us with the mental skills to be better shots.

We are thankful for all the professional marksmen (military, police, and security personnel) who have honed our skills and added variety and depth to our stories.

We are grateful to all the competition shooters and teams that we have coached and nurtured who helped us prove the effectiveness of these techniques.

We hope each reader of this book can identify with the stories and is enlightened and encouraged by their originator's own personal insight into the power of mental marksmanship.

— Disclaimers —

This book is intended for legitimate recreational and professional marksmen. The authors, publisher, and distributors of this book disclaim any liability from any damage or injury of any type that a reader or user of information contained in this book may incur from the use or misuse of said information. This book is for academic study only.

While we often use the male gender when referring to shooters in general in the text, the authors strongly support the development of marksmanship skills by both genders.

— Contents —

Contents

Contents

FOREWORD
SECRETS OF MENTAL MARKSMANSHIP

BY: LT. COL. DAVE GROSSMAN, AUTHOR OF ON KILLING, ON COMBAT, AND ASSASSINATION GENERATION

"This is the best book I have read in 30 years. If I could steal one book on the planet, put my name on it, and call it my next book, this would be the book!" For many years I have said this to every one of my presentations as I provide training to police in all 50 states and many foreign nations, all branches of the US military, and to all US federal law enforcement agencies. And now I finally have the chance to say it in this forward to the Second Edition of Secrets of Mental Marksmanship.

Here is why this book is so momentous. In two decades of war we have learned something profoundly important: if it works in the Olympics, if it works in the Super-bowl, then it works in combat! This is huge. Prior to the wars in Iraq and Afghanistan, there was essentially a ban on performance psychology or sports psychology in the US military. We simply did not know if it worked. There were those who said, "All that sport stuff will get you killed in combat!" And now we know that they were wrong.

This means that we can strip-mine the multi-trillion dollar realm of professional sports and apply it to military and law enforcement. In the military today we talk about "warrior athletes" and this book is the best resource for creating and developing these unique individuals. You can apply the information in this book to your child's soccer team or to any other area of physical endeavor. If I were teaching a Performance Psych 101 course this would be my textbook. For those who want to increase their shooting skills for competitive shooting, this book is the best possible resource. But for those who prepare for the life-and-death realm of combat, Secrets of Mental Marksmanship is a resource of unprecedented, lifesaving utility and value.

For every aspect of performance psych, the authors give us a military example, a law enforcement example, a hunting example, and a competitive shooting example. That, in-and-of itself, is an amazing achievement. I spent eight years writing my first book, On Killing. I spent ten years writing my next book, On Combat. If I could find one or two examples to make something come alive, I felt like I was doing well. To find four examples in four distinct fields, applied to each aspect of performance psychology, is an amazing achievement. I think you have to have written a book yourself to fully appreciate what Linda Miller and Keith Cunningham have accomplished in Secrets of Mental Marksmanship. And for me, those amazing examples just sucked me into the book. I read Secrets of Mental Marksmanship in one huge gulp, and in the wee hours of the morning, after finishing the book, I came up for air, having been mesmerized and deeply informed by this incredible book.

The final and most amazing thing about this book, is how truly qualified the authors are to address these four aspects. Linda and Keith are world champion level competitive shooters and coaches. They are law enforcement trainers, and they are both world class hunters and hunting guides. Kieth is a combat veteran and they have both trained and interacted with countless military personnel, police and veterans, while teaching in their wonderful, spacious mecca of shooting skills: the MilCun Marksmanship Complex and Training Center. I have had the honor to train under them, having made my personal pilgrimage to Milcun.

Thus, I welcome you to an amazing book. And I encourage you, I exhort you, to not just read it, but study this book, and apply it to your profession, your athletic endeavors, and to all aspects of your life.

WELL DONE, LINDA AND KEITH!

— Preface —

We have been giving lectures on the mental skills required for marksmanship for years (separately since the 1980s and together since the 1990s). We independently came to the same conclusion about these mental skills—you need them to shoot well.

Whether you're aware of them or not, if you're a top marksman, you're using them.

Whether you're a recreational or professional shooter, if you shoot well, you're using them.

You may not know that "they" are something, you may not know all the right terms for them, and you may not know how to call on them every time you need them. But when you shoot well, you're using them. And if you want to shoot well all the time, you need to learn how to call them up and use them all the time.

When we met, one of us was an Olympic-style smallbore shooter and the other was primarily a military service rifle shooter. What we discovered as we each learned each other's sport was this: while the technical and physical requirements were different, the underlying mental skills were the same.

You may not fully appreciate that no matter the kind of shooting you do, the underlying mental skills provide a single foundation. You may not fully appreciate the similarities between passing your annual qualification, competitive shooting, and an operational confrontation. But once you have mastered the mental skills required to fire a perfect shot, you will find that they're the same for any gun, anytime, anywhere.

The purpose of this book is to give you a different way to think about your marksmanship—your practice, your training, and your performance. The book describes the mental skills required to perform to the best of your ability and provides a set of tools that can be used to acquire and access those skills. This main theme of the book is illustrated with stories from the military, law enforcement, hunting, and competition realms. The reader who is most interested in only one of these areas can skip the stories from the other areas, but the reader who wants a complete picture will read all of them.

To our knowledge, this is the most comprehensive book of its type. It's the first time that all of the mental tools used by successful shooters have been brought together in a single place. And certainly, it's the first time the tools have been organized into constructive units that support a particular area of development. And it's the first time that the commonalities between operational and competitive marksmanship have been supported by illustrative stories from a wide variety of personal experience and expert sources.

Whether you're a soldier, a cop, a hunter, or a competitive marksman, you're certain to learn something that will improve your marksmanship skill. And if you're anything like most of our students, you will find something here that will improve your life skills.

— **Chapter 1** —

Introduction

SECTION 1-1: ONLY HITS COUNT

The soldier, the cop, the hunter, or the competitive marksman will all agree on one thing: only hits count. Depending on the game you're playing, it may be more important to be faster or it may be more important to be precise, but in the end it's the shooter who can achieve his aim—perfect shots on demand, anywhere, anytime, and all the time—who wins.

The bottom line is that both the professional and the recreational shooter want to do the very same thing. You both want to hit your target—the object of firing the shot in the first place—every time. And you have to be able to do it under stress.

We have all heard that marksmanship is a "complex skill." In order to fire a perfect shot, we need to bring together a mix of very specific conditions into a single magical moment. Some of the required conditions are technical, some of them are physical, but the requirements that are most interesting (as well as most important and most elusive) are the mental skills.

No matter the application (recreational or professional), you can never be too good a shot. From our point of view, here's how mental marksmanship fits into the picture:

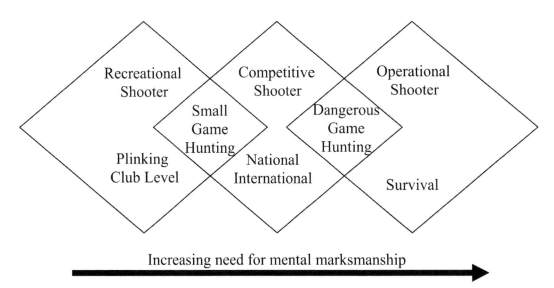

Increasing need for mental marksmanship

Secrets of Mental Marksmanship

Without any doubt, you cannot move from the recreational shooter to the competitive shooter without the use of mental marksmanship. And on your very best day in a firefight, you'll be lucky to be as good as you are on your worst day of training. We have gone through this, and we have trained hundreds of professional and recreational shooters and have seen them go through this.

We have read dozens of books on it too. Three famous ones leap to mind. In *A Rifleman Went to War*, Capt. Herbert W. McBride, an accomplished marksman, speaks of a World War I Canadian Expeditionary Force preparing itself to go to war. The primary skills needed by the riflemen of that day were to be able to march for long distances and be able to shoot when they got there. He noted that the soldiers were predominately backwoodsmen who were hardy and rugged and were accustomed to walking to most of the places they needed to go. They were also accomplished shots, having acquired that skill in order to feed themselves and their families. These were tough soldiers who needed little else than tougher NCOs[1] and hard officers to organize them and keep reminding them in which direction the enemy was now located. McBride noted that when these soldiers finally did meet the enemy, they would shoot from cover if possible, take up a proper fire position, and fire aimed shots.

As the war ground along, others with lesser background and experience eventually replaced these first soldiers. They had received less training in a hurry to get them to the front. They fired panicky shots, they didn't use support when it was available, and surprisingly enough, many did not shoot at all.

> "Every truth passes through three phases. First it is ridiculed. Then it is questioned. Then it is accepted as self-evident."
> —Arthur Schopenhauer, philosopher (1788–1860)

> "All things are ready, if our minds be so."
> —William Shakespeare in *Henry V*

> "The object of war is not to die for your country but to make the other poor dumb bastard die for his."
> —Gen. George S. Patton, soldier (1885–1945)

They didn't have the marksmanship skills, and they suffered as a result.

In *Marine Sniper: 93 Confirmed Kills*, Carlos Hathcock says that he learned how to read the wind that eventually supported his incredible achievements in Vietnam not from the U.S. Marines training program but from his experience at the national matches at Camp Perry, Ohio. There he was able to calibrate his thinking about how to read wind, because each and every shot he fired during competition required a wind decision. He was able to recognize all of the available wind indicators, confirm his thoughts by use of the range wind flags, apply the information to his rifle, and fire the shot. And each shot was immediately indicated so he could get feedback on that particular wind decision. It was a very logical approach to learning one of the most valuable skills required by a sniper on operations.

And Lt. Col. John George (*Shots Fired in Anger*), a member of the famed Merrill's Marauders in World War II, also an accomplished competitive marksman, speaks of how he had learned to fire perfect shots under pressure. He relates that this particular skill resulted in his surviving a close encounter of the Japanese kind. He tells of how he had become separated from his unit by a Japanese section that was determined to get him. He fired two well-aimed shots and killed two of his pursuers. This caused the remaining enemy to go to ground and take cover. George was then instantly up and running, trying to make his way back to friendly positions. The Japanese saw this and pressed the pursuit. George stopped and, using the skill learned in competition, was able to calm

Introduction

himself to fire two more well-aimed shots, killing two more enemy. The remaining Japanese troops quickly saw the futility in this pursuit and broke off the chase. George was able to make it back to friendly lines without further incident.

All three of these men were competitive rifle shooters who went to war and saw firsthand how the things they learned in competition helped them to survive in combat. More recently, we have received e-mails from our warriors in "the sandbox," saying that when the distances get beyond close-quarter battle, the guys in front call for rifle team members. One e-mail from a young soldier said simply, "That stuff you taught us on the rifle team works. Thanks." The fact is, you can never be too good a shot.

And this applies not only to survival situations on operations and in combat. Let's also apply it to your yearly qualification. In the military and in law enforcement, you have to qualify once a year with your personal weapon. It's surprising the number of people who are intimidated by the thought of going out and firing the weapon they're expected to use in war. It's surprising the number of police officers who are intimidated by the thought of going out and firing the weapon they're expected to use to defend the peace. They are intimidated by the thought of firing the weapon they're expected to use to protect themselves and others, to have their hits scored and published so all can see what bad shots they are.

Wrong way to think! If you're intimidated by the prospects of failure on the range, what must be going through your mind in an operational confrontation or a firefight?

"Give me good Generals and give me lucky Generals . . . and make my good Generals lucky."
—Napoleon Bonaparte, soldier (1769–1821)

"Funny thing about that . . . the more I practice, the luckier I get."
—Arnold Palmer, golfer (1929~)

"Only hits count."
—Sgt. Dave Oakie, soldier

"Skills are developed . . . by work!"
—Linda K. Miller, coach (1952~)

You should be eager to go to your qualifications so you can show everyone and especially yourself just what a good shot you are. Achievers like to be measured. You should too. You should ace your annual qualification, and if you don't, you should do something about it. You need to train. If you have to, you do it on your own. If you don't want to, you need to ask yourself if you are the right person for this job. Are you the kind of person your partner would want with him in a firefight?

If you don't have the desire to ace your annual qualification, then what? Do you figure the operational confrontation is going to be easier? It's not. You can score maximum hits on your qualification every single time and still find an operational confrontation the hardest thing you have ever done. You can never be too good a shot.

In this book, we're going to show you how you should think so that you will get the maximum effect from every training session you do. We will show you how to think to become a better shot—a better competitive shot, a better operational shot.

If you're good now, it's because you're using this mental marksmanship. In this book we will call it things and explain how it works so you can enhance your training time and call on these skills when you need them most—on operations, in the field, during qualifications, at a shooting match.

You can't get there from here without it.

We're going to spend the rest of this book discussing how you can mentally train for a physical skill. And although we're talking specifically about training for the skill of marksmanship, you can apply this same mental training to everything in life, from dealing with your children to improving your golf game.

Specifically, we're going to discuss:

➤ The power in your mind.
➤ The power in your world.
➤ The zone.
➤ Tools to increase your conscious power.
➤ Tools to increase your subconscious power.
➤ Tools to increase the power of your self-image.
➤ Applying advanced tools.
➤ The final power, the power of perseverance.

You may wonder: who is using this information?

We have given our mental marksmanship seminar (on which this book is based) to dozens of organizations, including groups of recreational and professional marksmen and even to an archery club. We include the basics of mental marksmanship in our technical marksmanship courses, which we have given to hundreds of police snipers, hundreds of military members, and hundreds of competition shooters.

When we give the seminar, we tune it to the type of person who is in attendance and we tell the stories that are relevant to them. When we teach it to professionals (law enforcement, security, and military), for example, we start the lecture a little differently than we do for hunters and competition shooters. Here's what we say:

> This lecture isn't for everybody. It is for the brotherhood, the fellowship, of arms. It is targeted for the serious professional, the officer who carries his weapons because he intends to use them when required to save his own life and the lives of others, the officer who can say, "This isn't what I do, this is who I am." By the end of the day, we can tell who's going to be in the driver's seat and who is along for the ride. The question you gotta ask yourself is, "Who do you want for your partner?" As Clint Eastwood said, "Do you feel lucky? Well, do yah?"

When we teach it to soldiers, they become the go-to person for marksmanship skill in their units. Many of our students are now successful unit rifle team coaches. When we teach it to teams, they become winning teams. We taught it when we coached a Canadian Army Reserve team which then became the only Reserve team ever to win the Canadian Forces Small Arms Competition and therefore the only Reserve team to represent the Canadian Forces at Bisley.[2] When we teach it to individuals, they become champions. We have coached 12 individuals to a Queen's Medal, the top honor for marksmanship in the Canadian Forces. A woman archer who took our seminar told us how other members of her club were intimidated by her desire to excel at the sport and would harass her and sabotage her mentally to keep her from getting ahead of them. We spoke with her and told her how to deal with this problem. Within a year she wrote us to say she had won gold medals at the nationals, and a year or two after that she wrote to tell us she had won gold medals at the world championships in Australia.

What we're finding out is that you cannot get there from here without it. You may call it something else—you may not even know it exists—but everyone who is good at some skill is using it. You must have it to get there.

We spoke with Warrant Officer Ron Surette, who is without a doubt the best Service Rifle shooter in the Canadian Forces at this time. We asked him what

---

"Strong people are made by opposition like kites that go up against the wind."
—Frank Harris, writer (1856–1931)

"When the going gets tough, the tough get going."
—Frank Leahy, coach (1908–1973)

---

he thought of this material based on how he was thinking when he was winning. He said that his learning to win was slowly developed over 20 years. He didn't know that this stuff was something. He didn't know that this stuff was called something. All he knew was that it worked. If he maintained the technical skills of firing a perfect shot and he had the right winning frame of mind, he would win.

We also spoke to Alain Marion, the best Target Rifle shooter in Canada today (and one of the best in the world and a retired police officer) when he attended a seminar. He smiled and said, "It's worth it to have everything I've been doing all these years confirmed."

Sgt. Ken Rodd, a member of one of Canada's police agencies, is also a believer in mental marksmanship. He used it to win medals at police competitions in Australia and Canada. He also has the highest score ever achieved on our Police Sniper 2 course, which has as its aim "to fire a perfect shot under stress."

Why would anyone on a rifle team, or in the profession of arms, or who is trying to compete and win as a champion, not want to do everything they could do to become a better shot? Sometimes older team members resisted, saying that they had always kept a spot on the team without this hocus-pocus mumbo-jumbo. The younger shooters, because they didn't know any different, thought that this was the way that it was done; they accepted and practiced the principles. Those

"Opportunity is missed by most people because it is dressed in overalls and looks like work."
—Thomas A. Edison, inventor (1847–1931)

"You can't miss fast enough to win a firefight."
—Author unknown

"Whether you think you can or you think you can't, you're probably right."
—Henry Ford, businessman (1863–1947)

"[Those who master a shooting skill in match conditions are] more likely to do well in a pressure situation."
—Rob Leatham, professional shooter (1961~)

"All power is from within and is therefore under our own control."
—Robert Collier, writer (1885–1950)

who resisted were slowly and sometimes sadly phased out based on performance. With their old-fashioned ideas, they couldn't be competitive.

Many shooters we teach are good from a physical and technical point of view, but they have reached a wall from the mental side. Mental marksmanship gets them over that wall. It's truly the big dark secret to better performance and better results.

The difference between whether you succeed or not will depend on how you think—and whether you think you can or you think you can't, you're probably right!

There's some good news and there's some bad news about mental marksmanship. The good news is that this book will tell you everything you need to know to immediately see an improvement. The bad news is that you will have to work at it to make it work. It will not just happen—you have to make it happen.

The hardest part for most shooters is this: first you have to figure out where you need to improve, and then you have to figure out what tools will help you get there.

We use our mental marksmanship map to guide us to our destination. As you can see on the diagram (page 6), your destination, the "zone," is in the middle.

➤ The circles that produce the "zone" are a balanced overlap of your conscious, your subconscious, and your self-image. Each of these circles has a "power" associated with it. These are the subject of Chapter 2.

➤ There are four additional building blocks, the powers that support your interaction with the outside world: the power of positive reinforcement, the power of focus, the power of achievement, and the power of the pack. These are discussed in Chapter 3.

➤ The "zone" is the subject of Chapter 4. Assessing your zone and determining areas for personal development are the main themes of that chapter.

➤ Chapters 5, 6, and 7 lay out the tools for developing your performance zone by increasing your conscious, subconscious, and self-image powers. In each chapter, the keys to developing the power, as well as many other mental marksmanship tools, are provided. The key to developing your conscious power is the mental program. The key to developing your subconscious power is perfect practice. The key to developing your self-image is self-talk.

➤ Chapter 8 takes the "focus on performance" theme and applies advanced tools. The chapter covers the power of planning, the power of preparation, power in the moment, and power after the moment.

➤ Chapter 9 is the conclusion of the book and discusses the final power, the power of perseverance.

Mental Marksmanship Map

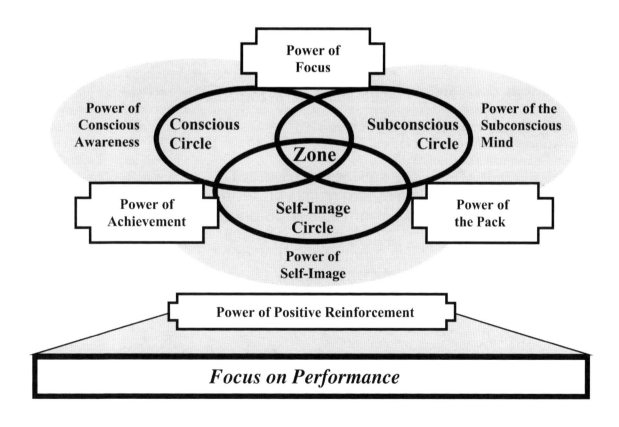

Introduction

MILITARY

Military Story—Vietnam Encounter
This is Keith's story, the one he tells when he starts our "Mental Marksmanship Seminar for Professionals."

I want to spend a few minutes and explain some things that will help you appreciate what I will be talking about. I'm not a psychologist. I was an infantry officer who was in combat, was shot at, shot back, and lived. I'm an international competitive rifle and pistol shooter and a coach qualified to the international level. I'm not going to talk to you about shooting techniques. I'm going to talk to you about how you should think—how you should think about your training, how you should think about your annual qualification, how you should think about shooting competitively, how you should think in an operational confrontation.

In November 1971, I was the point man for a recon team in Vietnam. (How I, a Canadian, found myself in such a situation is another story.) We had come across an area with recent signs of VC activity and decided to set up nearby to monitor. The team leader decided to set up booby traps (or "mechanical ambushes," to be politically modern) nearby to provide protection and early warning. Two team members were dispatched to do this.

About 15 minutes after they left, we heard shots and they came running back all excited, out of breath, and trying to explain how they fired up a couple of VC and there may have been more behind them. The team leader radioed in that we had made contact and that we would sit tight and continue to monitor the area. I was tasked to pick another guy and go nose around a little to see if I could confirm the bodies of the VC or locate the suspected larger enemy force.

We had gone about 100 meters when we came upon the body of a lone VC lying across the trail. I was carrying a Thompson submachine gun (which is another story), an easy-to-handle gun with a nice, slow rate of fire. I had it slung right side up, left hand on the pistol grip because I shoot left handed. I pushed it back around my side so I would have both hands free to search the body; my buddy would provide security while I was otherwise distracted.

I was just into the search when there was a burst of gunfire that made my ears ring. Dirt flew up into my face. I'm thinking, "*What the hell's happening here?*" After all that training, I still couldn't understand what was happening. My buddy fired a burst over me and yelled, "There's more behind him! Let's get moving!" I heard another burst of fire and there was more dirt flying.

As I blinked away the dirt in my eyes, I could see a young VC standing in the trail with an AK-47 and—MY GOD! HE IS SHOOTING AT ME. I finally remembered my own weapon. I reached back for it, found the pistol grip, and in extremely slow motion, brought it around.

MY GOD, HE'S GOING TO KILL ME. MAKE HIM STOP SHOOTING AT ME.

I could feel the recoil of the Thompson in my hands. BUT HE IS STILL SHOOTING AT ME.

I had no idea where my weapon was pointed. I just kept shooting and saying to myself, WHY WON'T HE DIE? WHY WON'T HE STOP SHOOTING AT ME?

I finally realized that a lot of the dirt that was flying around in front of me was from my own shots. I also finally realized that I had to walk my shots onto this target. I was shooting from the hip because of the LCV (look cool value); that's what all the really cool soldiers were doing around garrison, at the test-fire pit, and often on the ranges.

In a state of panic, such that I had never felt before, I was finally able to make this guy stop shooting at me. Thanks to the gun's slow rate of fire, I still had enough ammo left and was able to walk it up and onto my target. My Thompson finally ran out of ammo. I stood there in the middle of the trail mesmerized by the twitching body that had just seconds ago been trying to kill me.

The sound of more shots snapped me back to reality. I had found the larger enemy force. With an empty weapon and shots snapping past me, I ran back to the perimeter like the devil himself was after me. Low on ammo, and with darkness setting in, the team was able to hold the larger force off until gunships came and relieved the pressure so that we could be extracted.

And if I thought I was scared during that firefight, it didn't hold a candle to what I felt like afterward. Around base camp I was heralded a hero: I had met the enemy face-to-face and won. What a warrior I was!

However, I did have a few haunting thoughts. I didn't think heroes could get so scared. I didn't think warriors could screw up personal tactics so badly and live. How could I have done so much wrong and lived? I almost felt guilty for surviving this incident.

I was so incredibly lucky. I wasn't any braver than that VC. I wasn't any more skilled as a soldier. I wasn't any more of a warrior. I wasn't any better of a shot. I was luckier.

How many soldiers on both sides have died in their first confrontation because they weren't the lucky one? The one thing that I learned on the 37 recon missions that I did in Vietnam was that luck is always a factor in surviving. However, you need to develop and constantly practice your skills to improve your luck. This is the point I have tried to get across to every soldier I've ever trained from that point on. YOU CAN NEVER BE TOO GOOD A SHOT.

POLICE

Law-Enforcement Story—The State Trooper

A state trooper had pulled a car over for a routine traffic stop. As he approached the rear fender of the car, the driver opened his door and stepped out. He was holding a sawed-off single-barreled shotgun and fired at the officer, hitting him with a full charge of buckshot in the center of his chest.

The next thing the officer remembered was that he was changing magazines and scanning left and right. The perpetrator was lying against the hinges of his car door, dropped over backward. He was neatly stitched from belt buckle to throat with seven big .45-caliber bullets.

So where did this officer learn to shoot like that? Where did he develop the reflexes to respond to a threat like that? How did he know exactly what to do and how could he do it in such a way that he didn't remember doing it until it was done? Did he learn it at his police academy and develop it with continual practice at his agency?

Well, as it turns out, he was an accomplished ISPC[3] shooter. Nearly every weekend he was involved in competitions where this kind of reaction to scenarios was the norm. He had practiced drawing and firing his pistol hundreds of thousands of times. He had to be fast and he had to be accurate if he wanted to get close to the winners' circle. And although he didn't always win in these competitions, he did learn a skill that came to good use on his job.

We have been told by police officers that they have many fellow officers who don't like to shoot, will only shoot at their yearly qualification, and grumble because they have to do that. And then they grumble about having to spend time cleaning their sidearm. They won't do anything extra to develop their marksmanship skill because they figure if they can't do it on company time, then they're not going to do it. We find this kind of thinking hard to understand. Why would someone knowingly join the fellowship of arms and then not want to be as good at it as they could be? And if you ever find yourself in a very bad situation, which officer would you like to come to your rescue?

HUNTING

Hunter Story—First Subconscious Shot

From "The Performance Response . . . That Winning Feeling,"[4] this is Keith's story:

It was very late in the afternoon. I walked on the wheel tracks of the old logging road to avoid crunching the fallen leaves. I knew I was moving along too fast, but it was late to be getting to my deer stand and I was anxious to be there. I kept thinking that I should have been there at least 40 minutes earlier. Glancing left and right along the trail, I thought, "I could jump a deer anytime now and then what would I do?"

I was carrying my rifle slung over my right shoulder, muzzle down. Being a left-handed shooter, this allowed me to keep my right hand on the forestock, where it needed to be to fire a shot, and also where it needed to be to bring the rifle smoothly to the shoulder to fire an aimed shot in the least possible time. I had practiced this procedure many times in my basement and could mount the rifle without thinking about it.

As I walked quickly along, the trail broke into a small opening. The road traveled along one edge, which left about 40 meters from the track to the tree line on the other side. The entire time, I was running over in my mind how it would feel to react to a deer if I saw one.

My mind was so occupied with these thoughts that I didn't see it. My first realization that I had walked up on a deer was the snort, a very loud and very close snort.

Having felt it since then in other situations, I later realized that it was the moment I heard the snort that the "feeling" came over me. It was an incredible calm. It was an awareness that I was about to do what I'd been training to do and that I knew exactly how it was to be done.

On hearing the snort and before seeing the deer run from behind a small cedar tree, my mind was fully occupied with what the sight picture would have to look like before I could fire. The rifle had magically appeared on my shoulder as if handed to me. I wasn't thinking about the short 30 meters that the deer had to cover to make the tree line; I was thinking only of where the crosshairs had to be to cause a bullet to go through the lungs and exit the shoulder on the far side.

The rifle fired as if someone else had pulled the trigger. The deer stumbled and made the last jump to the tree line and disappeared into the bushes and the fading light. Someone cycled the action to reload the rifle. I listened . . . I wondered if I had missed . . . but I thought about how perfect the sight picture had been and what a perfect shot I had fired. Oh, yes, I had made the hit. I called the shot good.

It was the first time that I was aware of firing a truly subconscious shot and of the "feeling." This feeling is a hard one to describe, but once you have felt it and know what it takes to reproduce it . . . well, it just makes you feel warm all over, smile a knowing little smile, and then get down to business. It's a tremendous feeling of confidence; a quiet, deep-down feeling of total confidence that makes you know that what you're about to do is exactly right. It's as if you have your mind all neat and tidy, as if you've picked up all the laundry in your room and put it in a hamper, as if a bunch of little puppies are running about everywhere and you gather them up and put them into their pen. You're in control of the situation. You've created a plan, practiced, trained, and are now focused and concentrating. Your confidence is based on your preparation; you're in control and ready. This is the feeling.

All good shots are fired subconsciously. The "feeling" that Keith describes in this story is also called the "zone" or the "ideal performance state." The power of the subconscious and the tools to develop it are explored in later chapters of this book.

Competition Story—At the World Cup
Linda relates this experience at our mental marksmanship seminars:

In 1992 I was watching Sharon Bowes at the U.S. World Cup near Los Angeles. What a performance! She was shooting the standing portion of the three-position match, and she was shooting very well. She fired the last of the 20 record shots, put the rifle down, and came back behind the firing line where I was standing and watching. Her eyes were shining. There was a glow about her, one that seemed to come from deep inside. Her motions were fluid. Her voice was smooth, energized, and intense, unusually deep and eerily calm.

"That," she said, "is how it's supposed to be done. It was like it was in slow motion but not slow. The target was clear and right at the front sight. Every shot just happened; I don't remember shooting any of them. They just kept going in the middle, time after time after time. It was like I couldn't do anything wrong."

Later, she couldn't recall the conversation. She could remember going back behind the firing line to talk to me but couldn't remember a single phrase, not even the subject we had discussed. It was as though it were another person who had been there with me, savoring the moment.

That string of standing shots was a personal best for Sharon in competition, and it was the best standing fired on the range that day.

All good shots are fired subconsciously. I was lucky enough to catch a glimpse of Sharon when her subconscious was dominant. It was beautiful. The feeling she had is the thing that keeps most shooters coming back to train and to compete—just one more chance to feel that marvelous feeling one more time. The chapter on "the zone" explores this phenomenon, and the chapters following (all the tools) tell you how to attain that beautiful state any time, anywhere, whenever you want.

CHAPTER SUMMARY

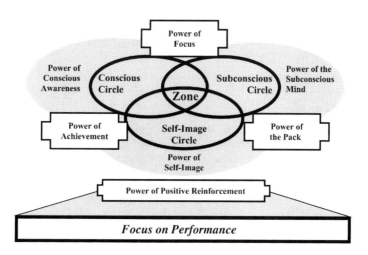

The soldier, the cop, the hunter, or the competitive marksman will all agree on one thing: only hits count. Depending on the game you're playing, it may be more important to be faster or it may be more important to be precise, but in the end it's the shooter who can achieve his aim—perfect shots on demand, anywhere, anytime, and all the time—who wins.

As Napoleon said, even his good generals needed to be lucky. And as Arnold Palmer said, the more he practiced, the luckier he got. In the first story, without much training, Keith needed a lot of luck to survive his Vietnam encounter. In the second story, the state trooper was sufficiently trained that his automatic response to being under fire saved his life. In the hunting story, the beauty and effect of a truly subconscious shot was described. And finally, the World Cup story illustrates the joy of being able to produce a series of perfect shots when it really counts.

NOTES

1. NCO stands for noncommissioned officer, the backbone of the army or any other branch of the armed forces.
2. Bisley refers to the range facility at Bisley, England, the "mecca" of the shooting world. The main civilian range is a multidiscipline facility that is home to the National Rifle Association of Great Britain, which hosts many important competitions. Commonly, the reference to Bisley also includes the annual service conditions competitions hosted by the Army Rifle Association and held at the Bisley facility as well as nearby military ranges.
3. IPSC stands for International Practical Shooting Confederation, a style of handgun competition that emphasizes reactive shooting, with speed being the primary factor and practical accuracy being measured on a body-size target.
4. "Performance Response . . . that Winning Feeling" by Linda K. Miller and Keith A. Cunningham was originally published in *Precision Shooting* (March 1997) and has been republished in *Favorite Stories on Winning*.

— Chapter 2 —

The Power in Your Mind

SECTION 2-1: DEFINITION OF MENTAL MARKSMANSHIP

The definition of mental marksmanship that we're going to use in this book is this: mental marksmanship is the process of improving the probability of having a consistent mental performance, under pressure, and on demand.

Do you think that this might help in your shooting? Does it apply to shooting? Do we need a consistent mental performance in shooting?

In competition, 90 percent of the medals are won by 5 percent of the shooters. In shooting (and in other endeavors), 80 to 90 percent of your physical performance will depend on how you think. You need a consistent mental performance only if you intend to win!

Do we really feel that much pressure in shooting? In competition and operational shooting, there's always pressure; every shot we fire has to count. We have to have all our equipment in the right place at the right time. We have to meet all our timings, get into the position in time, and fire the shot in time. Not only does it have to hit the target, it has to hit the right target. We have to fire shots in accordance with the rules of engagement, departmental policies, and hunting laws. Competitors, knowing that every shot they fire could win the match, may have to deal with noisy spectators and intrusive range staff. Hunters may have to deal with the excitement of finally

The Power in Your Mind

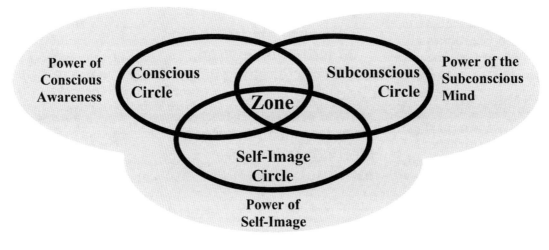

getting a shot at the trophy buck of a lifetime or even aggressive and dangerous animals. Police may have to deal with active shooters, excited civilians, and inexperienced superiors. Soldiers may have to deal with returning fire that will ultimately save themselves or fellow soldiers. They all find themselves in situations where one well-fired shot will make a lifetime of difference. Yes, we'd say that there's pressure.

Does it have to be on demand? In some Service Rifle competitions, the snap target appears for only three seconds, during which time you must acquire the correct fire position, estimate the wind hold off, locate the target, and fire a perfect shot. In an operational situation, you may have only a split second to fire. Clearly, a winning performance is pretty much needed on demand. The competitor can't say to a range officer, "Oops! Could I just have that exposure again? I really didn't feel like shooting just then." The cop can't say, "I wonder if you could herd that bad guy past the window just once more. I really wasn't ready to shoot on that last pass." Or the hunter, as he sidesteps the charging Cape buffalo: "I say there, old chap, would you mind terribly to just trot back about 50 meters and do that charging thing again and let me have another go? Now there's a good chap, eh what?" Yes, it has to be on demand.

When it's time to do it, it has to be done right, and it has to be done right now—if you want to win—whether you're in a shooting match or a gunfight.

"It's not about power over other people; it's about power over yourself. If you do not have power over yourself, then other people will have power over you."
—Anthony Robbins in *Unlimited Power*

"It is a rough road that leads to heights of greatness."
—Lucius Annaeus Seneca, writer (54 BC–39 AD)

"Train the mind and the body will follow."
—Keith A. Cunningham, soldier (1950~)

"Most athletes will acknowledge that 60 to 90 percent of success in sports is due to mental factors and psychological mastery."
—Charles A. Garfield in *Peak Performance*

There are other applications in life where you need such skills. You need them at work. Those of you who have had any military leadership training will remember when it's time for the Directing Staff (DS) to designate the next student to lead a patrol. You have just returned from the last one at 0300 hours, forced yourself to stay awake during the debrief, and can only think of when you might get something to eat. The next patrol is to go out in three hours, and the DS is about to announce the new leader as he shuffles through the papers on his clipboard. Everyone is looking down, afraid that eye contact might influence his decision. And finally the name is called out. Everyone else breathes a loud sigh of relief except the new leader—you. You feel as alone as a cartridge in a chamber as you hear the breach close behind you. Now would be a really good time for your mental skills to kick in so that it becomes clear just what it is you must do to get this patrol underway.

You need such skills in other sports. Keith tells a story of a senior NCO he worked with when he was in the military who wanted to make the army golf team. He complained that he had reached a plateau in his skill level and couldn't get past it. Keith had recognized this same plateau in his own shooting skills, and it was the desire to go beyond it that got him interested in mental marksmanship. Whenever the time allowed, Keith would talk with the frustrated golfer about the same mental skills that had worked for him—things like focusing on performance and letting the scores be what they may; realizing that it's this performance that will eventually get the scores you want; visualizing and imprinting on the subconscious mind what the perfect swing or putt should feel like; and more. And just as it had worked for Keith, it also worked for our golfer, who was, within a year, on the army golf team.

But the sports-related story that we really love to tell is one about a hockey team made up of eight-year-olds and coached by one of our students, a member of the Royal Canadian Mounted Police (RCMP). He mentioned he was having trouble getting the kids to work as a team. This reminded us of the U.S. Marine Corps sergeant who was teaching his squad unarmed combat. He said he taught them only three moves, and they practiced these moves over and over until they became automatic (or imprinted on the subconscious mind). He thought that it was better for them to do one of these moves really smoothly than to be able to do a dozen moves not so well. Smooth would soon become fast.

We suggested to our hockey coach that he focus on one of his plays until the kids understood it and could perform it smoothly. He could start the kids developing this play by having them visualize it as vividly as possible in their minds before they even got to the ice. As it turned out, the coach had a game that very night, and the next day he came back to our class clearly feeling like he had accomplished something. He didn't need much encouragement to tell how he got the kids to settle down and imagine in their minds how this play would go down.

"Johnny, you're on left defense, and when you get the puck I want you to automatically pass it to Georgie on right wing, waiting at our blue line. Georgie, as soon as you see that Johnny has the puck in our own end, I want you to drive hard to the blue line and expect the pass." Georgie nodded.

"As soon as you get it, I want you to pass it to Frank on the left wing at the center line, and Frank, when you see Johnny setting this play up, you make sure you're in position to receive the pass from Georgie." The coach waited to see that this had sunk in.

"Frank," he continued, "as soon as you have the puck, you take it over their blue line and get ready to pass it to Sammy, on center. Sammy," he said, looking directly at the young lad, "as soon as you see this play developing, you push hard to their blue line and wait there until Frank brings the puck into their end and then you drive hard to a position by their net and be prepared to receive the puck and put it into the net." Sammy smiled, understanding his role in the play.

"Once Frank has passed the puck to Sammy, then Frank and Georgie are to drive to the net to help Sammy and get any rebounds. This is the only play that I want you to even think about for the whole game."

Now, this might sound a bit complicated to those who aren't familiar with hockey, but to these kids it was a snap. Our coach went over and over this play with each participant sitting quietly with their eyes closed, visualizing the details.

So how did it go down on the ice? Well, the kids didn't win, but they did get a goal and several shots on

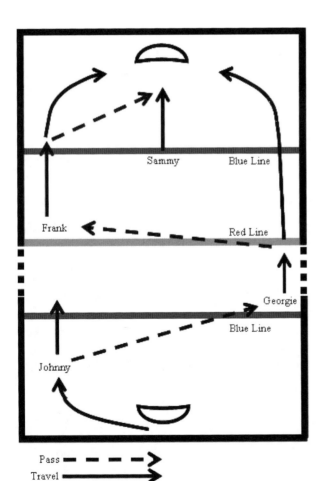

net as a result of the play. But the best part of all was what the kids talked about after the game. They talked about the play and the goal that they got and how they got it. They talked about how much fun it was to have a plan and know what they had to do and to know what the other team members were going to do. And they got smoother with the play and were excited about doing it again in their next game.

You need these mental skills when you're raising your kids. Keith tells this story about a parenting situation that required building a positive new attitude for one of his sons.

After one of my military postings, our younger son, Jesse, decided it was time to be rebellious. It was understandable since every time he was in one place long enough to make friends and get in a comfortable routine, we would move again. I hadn't appreciated there was any problem until I got a call from his teacher. It seemed that Jesse had hit one of the smaller boys in his class with a book, and the teacher wanted me to come in and talk about it.

Well, Jesse had got in with the bully crowd, and the little fellow hit with a book was the victim of the bullying. The teacher wanted me to do something about it. I assured her that he didn't hit anybody at home with a book and he didn't bully anybody, or else I would do my sergeant major act all over him. Unless they wanted me to sit in class with Jesse, they would have to be the ones to control him and I would support them in whatever action they deemed necessary.

We decided that Jesse would carry a form with him to each class and each teacher would record his performance for that class. The form would then be reviewed by the principal and then sent home with

---

"In the end, it is not about the hardware, it is about the 'software.' Amateurs talk about hardware (equipment); professionals talk about software (training and mental readiness)."
—Lt. Col. Dave Grossman in *On Combat*

"The one thing over which you have absolute control is your own thoughts. It is this that puts you in a position to control your own destiny."
—Paul G. Thomas, politician

Jesse to be reviewed and signed by me. This was working very well, but it was about this time that I noticed that Jesse would use his room as a sanctuary.

When confronted with one of life's problems, he would retreat to his room, where he would slam the door and leave the problem outside. Here he was surrounded with his posters on the wall and the music he liked and he wouldn't have to face the world. So, I removed his door from its hinges and set it to one side in the hallway. I took away his Nintendo and other favorite toys and told him he had to earn the right to have them back. Among other things, he could earn them back by speaking with respect to his parents and other figures of authority in his life, show better tolerance with his older brother, and do well in school.

I also had one more requirement of him. I insisted that he do one nice thing each day for the boy he had hit with a book. It didn't have to be a grandiose gesture; just some little discreet thing that no one else had to notice. I also emphasized with him that it didn't take much of a person to pick on the little guy, but it did take someone special to defend him. If he wanted to get into a fight, then the righteous fight was defending the right of others to exist.

All was going well, and as I reviewed his performance record for each day, I would ask him what he did nice for little Petey.

I got answers like, "The big guys were throwing his pencil case around the room and when it went by me I caught it and gave it back to him."

Good, Son, good!

And, "Today his pencils were all broken so I gave him one of mine."

Well, I can understand why they were broken. Well done!

And, "Today he was sitting by himself having lunch, so I went over and sat with him. Ya know, Dad, he's not such a bad guy."

I've got you now . . . and you are giving me a lump in my throat.

But then there was the day when I asked Jesse what he had done for Petey today, and he became quiet. I looked at him to see what was causing the hesitation, fearing the worst: a relapse back to bad behavior. We had had a couple of setbacks; was this another?

There was a quiver in his voice as he said, "I didn't do anything today, Dad. I thought about it all day and I just couldn't think of anything nice to do."

Well, you know what, Son, spending the day trying to think of something nice to do for someone has got to be the next best thing. You're doing just fine.

And Jesse has done just fine. We got him involved with Army Cadets,[1] with shooting and hunting. He is now a sergeant (soon to be warrant officer) medic in the Canadian Forces, and I see in him the kind of soldier that would fight whatever fight that was required to look after his men and his patients. And he still gives me a lump in my throat.

Military Story—Rabbits and Wolves

There is an excellent book called the *Three Day Road* by Joseph Boyden. It tells of two Canadian natives who volunteered to join the Canadian Army and fight in World War I. It follows these two as they come out of the backwoods of northern Ontario and get involved in the white man's war.

When they arrive in France, they, and the rest of the replacements, are timid and afraid of every sound. Their sergeant finally has had enough and tells them, "If you want to be warriors, then stop acting like rabbits and start acting like wolves."

Keith says that on reading this, he was reminded of his own experiences in Vietnam. When he first arrived, he thought every shot he heard was meant for him. "I felt like the enemy was hiding everywhere just waiting to get me."

This feeling persisted for a couple of months, and then one day he became tired of being scared. He had survived that long, and in the end he realized he really didn't have total control over his fate. "I had recognized that there was always an element of luck involved in surviving combat. I had no control over that, but I did have control over how I felt about it."

By playing the odds in his favor, he knew he could make his own luck. "If I were going to die, it would be as a wolf. I would apply the skills I had learned and the experience I was getting and take the fight to the enemy at every opportunity. I would look after my men, I would accomplish my missions, and to hell with the rest. It was from that day that I knew I would survive this combat."

Law-Enforcement Story—Remember the State Trooper

So how might this work for you as a police officer? Remember the story we told about the state trooper and his reaction to being shot?

He at first learned how to carry out the perfect draw. He had practiced it slowly until it was smooth. And then he kept on practicing the perfect practice until his "smooth" got fast. He tested himself in competition, where he felt pressure to do well and experienced stress that needed to be controlled. He refined his practice as required and continued to practice the perfect practice.

And then one day, with the channels of communication well defined between his conscious and his subconscious mind, it happened. His conscious mind recognized the situation and got out of the way so the finely imprinted subconscious mind could do its thing. He went on autopilot and it was easy. It was the same thing he had done thousands of times before. In the job that our police have to do these days, can you imagine being any less prepared?

Secrets of Mental Marksmanship

HUNTING

Hunter Story—Bull Moose

It's not hard to get Keith to tell a hunting story, and this one shows very well the mental side of firing one well-placed shot.

It was nearing the end of the moose season, and neither Linda nor I had seen any moose. I had worked my way into a tiny valley, which had bare rock ridges running down each side. The ridges had been formed during the Ice Age as the advancing ice had scraped the hard rock bare. They were about 30 to 40 feet high and too steep to climb in most places. I was looking for a game trail I had found some time before that ran perpendicular to the ridges and where the crest was not as tall and could be climbed more easily.

As I neared the trail and my attention was focused on finding it, a slight noise behind me caused me to look in that direction. And there, just then coming to a stop, was a huge bull moose. My rifle came up smoothly to my shoulder and my first thought was to hit the bull behind the front shoulder and through the lungs, the traditional game shot. I remember thinking what an incredibly large target he was, since he was only about 10 meters away.

But the bull had realized that the noise he had heard, and was moving toward, wasn't the cow moose he was envisioning. He immediately turned and began running toward the nearest little ridge, which was about 15 feet high and about 20 meters away.

This took away my lung shot, and I also realized that with every step he took he was getting further from any place where I could get a vehicle to recover him. Even if I had lung-shot him, he might have run several hundred meters before giving it up, and I would have to carry him out piece by piece every one of those extra meters. I had to shoot him in such a way as to drop him in his tracks.

The bull was now trotting up the little ridge about 30 meters away and in a few steps would be out of sight. The ridge he was climbing was steep enough to put him on a sharp upward angle, and now his head was visible. I remember the "feeling" coming over me as it became very clear what I had to do. The sight reticle moved up the body of the moose until it came to the ear and the rifle went off. The 1,000-pound moose crashed to the ground with such intensity that I was sure I felt the ground shake under my feet.

And, of course, the real work of the hunt could now begin.

But as wonderful a trophy as it was—and as wonderful as was the excitement of being so near such a large wild animal—the part that I remember most vividly was the calmness I felt, the get-down-to-business attitude I had, and how clear the plan to accomplish it had appeared to me.

In the Service Rifle matches I had competed in my entire military career, I had practiced just such a shot. In our Match 4 we have to run 100 meters and fire one shot at each three-second exposure. A three-second exposure isn't much time to recognize your target, acquire a sight picture, and fire a perfect shot, all from the standing position at a distance of 100 meters. The conscious mind must think only of the correct sight picture and then get out of the way so the subconscious mind can take over.

And that's exactly what happened when I shot the moose. It was just another shot, just like the ones I had already fired thousands of times. "Oh, hum, just another one," as my good friend and sniper coach Ron Surette used to say.

COMPETITION

Competition Story—Linda's ISSF Shoot

This is Linda's story, excerpted from The Challenge of Adversity.[2]

It was on the second day of the ISSF [3] (300-meter, 60-shot) match that controlling my own mental marksmanship was challenged. I shot on the first relay and, after firing a few sighting shots, my rifle misfired. I had sometimes encountered this in smallbore matches and had once shot an entire match with fewer than 50 percent of the rounds firing on the first try. It's a grueling way to shoot, and I was concerned about my endurance for 60 record shots of centerfire rifle.

The Power in Your Mind

I planned to try to continue and just shoot as well as I could under the circumstances. Then the rifle made the decision for me—it stopped firing altogether. I had taken up about 15 precious minutes of the hour and 45 minutes allowed for the match. What were my options? I could quit the match. I could try to borrow a rifle. I could put another barreled action into my stock. I could try to find Keith and see if he could fix the rifle. I thought through the pluses and minuses of each of the solutions and chose the last.

Keith was at another range about a kilometer away, shooting another match. I figured that by the time I got there, I wouldn't have to wait too long for him to finish his match (it being a 10-shot event). I explained my plan to the range officer, gathered up my rifle and the misfired rounds Keith would need to analyze the problem, and drove off.

When I arrived at the other range, I immediately headed for the shooting mound, asking everyone within earshot if they'd seen Keith. No one had. My heart sank. If I didn't find him quickly, I wouldn't have time to finish my match. Finally, someone said they thought he had already finished and had left. I wheeled immediately and scanned across the row of parked vehicles for his truck. It had been there when I arrived and . . . thank goodness, it was still there! It looked like there were a couple of people standing in front of it. Could one of them be Keith?

As I hurried over, I started to believe I might make it back to my own match with time enough to finish. Keith was a little surprised to see me, but he took my situation in hand calmly and quickly. I needed a little calm at that point, so I was grateful he was so very capable. He took my rifle over to the tailgate. He took out the toolbox. He took the bolt out of the rifle. So far, I was able to stay calm. But what he did next was really frightening. He started to take things apart. My heart sank again. I thought I wouldn't fire another shot, much less finish the match.

He performed minor surgery. He tested his work. I was slathering, quietly, inside. I just had to get back to the firing line! I had to control my feelings. I write magazine articles and books about this subject. I had no choice but to remain calm and focused on what I could control.

Finally Keith was satisfied. He gave me my rifle and I drove back to the match. He followed and stayed near-by throughout.

I had used up 38 huge minutes. I had just over an hour left to shoot. I thought about it. Yes, I knew I could shoot the match, and shoot it well in that amount of time. I just needed to stay focused. I didn't have time for any mental lapses or daydreams or anything. Just stay focused and keep shooting good shots.

I lay down on the line with my rifle. I had an outstanding butt marker who was swift and sure. I asked the range officer (RO) to notify the butts that Target Eleven was shooting again and would be shooting quickly. The RO said he'd already done so. Now I knew I had everyone on my side—my gunsmith and coach, my butt marker, and even the RO were being as helpful as possible. The rifle was as good as it was going to be; the rest was up to me.

I played my mental program, the short form. It's quick and helps me to focus and shoot quickly. I didn't have a lot of time to play, so except for significant wind shifts, I just made changes off my last shot. I was shooting quickly enough for that to be effective, even in tricky wind conditions.

I finished with 11 minutes to spare. I was breathless, ecstatic. I could hardly keep my feet on the ground. I had risen to the challenge, and it felt terrific.

I turned in the top score for the day and finished with a silver overall for the two-day aggregate.

My self-talk maintained an attitude of defiant success. I focused on the solutions available. I stayed with facts. I concerned myself only with those things over which I had control. It was my choice.

Section Summary

Mental marksmanship is the process of improving the probability of having a consistent mental performance, under pressure, and on demand. As you can see in the diagram on the following page, there are three primary powers that, like the legs on a stool, contribute to the strength of your mental performance.

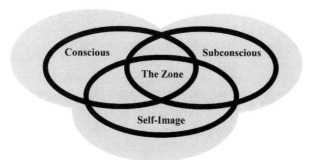

We will now explore each of these powers in turn: conscious awareness, subconscious, and self-image. Ultimately they interact to form the "zone," or as it's also known in sports, the "ideal performance state," which we cover in Chapter 4.

Now having said all this, it's not to say that you're going to win every time; there are too many variables beyond your control. But what it will do is improve the probability of success, and just that is more fun than losing any time.

SECTION 2-2: THE POWER OF CONSCIOUS AWARENESS

You are here

Power of Conscious Awareness — Conscious Circle — Zone — Subconscious Circle — Power of the Subconscious Mind

Self-Image Circle

Power of Self-Image

The power of the conscious mind, or awareness, is sometimes called "the principle of the picture." It's not important what you say; it's only important what you cause someone (including yourself) to think.

Think back to the mental pictures you had the last time the boss said, "I'm not saying that it's a bad idea . . ."

Our conscious mind controls our thoughts, sets our goals, distracts us, and sets us dreaming. It can conjure up a most imaginative picture and then propel the rest of our life patterns toward that picture.

The conscious mind can picture more than 2,500 pictures per minute, but only one picture at a time. You can think only one thought at a time. You can flick back and forth very quickly from one thought to another, but you can have only one thought at a time. Therefore, the picture with the most "pay value"—the one that means the most to you—will dominate your mind.

What picture are you allowing to dominate your mind when you're shooting? For example, if you're shooting your annual qualification and have just missed a target, you might think, "My God, I've just shot a miss. There goes my score. I just can't shoot another miss. Whatever you do, don't blow this next shot! What if I do shoot another miss?" What picture is dominating your mind?

What if, instead, you thought, "Okay, what do I have to do to get another hit? I need to remember what I did to get the last hit." Which picture do you think will improve the probability of your having a more consistent mental performance, under pressure and on demand, and therefore improve the probability that your next shot will be a hit?

Remember this principle the next time you have to give instructions or orders to someone. As you're speaking, ask yourself, "What did I just cause them to think? Are they picturing the same picture that I'm picturing?"

The conscious mind is responsible for our situational awareness. Everyone in the fellowship of arms needs to develop and maintain their situational awareness, which is that ability to be aware of what is happening in your area of influence. It sees what is happening to you, or about to happen to you, and sends signals to the right places.

The conscious mind filters what our senses bring to us. Those things that aren't immediately required for survival are

"Consciousness is a phase of mental life which arises in connection with the formation of new habits. When habit is formed, consciousness only interferes to spoil our performance."
—W.R. Inge, writer (1860–1954)

"The real voyage of discovery consists not in seeking new landscapes but in having new eyes."
—Marcel Proust, writer (1871–1922)

"Men are wise in proportion, not to their experience, but to their capacity for experience."
—George Bernard Shaw, writer (1856–1950)

"A moment's insight is sometimes worth a life's experience."
—Oliver Wendell Holmes, writer (1809–1894)

diminished. This can cause such phenomena as auditory exclusion, tunnel vision, slow-motion time, and memory distortions.[4] The important point here is that if you know about and understand these things, when they happen you won't be surprised or think you're going crazy. You need to train for them with realistic simulations and train for the antidote as required. The one that is the most lethal to operational marksmen is tunnel vision; that's why you're trained to scan after each engagement. It isn't just to look for more bad guys but also to more quickly minimize the effects of tunnel vision. (Interestingly, competition shooters also need to include the "broad scan" so they don't get mesmerized by pretty sight pictures and they remember to look around and pay attention to wind conditions.)

The conscious mind is our "orchestra conductor." Just as an orchestra conductor brings together all the various instruments into a coordinated effort and produces the desired results, so does the conscious mind bring together all the required skills to fire a perfect shot and produce the desired results. It's through the conscious mind that we start our journey to learning a required drill. We first must recognize what we want to be able to do, and then we must break that down into its various components. Each piece is then practiced individually until it's right and it's imprinted onto the subconscious mind. Then the pieces are put together and prac-

"The practical and theoretical life of all people, as well as of individual human beings, results from the habitual direction their attention involves . . . each of us literally chooses, by his way of attending to things, what sort of universe he appears to inhabit."
—Edward F. Etzel, Jr., Olympic gold medalist for shooting, 1984

"Researchers say we have about 60,000 thoughts a day . . . our thoughts cause our feelings . . . your thoughts and your feelings create your life . . ."
—Various commentators in *The Secret DVD*

"'The Secret' is the law of attraction. Everything that's coming into your life you are attracting into your life. And it's attracted to you by the images in your mind."
—Bob Proctor, philosopher

ticed as a whole until the entire movement is smooth and consistent. And just as the orchestra conductor must know what a well-played piccolo must sound like and when it's to be heard, the conscious mind must be aware of what the perfect shot should look like and when it needs to be fired. When so signaled, it gets out of the way and lets the subconscious mind fire the shot.

The conscious mind can be a "control freak." It will want to micromanage and be in control of each of the steps toward firing a perfect shot. This may be a result of the requirement of the conscious mind to be in control of the learning steps. But in the end, all we want the conscious mind to do is picture what is to be done and then get out of the way. One of the best ways to do this is with a mental program.[5] It keeps the conscious mind busy so it will let the subconscious fire the shot.

The conscious mind is the goal setter for the subconscious mind. It simply pictures what needs to be done, which triggers the subconscious mind into action. This is how we train for a conditioned response (i.e., go on "autopilot"). So we must be careful what we have the conscious mind picturing. Because, as Lt. Col. Grossman said in his book, "Whatever you drill for ahead of time will be there for you in combat. No more or no less." And as we like to say, "Your best day in combat will only be as good as your worst day in training."

MILITARY

Military Story—Heightened Senses
Soldiers who spend time in combat situations will notice that all of their senses become heightened. They can smell better, they can hear better, they can see better.

Keith says that he can recall in great detail when he noticed this in Vietnam. "The Viet Cong had a smell about them that was unique. This, of course, had to do with their diet, hygiene, and living areas. But when we came onto sites where there were signs of recent activity, I could tell how long since they had been there by the smell."

He says that some of his fellow soldiers could do this as well, while others couldn't. One of his team members once prevented the team from walking into an ambush because, with the wind in his favor, he could smell them. The team backed away from the area and called in artillery— and he was right.

"I also vividly remember how, once I got back home, these heightened senses started to fade," Keith says. "I would go hunting as often as I could, hoping to keep them sharp and a part of me. But it was to no avail. I soon lost them simply because everyday life isn't 'life and death.'"

The Power in Your Mind

POLICE

Law-Enforcement Story—Hitting the Wall

There is an excellent story of a police sniper who had taken up a position overlooking a cement wall, which was about 10 or 15 meters in front of him.

He eventually got the green light on a bad guy who was about 100 meters on the other side of the wall. He carefully adjusted his position so he could just see his target over the wall to his front and fired his shot. Nothing happened. The rifle fired, but the bad guy was still holding his hostage and, after a quick look in the direction of the shot, returned to his threats.

The sniper fired a second shot and still nothing happened. As he readied to fire a third shot, a nearby tactical officer came up to him and pointed out that he was hitting the top edge of the wall to his front. The sniper adjusted his position to take this into account, and on the next shot the hostage situation was resolved.

It's indeed lucky that the bad guy was otherwise distracted and waited. Our sniper was too focused on his target and his downrange results. We have to train the conscious mind to see the details of making everything right at the rifle end and then let the rifle take care of the other end.

HUNTING

Hunter Story—Expecting the Game

Hunters will sometimes become so focused on their target that they don't take the time to line up the sights properly. After the buck or bull of a lifetime has bounded off into the tree line, they sit and wonder how they could have missed such an easy target. They will spend the rest of the day looking for blood trails because they're sure they had hit it since it was so big or it was so close. What they actually did was look over the sights and hit very low. (You might recall a similar story we related earlier of this same thing happening to Keith in combat.)

You must train for just such events. (You're going hunting. What, did you expect not to see any game?) It's simple practice, which can be done at any range. From a carry position, bring the rifle to your shoulder, release the safety, establish a sight picture, and fire a shot. You do this over and over again until it becomes smooth.

This same procedure can be practiced in your living room by dry-firing it.

And during the hunt, whether you're doing a "sneak and peek" or sitting in a stand, you can spend some of your time imagining your quarry suddenly appearing in a particular spot and practice raising on that animal.

This helps you develop your situational awareness and improves your expectations that you just might see some game, and then increases the chances that you'll have the correct picture in your mind when you do see the game you're after.

COMPETITION

Competition Story—How Good Shooters Think

The following is an excerpt from an article called "How Good Shooters Think."[6]

Have you ever wondered if there's a difference between how you think when firing a shot in competition and how everyone else thinks? We're especially interested in how good shooters think, and specifically, what separates the champions from the rest.

In a study of this question, Edward F. Etzel Jr.[7] identified and tested the following mental skills:

➤ Duration—The ability to think/concentrate for an extended period of time.
➤ Capacity—The ability to think about complex things.
➤ Flexibility—The ability to change the focus or topic of thought easily.
➤ Intensity—The ability to be alert and focus intently on a subject.
➤ Selectivity—The ability to focus on only the few things that are directly relevant to the task at hand.

Of these, Etzel's study of top shooters found that selectivity appears to be an indispensable asset in that they must be able to repeatedly focus on only a very few sources of critical information (e.g., the sight picture) while simultaneously disregarding nearly everything else (e.g., range staff, other shooters, the weather, the past, the future). In shooting literature, Gary Anderson[8] perceptively noted the significance of selectivity:

> "The number of things the shooter must be consciously aware of when he fires a shot are an indication of the state of his training. Performance is generally best when active concentration is needed on only one phase of the shooting act."

With any complex skill (such as driving a car or playing an instrument or target shooting), it takes a large volume of quality practice to develop a successful performance level. The new shooter has not trained long enough to involve the subconscious and must think through each detail of firing the perfect shot. The trained shooter has committed many details to the subconscious and can therefore focus only on the critical points.

In fact, in predicting a shooter's success, as we mentioned earlier, the most important attention skill appeared to be selectivity, the ability to distinguish relevant information as well as to screen out irrelevant information. Research has generally indicated that human beings are extremely limited in this ability. Since it's a rare skill and it's the most important skill identified in Etzel's study, selectivity is possi-

"Our job as humans . . . is to invoke the law of attraction. You become what you think about most, but you also attract what you think about most."
—John Assaraf, entrepreneur

"You create your own universe as you go along."
—Winston Churchill, statesman (1874–1965)

"In three simple words: thoughts become things."
—Mike Dooley, writer

bly the defining skill for champion shooters. Perhaps this is the skill that separates the shooter from the nonshooter, the recreational from the competitive, the club level from the world class. If all other factors were equal, would this one factor make a shooter a champion?

In the survey, selectivity scored over one-and-a-half times more important than the next nearest factor.

It's also a skill that not too many people talk about. When you talk to a champion shooter after a well-shot match, he doesn't always have a lot to say. It may be that the shooter just isn't able to verbalize the answer. When you ask a coach, "What's the most important thing for me to be watching or thinking about?" few coaches have a specific answer.

When we train our police snipers and competitive shooters, we spend a great deal of training time getting them to observe and verbalize and reinforce exactly what they were thinking when they fired perfect shots and produced "pretty little groups." One of the things we notice is that in the beginning they don't know what they're thinking. As the days and the training progress, they start to be able to verbalize what they're thinking and then finally they start to be able to control what they're thinking during the shooting session.

Mental skills are skills. They can be learned, trained, and practiced. Certainly each individual will have his own strengths and limitations in mental skills, just as he does physically and technically. And just as physical and technical skills can be improved with the correct training program, so can mental skills.

SECTION 2-3: THE POWER OF THE SUBCONSCIOUS MIND

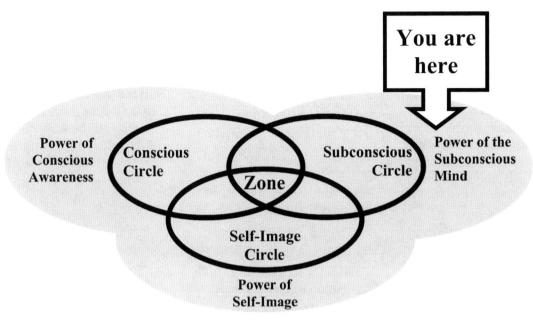

The subconscious mind moves you to do whatever the conscious mind is picturing.

Let's imagine we have placed a 4-inch beam on the floor and have offered to buy you the best meal in town if you can simply walk from one end to the other. While you walk the beam you might think, "Well, this is easy. I think I'm going to have a big steak about 2 inches thick, with a big baked potato and that salad that I really like."

You walk the beam easily because the conscious mind created a picture of how easy it would be and then was kept busy thinking of other things, staying out of the way so that the subconscious mind could do its job.

But what if we offer you the same deal, only this time the beam is extended off a 10-story building. So now the pay value to you is different—you could fall and kill yourself.

> "The unconscious self is the real genius. Your breathing goes wrong the moment your conscious self meddles with it."
> —George Bernard Shaw in *Man and Superman*

> "Advanced shooters relegate the shooting process to the subconscious and their concentration is a strong nonverbal nature termed the 'alpha state.'"
> —William Krilling, *Shooting for Gold*

The conscious mind tries to micromanage the situation and is continually picturing how far down it really looks from way up there. Your conscious mind thinks the pavement down there looks pretty hard. "I wonder how high I will bounce when I hit that pavement?"

The subconscious mind has no understanding of fear; it simply keeps moving you in the direction the conscious mind is picturing. So, the subconscious says, "What's he picturing?"

And the conscious mind replies, "Well, you're not going to believe this, but he's picturing falling off."

So now you get nervous and anxious. You fret about falling instead of what you have to do to get to the other end of the beam. You keep focusing on end results instead of what you have to do to get your desired results.

The subconscious mind is a

powerful tool. It would be nice to have it working for you.

The firing of a perfect shot involves many skills and activities all taking place at the same time. The conscious mind can do all these activities, but only one at a time. Each action needs its own thought because we can only think one thought at a time. However, the powerful subconscious mind can perform almost limitless functions at the same time, leaving the conscious mind to picture only the right thoughts.

To be successful at any complex skill, you must develop the subconscious mind to deal with all the functions that go toward the correct execution of that skill. All successful shooters shoot subconsciously. Conscious activity becomes a subconscious action through repetition. Once it's in the subconscious, it's right because it feels right.

In the beginning, to get it there, each individual action must be done separately, with the conscious mind picturing each one. As we practice, each action becomes a subconscious action.[9] For example, when we were first learning to drive a car, we had to think out each action either before or as we were carrying it out. The conscious mind tells us we need to make a right turn. It then tells us we need to be in the rightmost lane; it tells us to put on our signal light, look in the mirror, and to start slowing down. It tells us that we're at the right place to start turning the steering wheel and that we're turning too much or not enough.

> "While we stop to think, we often miss our opportunity."
> —Publilius Syrus, writer (1st century BC)

> "If one really wishes to be master of an art, technical knowledge of it is not enough. One has to transcend technique so that the art becomes an 'artless art' growing out of the Unconscious."
> —Daisetz T. Suzuki in *Zen in the Art of Archery*

> "All successful shooters shoot subconsciously."
> —Linda K. Miller, coach (1952~) & Keith A. Cunningham, soldier (1950~)

> "Only perfect practice makes perfect."
> —Cal Ripken Sr., coach (1935–1999)

It tells us that we have completed the turn and that it's time to straighten out and drive forward.

By now, you've made thousands of right turns. The conscious mind has to only picture an upcoming right turn and then get out of the way. You make all the right moves to accomplish the turn while at the same time you might be adjusting the tunes on the radio or even grabbing that coffee that is splashing in your cup holder.

Or how about learning to type? (At least it was called typing when we were taught how to do it.) The first lesson was the letter "a". A large letter "a" was displayed on the chalkboard, and we had to fill a page using the little finger of our left hand. We were creating a conditioned response to the symbol "a". And we created this conditioned response for each of the letters in the alphabet. No longer did we have to stop and think of where that letter was; the conscious mind pictured the symbol and turned it over to the subconscious to react accordingly.

But here's where we have to be real careful. We must ensure that we're practicing the right thing, because whatever you're practicing—good or bad—you're going to learn to do it that way. What you feed into your subconscious computer is what you're going to get out in action or skill level. Practice doesn't necessarily make perfect if we're practicing the wrong thing. Only perfect practice makes perfect.

One of the best ways to practice perfect practice is through dry-firing. All good shooters spend more time dry-firing than they do firing live. You can do this almost anywhere, anytime. You don't need a range or a range officer. You need only your equipment and an aiming point. You can fire thousands of perfect shots. You never need your ear defenders. And the real good news is that the subconscious mind doesn't know the difference between a dry shot and a live shot. It sees the sight picture and reacts accordingly—the essence of firing a perfect shot. With the subconscious mind correctly trained and working for you, you'll fire a perfect shot every time because that's the only way you know how to do it.

When in competition or training, you must be careful what you're picturing. You must always picture the performance you must produce to fire a perfect shot. When coaching, you must always ensure that your students are focusing on performance. As coaches, if all we did was point out mistakes, then that is all that would imprint on the subconscious mind.

For example, if we had the objective to get you to stop thinking about elephants, we might say, "Okay, for the next few minutes I don't want you to think about elephants. Elephants represent bad shots and the mistakes you make when you shoot bad shots. You may think about anything else so long as it isn't elephants. Okay? No elephants!"

Then we would continue on the lecture:

"We recently watched a very interesting story about elephants that live in a desert. We thought this most unusual because we thought that elephants would need tons of forage and water. But these elephants were thriving very well. In fact, they're among the largest elephants in the world. *No one is thinking about elephants, right?* We watched another TV show about this couple in Africa who would camp out by the river just to watch the elephants come down to get water. They tell the story of one dark night when one of them comes out of their brightly lit tent and, unable to see properly in the dark, walks directly into the behind of a huge elephant. Both elephant and man were frightened by this unexpected encounter, and each ran off in different directions. Once back in the tent, they were amazed at how rough was the elephant's hide. It had, in fact, left a road rash on the man's face. *Excuse me, I thought I had asked you not to think about elephants?"*

If we wanted you to stop thinking about elephants, we could do that better by talking more about something that we *do* want you to think about. So, let's say we want you to think about giraffes and not elephants. Giraffes represent all the things you must do to fire perfect shots. So here's what we might say:

"Did you know that giraffes have the same number of vertebrae in their neck as do we humans? It's just that each of theirs is about 18 inches long. And did you know that the pattern on each giraffe is as unique as a fingerprint? Researchers use this to identify the giraffes they're studying. When we were in South Africa with the Canadian Long Range Championship team in 1999, one of the things we most wanted to see was a giraffe. We were able to drive to a local park that allowed us to drive through and see the animals from the vehicle.

> "Practice is the best of all instructors."
> —Publilius Syrus, writer (1st century BC)

> "It is not important what you say, it is only important what you cause someone to picture."
> —Lanny Bassham, Olympic gold medalist (1947~)

> "Whatever your mind can conceive and believe, you can achieve."
> —Linda K. Miller, coach (1952~) & Keith A. Cunningham, soldier (1950~)

> "What you can picture is what you can be."
> —Linda K. Miller, coach (1952~)

And sure enough, we were able to drive right up to a giraffe. It's a huge animal. We felt that we could have driven the vehicle right through under its belly. *Did anyone have a problem thinking about giraffes just now?"*

If we write about giraffes, you think about giraffes. When we coach, we talk about "giraffes" (all the things that the shooter must do right) so students think only about what they must do to fire perfect shots. Focus on the things that must be done correctly, analyze those things, and ignore the bad things. The "elephants" (the bad things) are then simply pushed out of the way by the "giraffes" (the good things).

If you want to perform a skill a certain way, you must picture that performance all the time and eventually you will develop the subconscious skills to carry it out.

Military Story—"I Love a Parade"

One of the things the military can do really well is a parade. They're always enjoyable to watch because they're always done so well.

The reason for this is the way that they train for a parade. They don't start by simply putting the soldiers on a parade and let them stumble around trying to accomplish the different movements. They start by breaking the parade into separate drill movements. Then they break each of the drill movements into individual pieces. To teach these individual drill movements, the drill instructor (DI) demonstrates and then explains the complete movement so the student can picture the required end results. Then the DI demonstrates the first portion of the movement, breaking it into logical learning parts. Then he has the student perform this same portion while he coaches to ensure each detail is right. The remaining parts of the movement are taught in the same manner. Then the parts are put together and the complete movement is practiced while being coached.

Each of the drill movements to perform a parade is taught this way, creating a conditioned response to a drill command. And whether it's drill on a parade square or successfully carrying out a counterambush drill while on operations, it's a conditioned response to a command or situation.

Law-Enforcement Story— Train to Survive

Police, training for a survival situation, must be very careful how they train. A number of years ago we heard a story from several police colleagues (and then read the same

"Our subconscious minds have no sense of humor, play no jokes, and cannot tell the difference between reality and an imagined thought or image. What we continually think about eventually will manifest in our lives. Unfortunately most of us are completely unaware of this fact, and we do not monitor our thoughts with the care needed so that we can create in our lives the results we say we want. Since the great majority of people do not feel worthy and deserving of abundant good fortune, radiant good health, and total success in all areas of their lives, that overriding thought pattern controls the results people get. The first order of business of anyone who wants to enjoy success in all areas of his or her life is to take charge of the internal dialogue they have and only think, say, and behave in a manner consistent with the results they truly desire."
—Sidney Madwed, businessman

story in Lt. Col. Grossman's book[10] of how, in the days of the revolver, police would dump their empty casings into their hands and then put them into a pocket so they wouldn't have to pick up brass at the end of training. They later found out that these officers were, while in a gunfight, taking the time to do the same thing with their empty casings. And some officers were even found dead with empty casings in their pocket.

Lieutenant Colonel Grossman also tells the story of a department that wanted to train its officers by using a drill to draw and fire their weapons. They, of course, had to have the weapon in the holster at the start of each drill, so they would draw, fire two shots, and holster. This they practiced thousands of times. And this is exactly how the officers reacted in a gunfight: they drew, fired two shots, and holstered.

The point here is that the most innocent of drills have to be thought out carefully, to include how you want the officer to finish when he applies the drill on operations. If we think back to the story about the state trooper and how he performed under stress, he also reacted exactly as he had practiced, which included an operationally logical finish—change magazines and scan.

HUNTING

Hunter Story—Cycle That Action

Remember we said that only perfect practice makes perfect. We once heard a story about a hunter who wanted to get ready for his upcoming trip. He decided he would practice cycling his rifle, just in case he needed a follow-up shot. He loaded his rifle with dummy rounds and, with the rifle in his shoulder and while maintaining a sight picture on a lifelike deer target, he would cycle each of the dummy rounds through his rifle. He would then reload and do this over and over.

On the day, when finally presented with a trophy buck while hunting, he carefully brought his rifle to the shoulder and established his sight picture and then . . . he cycled each of the cartridges through his rifle until it was empty and didn't fire a single shot.

Under the stress of the hunt, he carried out what he had trained to do in faithful detail.

COMPETITION

Competition Story—Rapid-Fire Pistol in the Dark

What you do in training is what you will do under stress, because that is what's imprinted on the subconscious mind.

One of the competition disciplines we have been involved with is rapid-fire pistol. Here the competitor must fire one round at each of five targets in progressively faster time limits. The first series of five-round strings is fired in eight seconds, the next series in six seconds, and the final series in four seconds. One must develop a smooth swing through each target, firing at the exact right moment so the pistol never stops moving but fires as the shooter is moving on to the next target. The targets are always the same distance apart and at the same height, so the competitor develops muscle memory as to the exact height to hold the pistol and when the trigger needs to be pressed.

This was demonstrated in a match one time when, just as the first shot was fired in a string, the lights went out. Our well-trained competitor completed the string in total darkness and scored as well as he was accustomed to doing. The conscious mind started the string and the subconscious mind finished it.

SECTION 2-4: THE POWER OF THE SELF-IMAGE

When you develop the subconscious habits and the attitude of a champion, you must become that champion: self-image and performance must equate.

Our self-image is composed of our habits and attitudes. If we have the habit of training and the attitude of a winner, we improve the probability of winning. If we change our self-image from an average shooter to a winner, we're going to want to change our performance to accommodate this winning self-image. If we improve our per-

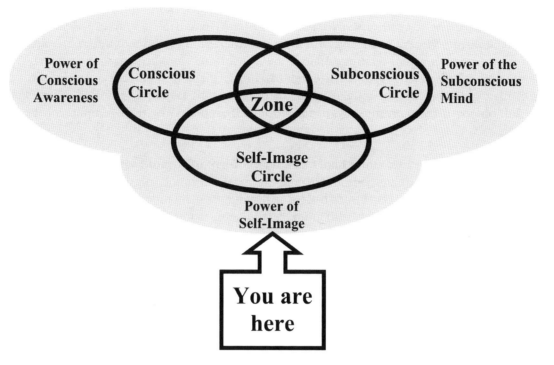

Power of Conscious Awareness

Conscious Circle

Zone

Subconscious Circle

Power of the Subconscious Mind

Self-Image Circle

Power of Self-Image

You are here

formance and start producing winning scores, our attitude will change to one of a winner. Our self-image and our performance must equate.

A method to check your self-image is to become aware of your "comfort zone." Are you comfortable shooting in international events, or national or provincial or club shoots? Or are you most comfortable to just plink in a gravel pit or out on the farm where others can't watch you?

A student in one of our competition rifle courses kept asking for an opportunity to have some fun shoots, to just do some plinking. This was because he didn't see himself as a competition shooter. He was out of his comfort zone with others watching him and knowing his results.

If you want to become a better shot, you must move your comfort zone up a notch. You

"The value of self-esteem lies not merely in the fact that it allows us to feel better but that it allows us to live better—to respond to challenges and opportunities more resourcefully and more appropriately."
—Nathaniel Branden in *The Six Pillars of Self-Esteem*

"It is not your aptitude, but your attitude determines your altitude."
—Zig Ziglar, writer (1926~)

must aim at a better performance, which will give you better results, and you must develop the confidence that you can perform this way no matter the level or situation. Self-image and performance must equate.

Another method to check your self-image is to listen to your own "self-talk," or your "interior monologue," as a sports psychologist would say. You can adjust your self-image by adjusting your self-talk. You can develop a positive self-image by saying positive things to yourself:

➢ I know what I have to do to fire perfect shots.
➢ It's like me to shoot perfect shots.
➢ It's like me to put in a winning performance.

If you persist and you're consistent, you will push other thoughts out of your mind, removing any traces of self-doubt. You'll eventually see yourself like this. Your self-image will change, with performance soon to follow. They must equate.

Military Story—Rangers Lead the Way

Anyone who has been in any military will remember the gung-ho instructors, the ones who know every amusing and hard-nosed saying that ever was said. There is a reason that military training emphasizes the idea that soldiers are "ass-kicking, name-taking, and heart-breaking." They want you to have the self-image of someone who can win against all odds in a game where there are no second-place finishers, where absolute victory is the only option. One very good example of this is the motto of the U.S. Army Rangers: "Rangers lead the way." Keith spent most of his time in Vietnam with "G" Coy 75th Rangers (Ranger Team Miami). Later he came back to Canada and joined the Canadian Army; however, it's his first military self-image, built during his time with the Rangers, that he most closely identifies with.

Another outstanding saying to create a positive self-image was the one used by Gunny Highway in the movie *Heartbreak Ridge*: "Improvise, adapt, and overcome." Later, we heard a very good friend of ours, Doug Peel, a retired regimental sergeant major with the Queen's York Rangers, use this saying with an adaptation that further enhances the picture of how a soldier should see himself: "Improvise, adapt, persevere, and overcome."

Law-Enforcement Story—Qualifications Are a Snap

We once had a member of a provincial police agency come to us with a fear of doing her annual qualification. Although she had never failed it, she was always concerned that one day she wouldn't make it. The instructor would natter at and harass her during the qualification, acting more like a frustrated drill sergeant than a marksmanship instructor.

The procedure with this agency was that when an officer failed the qualification, his sidearm was immediately taken away. The officer had to go back to the detachment in a patrol car, in uniform and without a sidearm. He was required to return in two weeks to be retested and had to pass before the sidearm was returned. The officer's self-image was falling quickly into negative territory, and with no sidearm to practice with, he was expected to somehow magically improve his chances of passing on the next test.

So, we started by teaching the officer how to shoot a perfect shot, how to use her pistol with its heavy and long trigger pull to hit a target. We practiced this until she was good and then got her to fire two good shots, one after the other. We talked to her about how to deal with the instructor harassment. This little course lasted for

"Whether you think you can or you think you can't, you're probably right."
—Henry Ford, businessman (1863–1947)

"If you aren't your own best friend, who the hell is?"
—Author unknown

"What you think is how you feel. And you are in charge of what you think."
—Author unknown

"So you end up attracting to you the predominant thoughts you are holding in your awareness, whether those thoughts are conscious or whether they are unconscious. That's the rub."
—Rev. Dr. Michael Beckwith, DD, visionary

about two hours, and when she showed signs of enough for one day, we stopped. Only perfect practice makes perfect, and if the performance is starting to disintegrate, then it's time to stop. Later, this officer came to one of our pistol clinics and continued her training. She did well in the little end-course shooting test, and we could see by her body language that she had more confidence. Performance and self-image must equate.

Later she e-mailed us that her next qualification was the easiest thing she had ever done. She focused totally on what she had to do to fire a perfect shot, and she so completely ignored the nattering instructors that they eventually left her alone. This is why we have the motto, "Focus on Performance." If you do this, the rest will fall into place.

HUNTING

Hunter Story—To See Yourself as a Good Shot

We do a lot of hunter marksmanship courses, and the one thing we try to do on these is get the student to see himself as a good shot. They're on this course because they aren't good shots or not as good as they think they should be, and their self-image is the first thing we have to fix.

The firing of the shot, on any hunting trip, ought to be the easiest part of the whole trip. We, of course, start their training by doing what we can to make the rifle fit them better, make sure the scope is set up correctly with proper eye relief, and teach them how to apply the marksmanship principles. Once they realize what a perfect shot should feel like and they are getting some better downrange results, their self-image will improve. Self-image and performance must equate.

COMPETITION

Competition Story—The Winners Have Arrived

This is a story that Keith likes to tell from when he was coaching and shooting on an army rifle team. It shows how self-image can help you or hurt you.

I was coaching and shooting on a rifle team that was training for the Canadian Forces Small Arms Competition at Connaught Ranges, near Ottawa. We had been training for several weeks and I was pushing the mental side of the game.

On the weekends, most of the team went home. On this particular weekend, however, a shooting club located at the range was running a sniper rifle shooting match and I wanted to shoot in it. These matches are shot in two-man teams; one member of the team shoots while the other calls wind and watches swirl and splash, and then they switch around so both members have to do both jobs. I needed a partner to enter in these matches and one of my students volunteered. We would both use my rifle.

On the morning of the match, we were getting organized and I was running over some of the communications we would be using on the firing point. My young student seemed nervous and unsure of himself. I had seen this guy shoot during the past several weeks and knew he was capable as long as he kept thinking positively.

As we walked out to the range for the start of the match, a small crowd of competitors had gathered around to chat with each other before the match started and while waiting on the organizers to finish their range preparations. As we walked past, I said good morning to several who I knew. They returned my salutations and joked with me that they might as well go home, the match winners had likely just arrived. The crowd laughed nervously and shuffled about a little. I also laughed at the jokester's comments and assured them that the match wasn't over until the last shot was fired. I could hear the crowd whispering about who I was and whether I was a good shot. The jokester assured them that I was the one to beat and would likely win the match.

My student could also hear the whispers and said to me, "They think we're going to win this match; that's all they're talking about. One guy said he figures he's just wasting his ammo. You talked about this

> "Oh, what a tangled web we weave when first we practice to believe."
> —Laurence J. Peter, educator and writer (1919–1988)

kind of attitude just last week. They're doing everything they can to have an excuse to lose this match before they shoot it."

I was pleased my student had remembered what I had told him and that he recognized it now. I told him that we weren't going to do anything special for this match, just have fun. We were going to read the wind the best we could, shoot perfect shots as fast as we needed to, and then go see how we did.

As it turned out, we had a good match and dominated the prize list. My student was elated, and I was pleased that I could prove the point I was trying to get across. Our relaxed mindset and get-down-to-business attitude had won this match. We simply fired as well as we could and let the rest of them lose the match.

Keith's self-image in this case can best be described as this: "I'm capable of shooting good shots, and I'm here to shoot as many of them as I can." The other competitors' self-images can be characterized as follows: "We aren't confident that we can shoot as well as this guy, so we're going to kind of give up just in case he beats us."

CHAPTER SUMMARY

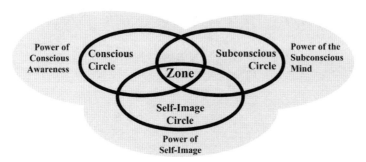

The definition of mental marksmanship is this: mental marksmanship is the process of improving the probability of having a consistent mental performance, under pressure, and on demand. There are three components of your mind that you need to develop in order to perform well: the conscious mind, the subconscious mind, and the self-image.

The power of the conscious mind, or awareness, is sometimes called "the principle of the picture." It's not important what you say; it's only important what you cause someone (including yourself) to think.

The subconscious mind moves you to do whatever the conscious mind is picturing.

When you develop the subconscious habits and the attitude of a champion, you must become that champion. Self-image and performance must equate.

By understanding and then developing these three areas, we develop our ability to acquire and expand "the zone," that magical place from which all our best performances spring. Starting in Chapter 4, we explore the zone and then we focus on the tools that will help us develop each of these component parts of our mind's zone. Before we get to that, though, we'll take a moment to explore "The Power in Your World" in Chapter 3.

NOTES

1.   The cadet organization in Canada is segmented into army, navy, and air force cadets. Each of these runs a program that teaches young people (up to the age of eighteen) some of the discipline of the military, along with some of the military skills (like drill, glider flying, winter camping, etc.). The army cadet marksmanship program develops young shooters and ultimately supports the National Cadet Rifle Team to compete annually in Bisley, England.

2.   "The Challenge of Adversity" by Linda K. Miller and Keith A. Cunningham was originally published in *Precision Shooting* (October 1996) and has been republished in *Favorite Stories on Attitude.*

3. ISSF stands for International Sport Shooting Federation, the name that replaced the ISU, International Shooting Union (also known as UIT, Union Internationale de Tir).

4. These phenomena (perception alterations such as auditory exclusion, tunnel vision, slow-motion time, and memory distortions) are discussed in Lt. Col. Dave Grossman's book *On Combat* (with Loren W. Christensen) as well as most books on post-traumatic stress and many books on battle stress.

5. The mental program is thoroughly discussed in Chapter 5, "Tools to Increase Your Conscious Powers."

6. "How Good Shooters Think" by Linda K. Miller was originally published in the *CoachNet* newsletter (July/August 1999) and has been republished in *Favorite Stories on Attitude*.

7. Edward F. Etzel Jr. examined the question of "how good shooters think" (our phrasing of his more complex question) as a part of his Master of Science in Physical Education at West Virginia University. His findings were published in the *Journal of Sport Psychology* (1979) under the title, "Validation of a Conceptual Model Characterizing Attention among International Rifle Shooters."

8. Gary Anderson wrote an excellent book called *Marksmanship*, published in 1972. He also wrote many articles for various magazines during the early 1970s. For smallbore shooting particularly, Anderson was a favorite reference.

9. While the trained psychologist will probably cringe at our loose use of terms and might prefer us to use semiconditioned response, we are striving to communicate effectively to our readers rather than to be exactly correct in the technical use of terms.

10. *On Combat* by Lt. Col. Dave Grossman.

— Chapter 3 —

The Power in Your World

This chapter is about how you operate in the world and how you interact with the people in your life. It includes four important powers that, once you acquire them, will help you control the way you function in the world, the way you perceive the world, and, therefore, the way you succeed in the world. The four powers we discuss here are:

➢ The power of positive reinforcement
➢ The power of focus
➢ The power of the pack
➢ The power of achievement

Mental Marksmanship Map

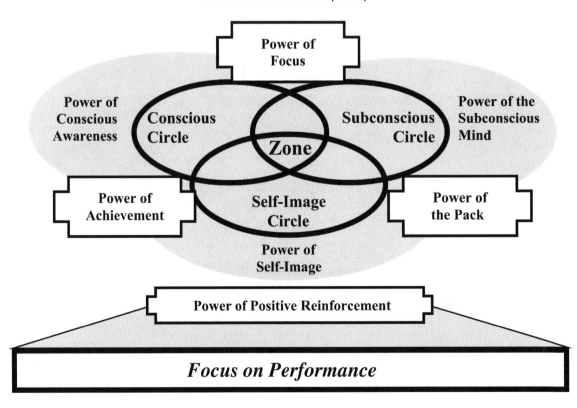

SECTION 3-1: THE POWER OF POSITIVE REINFORCEMENT

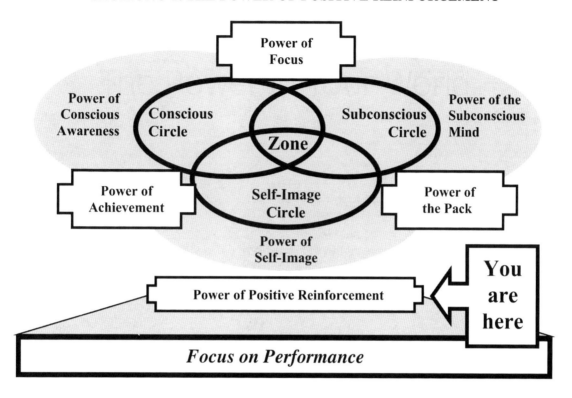

The more we think about, talk about, write about, or hear about something happening, the more we improve the probability of that thing happening.

This is the single most important principle of mental marksmanship. You will get more results from applying this principle than from any other. If you can change only one thing in your world, make it this one. Once you have mastered it, the others will get easier.

What do you talk about or listen to after a match or training session? Do you talk about all the successful shots you made? Or do you relive, retell, and reinforce the one or two mistakes you made? Do you tell everyone who will listen (and some who won't), over

"Act as though it were impossible to fail."
—Dorothea Brande, writer (1893–1948)

"The more we think about, talk about, write about, or hear about something happening, the more we improve the probability of that thing happening."
—Linda K. Miller, coach (1952~) & Keith A. Cunningham, soldier (1950~)

and over, every gruesome little detail about some mistake? With each thought, each repetition, you are increasing the probability of repeating the same mistake, not just for yourself but also for everyone who is listening to you.

Several years ago, Keith was a member of a Canadian national Target Rifle team going to Australia to compete in the World Long Range Championship. One member of the team loudly proclaimed that he cross-fired a lot. (For those who aren't familiar with this term, it's one of great importance to both the competition and the police world. It simply means that the wrong target has been hit. To the competitor, he loses some valuable points and it will likely cost him the match. To the cop, it means his life will likely never be the same.) We think this competitor was talking this way because he didn't have a solution for cross-firing and if the coach put him on a team and he cross-fired, he could say, "There, I told you so. You shouldn't have put me on that team." This guy even had a campaign-type button made up that said, "I am the Crossfire King." He wore this button everywhere, including on the range and at the social functions put on by each of the local clubs. Many would ask him about this huge button, and he would relish the opportunity to tell everyone around him about every cross-fire he ever made. At no time did he relate the solution to cross-firing, but over and over we heard all the ways to cross-fire, each time improving the chances that each of us who were forced to hear this would cross-fire ourselves. The only thing we could do was walk away from this guy and fill our heads with the solution to cross-firing.[1]

Instead of talking and thinking about what mistakes can be made, you should be reinforcing the things you do right. You should be talking about the center hits you got, how good your position feels when you shoot from around a barricade, or the good hits you got with your support hand. You should be listening to others tell about the things they did right. If a fellow officer isn't talking and reinforcing something positive, you should walk away. They'll get the picture: it's lonely being negative.

When someone comes off the firing line, the question you should ask him is, "What went well for you?"

> "Act as if you expect to succeed."
> —Keith A. Cunningham, soldier (1950~)

> "We are what we repeatedly do. Excellence, then, is not an act, but a habit."
> —Aristotle, philosopher (384 BC–322 BC)

> "Start by doing what's necessary, then what's possible and suddenly you are doing the impossible."
> —St. Francis of Assisi, friar (1181–1226)

> "The thing always happens that you believe in; and the belief in a thing makes it happen."
> —Frank Lloyd Wright, architect (1867–1959)

You should fill your mind with success. You must develop the ability to feast or forget. When you shoot a nicely centered hit, you should feast:

➤ Look at it good and long.
➤ Tell yourself, "It's like me to shoot like that."
➤ Remind yourself what you did to shoot that beautiful shot.

When you shoot a miss, you should:

➤ Learn what you can from the data it provides.
➤ Get your mind back on to what it takes to shoot centered hits.

Dig for success from every shot. There has to be something you did right or something you can learn from it. If there isn't, then forget it. Set it aside and move on.

Be careful analyzing what you're doing wrong. Instead, analyze what you're doing right. Then repeat what you're doing right, over and over, and what you're doing wrong will simply get pushed aside and disappear.

Don't be your own worst enemy; be your own best friend. Don't cut yourself down; give yourself a pat on the back. If you hear your interior voice saying things like, "Oh, I'll never be able to do that" or "I'm not smart enough to do that," or "I'm not good enough to try that," then you have an enemy on the inside.

On our police sniper courses, it takes us three days to get the officers to stop cutting themselves or others down. They defend their nega-

> "Most people are thinking about what they don't want and it shows up over and over and over again."
> —John Assaraf, entrepreneur

> "It has been proven scientifically that an affirmative thought is hundreds of times more powerful than a negative thought."
> —Rev. Dr. Michael Beckwith, DD, visionary

> "For 18 months before the Olympics, Linda Thom wrote in her diary every single night, 'I am the 1984 Olympic gold medalist in the Ladies Match Pistol,' and it came true."
> —Terry Orlick in *In Pursuit of Excellence*

> "Learn it until you forget it."
> —Bruce Lee, martial artist (1940–1973)

tivity by saying, "Oh, it's a joke. It's just how we talk." But it's not productive. It's not positive reinforcement. In fact, it's negative reinforcement, and it's destructive. Instead, we want them to build others and themselves up. We continually coach them to find other ways to say certain negatives and soon they are doing it on their own and, more importantly, with each other.[2]

No one controls the way you think about yourself. You have two choices—good or bad. It takes the same amount of effort to think either way. So get the benefit of thinking about yourself in a good and positive way.

So, here's where we get the most resistance from people who are new to this type of thinking: "How do I look at a problem if I can't analyze what I did wrong?" It's simple. You don't avoid the problem, but you approach it with the attitude that "I need a solution to . . ." For example, if the problem is that you're flinching, you can use two approaches:

➤ "Dammit! I keep flinching!"
       or
➤ "I need a solution to flinching."

Which of these approaches conjures up the better picture of how to solve the problem? The first statement leaves you kind of stuck. No further thoughts come to mind, except possibly a barrage of negative self-talk. The second statement can help you start thinking in a constructive way, looking for a solution.

MILITARY

Military Story—Exploit Success

Reinforce the positive. In the military, one of the basic tactics is to always keep a reserve. Normally a commander has several subunits under his control, and he tries always to keep at least one of them in reserve. This reserve allows him to have some flexibility to adjust to the flow of the battle.

In a defensive situation he might use them to stop the enemy from exploiting a weak point that they have by chance found.

In the attack, you might think that the reserve is used to help that part of the attacking force that is having trouble. But in fact, they're more wisely used to exploit success. Once the attack has found the weak point in the enemy's defense and has broken through, you can expect the enemy to plug the hole with his reserve. If the attacking reserve is assigned here, they can strengthen the existing unit and capitalize on their success. This will also boost the resistance to the counterattack that is surely to follow from the enemy. Once successful, the attacking force can deal with the enemy bit by bit.

The same principle applies to your training. Figure out what is working, analyze what you're doing right, and focus on exploiting that.

The Power in Your World

POLICE

Law-Enforcement Story—Get Your Hits Faster

We were recently hired to help train a security agency that wanted to compete in the U.S. SWAT Nationals. We were excited about this job, as we both have a lot of competition experience and feel it is a great way to develop operational skills.

To get a better idea as to where our students were in their skill level and to see where they had to go, we watched videotapes of the team competing in the previous year's competition.

It was very clear to us that what they had to do was get their hits on target faster. They were all in excellent physical condition and could do all the physical requirements as quickly as was needed. They could get their hits on target if they took deliberate, aimed shots, so what was needed was to speed up those deliberate shots.

At first we met some resistance. Some were certain that if they shot any faster they wouldn't get the hits, and that it was better for them in the long run to slow down and guarantee the hits. We certainly agreed with them there, that a hit beats a miss any time, but we believe that a fast hit beats a slow anything, anytime and anywhere.

Our training technique here was to bombard them with all the positive ways to shoot faster. Being smooth was the key to being fast. We went through the videos, showing them where any of the teams could have picked up time if they could have gotten their hits faster. One of the students complained that he knew one of the competitors on another team was an IPSC shooter and that hardly seemed fair. Here we had to bite our tongues, swallow the blood, and be very patient with our response. Yes, to be a good IPSC shooter you need to get your hits faster than the other guy, but wasn't that a good operational skill to have? And if you think it might help in these competitions, you could get involved with IPSC yourself. We gave this concept of getting your hits faster a day or so to gel.

We introduced practical exercises, shot at close range with large targets to give them the feel of shooting smooth and getting hits. We then made the targets smaller and finally we increased the distance. Throughout we gradually decreased the time to complete the exercise, all the while focusing on being smooth.

We got DVDs of the U.S. Steel Challenge and showed them to the students, pointing out how quickly these competitors were getting their hits and the smoothness of their shot procedure. We downloaded the "pro tips" from the Shooting USA television show. These tips are often given by the marksmen trained at the U.S. Army Marksmanship Unit at Fort Benning, Georgia. We were interested only in the ones that showed how to shoot faster and how being smooth resulted in fast. We wanted the students to notice the facial expressions, or lack thereof, that were demonstrated by these professional shooters. One could easily see the intensity of the focus required to perform at this level.

Each day we fired exercises that let them slow down and fire deliberate, perfect shots to remind them what every shot (fast or not) has to be like when it's fired perfectly. They were coached to keep the shot process smooth and to go only fast enough to stay in control, as being in control meant getting hits. But they were also encouraged to push the limits of control, and they were becoming faster without even trying.

We weren't able to accompany our students to the match, but we were grinning ear to ear when we heard they had won the 2008 U.S. SWAT National championship. We were very proud of them.

> "I'm a firm believer in training, that dull, boring 'if I have to do this one more time I'll scream' training that every GI hates. It lets people like me perform in combat when common sense was telling me to run like hell."
> —Vietnam veteran, quoted in Lt. Col. Dave Grossman's *On Combat*

Secrets of Mental Marksmanship

HUNTING

Hunter Story—Practice Your Raise

In our area, deer hunters can shoot only a buck unless they have a specific doe permit. And moose hunters can only shoot a calf unless they have a specific cow or bull permit obtained by a draw. So there are often times during the hunt when you're sitting in your hide and watching a game animal that you cannot take. We teach our hunter marksmanship students to make use of these opportunities by reinforcing a positive.

Whether you're hunting with a bow or a rifle, practice raising on the animal and establishing a sight picture as if you were going to shoot. If you can do this on a doe or a lesser buck so that the animal is unaware of your presence, then when it's time to take the shot on your trophy, you will know exactly how to do it. You'll have practiced and gained confidence by reinforcing what you can do and thereby gradually making what you can do more powerful.

COMPETITION

Competition Story—Two Bull's-Eyes, Back to Back

During a match when we aren't firing, we like to walk the firing line and watch competitors as they shoot. It often provides us with interesting stories to illustrate points in our lectures and books. Just like the one we're about to tell.

In this particular match, the range was 900 meters and the winds were about as tough as they could be to shoot in. They were running at about 25 kph[3] and were fishtailing from 10 o'clock to about 2 o'clock. Shooters were getting lots of wide shots, and many were getting misses.

As we walked the line, a nearby commotion grabbed our attention. A competitor who had finished shooting was packing his equipment to leave the line. He was being loud and was definitely angry about something. The range officer was trying to settle him down and get him off the line before he did much more to disturb the other shooters. Behind the line, he threw his gear down on the ground, and we could clearly hear his rants as he tried to explain his bad score to anyone who would listen. It seems that his relay always got the hardest wind, his shooting partner was slow and was getting misses, and by the time that was sorted out, he was out of step with the wind. And that damn marker on his target was slow and even had the audacity to give him several misses, and he had been shooting enough years to know when he missed and when he didn't. We left him there in the middle of his rant, hoping no one thought this was an example of how to behave on the firing line.

A short distance further on, we noticed another competitor packing up his equipment to leave the line. He was clearly in a good mood; he wore a broad smile and his body language was light and springy. We approached him and asked, "What went well for you?"

This shooter was bubbling with excitement. "Just wait till I tell ya!" he said as he withdrew from the firing line and turned to put his equipment on the ground. But he was already starting his story. "That wind is the worst I have ever seen. Today it was worse than anything ever felt at Trentham.[4] It's fishtailing through 12 o'clock and shifting fast. You can have your sight set for the left wind and get caught in the aim with a right wind. And that will get you a miss, just like that!" he said, snapping his fingers.

"But wait till I tell ya. I got several wide shots and a couple of misses, but I finally figured out that when the wind was blowing hard from the left . . ." he waved his fingers to demonstrate a hard wind from the left . . . "I needed 10 minutes to get a bull. And when it was blowing hard from the right . . ." he waved his fingers from the right . . . "I needed eight minutes to get a bull. So then there I was, ready to fire my second-to-last shot, when I saw the wind picking up from the left, so I waited a few seconds to see if it would settle a little. Sure enough, there was that 10-minute left wind. I put it on my sight and fired as fast as I could and got a bull.

"The wind held steady from the left while my shooting partner fired his shot. He got a miss and I had to wait while he had them check for a hit. It took a long time, and all the while I was wishing they would hurry up because I had the wind pegged.

"Finally I got to shoot. The wind was the same, and I had 10 minutes left on the sight. I was in the aim with pressure on the trigger when I felt a wind change. And there it was—it was shifting to a right wind. I kept changing the sight as I watched the wind until I had eight minutes right. I fired, and I'll be a monkey's uncle if I didn't get another bull."

Someone nearby asked, "Yeah, well, what did you score?"

As our shooter, still sporting a huge grin, picked up his gear and turned to go, he stopped just long enough to look back and say, "Two bull's-eyes, back to back with an 18-minute move."

Now you just have to ask yourself, which one of these two competitors do you think has improved the odds of a better performance in their next windy match?

Competition Story—I Can't Believe I Shot a Six!
From "Can I Give You a Little Honest Feedback?"[5]

For several years, Linda was the provincial team manager and coach at the same time as she was a national team competitor in smallbore. Her protégés on the provincial team knew that they were only to talk to her about successes before a match, and if they had to talk about outcomes, they could only talk about 10s—how many 10s they had shot, and how it *felt* to shoot a 10.

At the Crosman International Airgun Grand Prix one year, Linda was enjoying the company of several provincial team members when a shooter came up to the group and said, "I can't believe how horribly that went. I shot a 6! I can't believe . . ."

One of Linda's team members interrupted. "You can't say that. Linda hasn't shot yet," and with that, grabbed the newcomer by the arm and propelled her away from the group, explaining our prematch code of behavior. There's nothing like a converted believer!

SECTION 3-2: THE POWER OF FOCUS

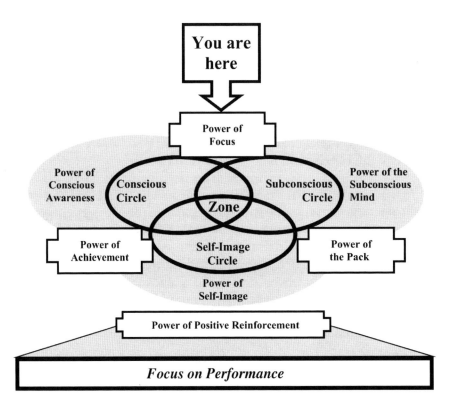

Wherever you are, be all there.

If you're in the classroom, there is nothing more important than what you're learning at that moment. If you're at home, right there and then, there is nothing more important than your family. If you're on the range or on duty, then there is nothing more important than getting down to business and doing your job until it is time to go home again.

Focus is a force multiplier. If someone were to take a couple pounds of C-4 explosive and smear it on the side of an armored vehicle and then set it off, it would barely singe the paint. But if you were to form the same charge into a shape like a cone and apply it to the same vehicle, you would blow a little hole right through the armor. This is because all the energy of the charge is focused in one area. This is how you must train, with all of your focus on the task at hand.

When you're firing shots, shoot only one shot at a time. Do what you must to give the shot in the chamber maximum opportunity to hit the target. Previous shots are gone; there is nothing you can do about them now. The next shot in the magazine will have its turn, but right now, be in control of this shot and make it do what you want. Focus in shooting is easy because there are only two basic steps:

➢   Step 1—Lear n what it takes to hit the target.
➢   Step 2—Repeat step 1.

> "Wherever you are, be all there."
> —Author unknown

> "To do two things at once is to do neither."
> —Publilius Syrus, writer (1st century BC)

> "Quiet minds go on at their own private pace like the ticking of a clock during a thunderstorm."
> —Robert Louis Stevenson, writer (1850–1894)

> "When you come to lessons . . . collect yourselves on the way here. Focus your minds on what happens in the practice hall."
> —Eugen Herrigel in *Zen in the Art of Archery*

MILITARY

Military Story—Designated Marksman Saves the Day

This is an interesting story with two themes: what you can do if you focus your efforts, and what you can do if you focus on firing individual well-aimed shots.

While training military rifle teams, we have often discussed the relationship between the number of rounds fired in combat and the number of casualties produced. We often wondered how long a battle would last if the hit ratio was something as simple as 50 percent; that is, for every two rounds fired, one member of the enemy force could no longer fight. Well, maybe this story sheds some light on this concept.

One of our rifle teams (five riflemen) was once tasked to be enemy force while platoon-sized elements attacked their position (about 30 attackers). Both sides were wearing laser sensors and had laser firing devices attached to their rifles. When hit with the laser pulse that was emitted when a rifle was "fired," the sensors gave off a loud tonal sound that would only stop when the casualty lay down on his back. An umpire would come around later with the "God Gun," which would reactivate the sensor and allow them to become alive again.

The attackers were devastated, largely because the rifle team members were accustomed to firing aimed shots and actually intended to hit their targets. Adapt, improvise, and overcome—the attackers kept trying, adjusting their tactics until they finally were able to overrun the position, but only after taking so many casualties they were rendered ineffective to continue.

The Power in Your World

So that was "just a training exercise." What about reality? We read an outstanding example of reality. It took place in Farah Province, Afghanistan, in the city of Shewan. Approximately 250 insurgents ambushed 30 U.S. Marines.

The ambush started in the usual way, with the Marine vehicles coming under a barrage of enemy rocket-propelled grenades (RPGs) and machine gun fire. The Marines responded and an intense eight-hour battle resulted. During the battle, a designated marksman single-handedly kept the odds in their favor by reportedly killing 20 enemy fighters with his devastatingly accurate precision fire. He stayed cool in battle and applied his marksmanship skills to kill any enemy combatants who attempted to engage or maneuver on the Marines. What made his actions even more impressive (although expected) was the fact that he didn't miss any shots.

Now here is where the power of focus comes in, as quoted from the *Marine Corp News*: "I was in my own little world," the young corporal said. "I wasn't even aware of a lot of the rounds impacting near my position, because I was concentrating so hard on making sure my rounds were on target."

Law-Enforcement Story—The Stack

When tactical officers are about to make an entry into a confined area such as a house, they line up in what is commonly called "the stack." Each of the officers has been assigned a specific job to do once inside. To make this technique effective, they must organize, coordinate, and focus their efforts. Once entry starts they have no time to duplicate effort, as duplication in one area means that some other area isn't being secured. In the stack, they mutually support and amplify each other's efforts. They enter just like a shaped charge through armor, and once inside, they expand to do their specific jobs.

Hunter Story—Flock Shooting

In hunting, there is a term called "flock shooting." It's used primarily in reference to game bird hunting but can apply to any situation where there are multiple targets. In these situations, the hunter tries to hit all the targets and is in such a panicked state of mind that firing perfect shots is quickly abandoned. The result is that in almost all cases, none of the targets are hit.

The solution to this is to pick your target and fire properly at it and then pick another target. In this manner you may not get all of the targets, but you will get some and likely more than with the flock shooting method. The point here is to focus your efforts each time, giving the shot in the chamber maximum opportunity to hit its target.

> "Along with the expectation of success, peak performers say that the everyday world recedes into the background and that they have a feeling of being surrounded by an invisible envelope in which only the action they are engaging in seems to exist. At these times the athlete is so focused as to become largely unaware of himself."
> —Charles A. Garfield in *Peak Performance*

> "Where the mind goes, everything follows."
> —Terry Orlick in *In Pursuit of Excellence*

COMPETITION

Competition Story—Two and Five-Sixths Minutes of Wind

At Bisley, England, in the Target Rifle competition, there's a match called the Kolapore. It's a team event and a very prestigious match, the original prize being a statue of a gold elephant given by the Rajah of Kolapore. The rivalry amongst the international teams competing is always taken most seriously. Each stage of the match consists of one sighter and seven on score (fired by each member of the team and repeated at various distances).

As Keith was getting ready to shoot this match on one occasion, he was joking with his wind coach. In these matches, the wind coach focuses on the wind and calls for the appropriate adjustment to the sight. The shooter is only required to deliver the very best shot, on command. The wind coach in this case was Jim Bullock (who had spent a short time in the air force), and he and Keith (whose blood ran army green) frequently bantered back and forth in a friendly rivalry. This occasion was no different.

For the first and only sighter, Jim gave his wind call of 2 and five-sixths minutes of left wind. Those who know this game might think that this sight setting must be a misprint. But Keith was using a Central sight, which had 1/3 MOA clicks, and he modified it so that there was a minor click between the major clicks. As Keith applied this windage to his sight, he commented that this must be the first time the air force ever made such an exacting call. Jim glanced through his spotting scope to confirm the wind setting and wondered aloud if the army still issued watches with hands that didn't move so they only had to teach their soldiers to tell time for twice each day. Keith settled into his shooting position and as he dry-fired several shots, he commented how fortunate it was that the air force had gravity on their side or they wouldn't have been able to hit anything.

It was now time to fire the sighting shot. The shot was fired and the target indicated, showing a hit that barely caught the right edge of target, perfect for height. Jim very casually asked about the quality of the shot and if the sights were tightly installed on the rifle. Keith assured him that this had been done correctly. Jim then took a careful look at the sight setting using a magnifying glass. He sat back in his chair and smiled. "Well," he said, "your army left didn't work; try your air force left."

Keith then looked carefully at the sight setting and saw that he had put on right windage instead of left. He wound off the 2 and five-sixths minutes of right wind and put on 2 and five-sixths minutes of left wind. Keith took these matches as seriously as he had taken his sniping in Vietnam and was extremely embarrassed to have let his focus be interrupted during the important procedure of setting the sights. You don't make mistakes like this at Bisley and survive for very long.

He then became incredibly focused, very determined to somehow overcome this mistake. As he put the next round into the chamber, he said to Jim, "Okay, that's a lick on me, so now if you can keep up with the wind, I will absolutely give seven of the most perfectly fired shots there ever were." He fired the first shot on score and it was a V-bull. He then followed it with six more V-bulls for a perfect score. He completely redeemed the score, but he has yet to live down that sighting shot.

Wherever you are, be all there. When it's time to make a sight adjustment, focus on it and ensure it's correct. When it's time to fire the shot, focus on it and ensure it's correct. There is a time to joke around and a time to be serious. Be professional enough to recognize the difference.

SECTION 3-3:
THE POWER OF THE PACK

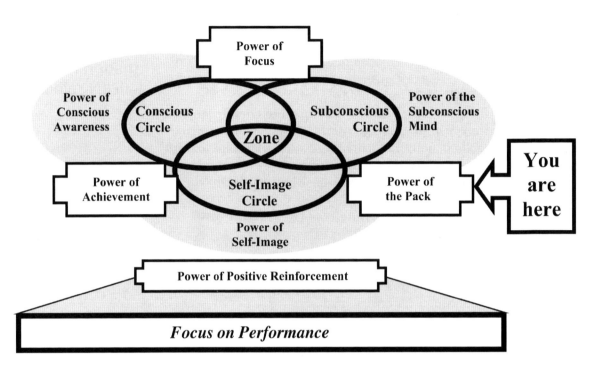

As Lanny Bassham says in his seminars, "We raise or lower ourselves to the standard we're around. We tend to copy the group. Therefore, surround yourself with people who are where you want to go."

Your performance won't improve until you change to a higher standard. You must be around winners. When we're at a match and we haven't won, we make it a religious rite always to congratulate the winner. We talk to him. We comment on some particularly fine score or performance that he turned in. We point out how well he performed despite the bad weather. We ask what was going through his mind when he shot so well.

Make conversation with the

"If you want to soar like an eagle, then don't fly with the crows."
—Author unknown

"We raise or lower ourselves to the standard we are around. We tend to copy the group; therefore, surround yourself with people who are where you want to go."
—Lanny Bassham

winner. At the very least shake his hand and congratulate him.

Whenever you're at a training session or just in from an operation, you should seek out the individual who put in the best performance and talk with him as we just described. And if this doesn't fit well with what you do, then get involved with competition shooting and be around the winners.

And get used to this congratulating thing. It won't be very long until they will be coming up to you and congratulating you on your performance.

Be careful who you hang out with.

If you want to be a winner, be around winners and those who think like winners. This is also good advice for life, as well.

"If you don't want to get shot at, then don't fly with the crows."
—Keith A. Cunningham, soldier (1950~)

"If you're not pulling with me, you are pulling against me."
—Linda K. Miller, coach (1952~)

"The greater the loyalty of a group toward the group, the greater is the motivation among the members to achieve the goals of the group, and the greater the probability that the group will achieve its goals."
—Rensis Likert, organizational psychologist (1903–1981)

"The power in each of us is the power in all of us."
—Canadian rowing coach

MILITARY

Military Story—The Canadian Airborne

Several years ago, the Canadian Army suffered an embarrassment when its airborne regiment was disbanded. There are a lot of reasons why this happened, most of them political, as well as lack of good leadership from all levels. But it all started from within when some "bad apples" were given the opportunity to do as they wished in the name of being rough and tough airborne troopers. They intimidated their leadership, and good, quality soldiers were swayed in their direction, thinking that this was the way it was in the Canadian airborne regiment. In the end, these losers caused the shame and demise of the regiment.

POLICE

Law-Enforcement Story—What's "Normal"?

Law enforcement has a very strong fellowship, first with your immediate partner, then with your department, and finally with anyone in the uniform. This, of course, is a good thing when you need to depend on someone providing you with operational support. But within this fellowship there are the losers and the whiners, and here is where you have to be careful.

You'll remember that, when we talked about training the subconscious mind in an earlier chapter, we said that the subconscious mind doesn't know the difference between doing something right or wrong; it just imprints whatever you're doing. So you need to ensure that you only imprint good things like perfect shots. Similarly, you need to associate with the good personalities within the fellowship.

This came to light for us when a student of one of our police sniper courses told us that before taking our course, he thought that the guys he was hanging out with were "normal" and he didn't realize that they were really the losers and the whiners. Once he had a week (the duration of the course) of constructive support and positive reinforcement, he realized just how negative these guys were. He made a vow to hang with the more positive guys and to be more positive himself, at work and at home.

HUNTING

Hunter Story—Hunt Camps

In our hunting area there are a number of hunt camps. These camps have been in use for several generations and normally consist of a cabin and a hunting area on Crown Land (land owned by the government). There are two types of camps: those that hunt seriously and those that don't.

Those that don't hunt seriously spend their

time drinking, playing cards, and complaining that there are no deer in their area. Those camps that do hunt seriously don't allow drinking in camp, organize where each of the hunters are to hunt, and usually bag their limit. So, if you are a serious hunter, associate with others who think (and act) the same way.

COMPETITION

Competition Story—On Winning

Competition shooters need to be careful with whom they hang around. This game certainly has its share of losers and whiners. These kinds of people can literally suck out of you any competitive spirit you might have as they try to drag you down to their level. If you're a serious competitor, one who wants to gain the most amount of good, positive training from your competition experience, then you need to avoid these types like they are the plague. Instead, you need to hang out with the winners, those who are taking the experience as seriously as you should be.

You don't always win every match you enter, but you can still feel like a winner and you can certainly associate with the winners. Mingle with them, congratulate them, shake their hands, and talk with them. Get them to tell you the story behind their win; there is always a story.

Alain Marion is currently Canada's top Target Rifle shot. When Keith was first starting out in this mental marksmanship game, it was easy to see who was winning most of the matches. In order to establish this power of the pack, he watched Alain whenever he could to see how he conducted himself on the firing mound. Later he would ask questions and get into conversations with Alain. He also congratulated him and shook his hand when he won. And if there were pictures being taken, Keith would try to be in a picture with Alain—anything he could do to be in the aura of the winner. Keith often talks about the time when he finally beat Alain at a match. Alain was the first one to congratulate him because Alain also understood the power of the pack.

We recently attended a sniper competition. The winning sniper pair were gracious in their acceptance speeches, but they clearly hadn't been coached in this winning thing. Before they walked away from the presentation area, they should have paused and allowed the rest of the competitors, the organizers, and the spectators to come forward and congratulate them. Instead, they allowed an equipment salesperson to monopolize them. (We wouldn't expect the salesperson to understand that wasn't the time, although it would have been helpful if he had.) We stood by for about 10 minutes, waiting for an opportunity to congratulate them, and eventually gave up.

So the next time you're at a match or any other competition, make sure you congratulate the winners, and if you're one of the winners, make yourself available to be congratulated.

"The instant formal government is abolished, society begins to act. A general association takes place, and common interest produces common security."
—Thomas Paine, philosopher (1737–1809), in *The Rights of Man*

"In my wide association in life, meeting with many and great men in various parts of the world, I have yet to find the man, however great or exalted his station, who did not do better work and put forth greater effort under a spirit of approval than he would ever do under a spirit of criticism."
—Charles M. Schwab, businessman (1862–1939)

"A team of champions does not always produce a champion team."
—Arthur E. Clarke in *Double Palma Gold* (1997 *Precision Shooting Annual*)

SECTION 3-4: THE POWER OF ACHIEVEMENT

If you want to achieve it, you will work to accomplish it.

The emotion of really wanting something is a powerful driving force. Think back in history about those individuals who strived to rule the world. Hitler, for example. Think of the power he possessed, the millions of people he influenced, and the success he nearly obtained.

On a lesser scale, but just as powerful, you worked to get your first bicycle, your first car, or your first rifle. Maybe your first bicycle story went something like this . . .

You may have spent hours looking through the Canadian Tire (or Sears Roebuck) catalog trying to decide on the exact bicycle you wanted. When you finally decided, you circled it with a pen and kept the catalog open to that page and put it in an obvious place so your parents would see it. You might make the point with your parents as to how much faster you could do some errand or other if you had a bicycle. And if that catalog on the coffee table ever got closed in your mother's effort to tidy up, you saw to it that it got reopened to the right page. And so this might go on until eventually, you got your bicycle.

Somewhere in our lives we have wanted something strongly enough that we were willing to spend every moment of every day focused on how to obtain it. In almost all cases, we were successful.

If you want to become a better shot, then want it strongly enough to make use of this powerful force of desire . . . and then get to work and achieve it.

"Successful people believe that there are no failures, only results."
—Anthony Robbins in *Unlimited Power*

"If you want to achieve it, you will work to accomplish it."
—Author unknown

Military Story—That's Not a Failure Rate, That's a Success Rate

All good militaries in the world have difficult courses that soldiers must attend to become properly qualified and to become professional and proud fighting men. The knowledge learned on these courses is only part of the reason they're so challenging. The other most important factor is the sense of achievement from having successfully completed a course that so many others have failed. Graduates automatically join a fellowship that spans many generations.

Keith, who has spent time in the U.S. Army and a career in the Canadian Army, attended many courses, but there are only two that cause him to stiffen with pride: the U.S. Army Ranger course and the Canadian Army sniper course. Both of these courses are hard, with a failure rate of over 50 percent. But it's that sense of achievement, the feeling of rising to the challenge and meeting it, and belonging to that group, that keeps them foremost in his memory.

Law-Enforcement Story—A Select Group

Members of law enforcement must go through very strenuous selection requirements to even be considered for a position on the tactical team. Once through the selection, they then must undergo challenging training before they're considered a true member of the team. Here, too, there is a tremendous sense of achievement having met a challenge that not everyone can accomplish. And if we ever thought the blue fellowship runs deep, it runs even deeper among the tactical teams.

Hunter Story—Building the Dream

We like to hunt, and when we decided to buy a large property on which to build our ranges, we naturally hoped there would be lots of game to go with it. The first few years were pretty much a flop, as the deer, right at the start of the hunting season, would quickly go nocturnal. If you didn't see a deer in the first couple days of the season, your chances decreased with each day that passed.

The entire property was covered with thick forest and rugged terrain. Never ones to give in easily, even where Mother Nature is concerned, we decided to try to do something that would give us a deer hunt like the ones we see on the "Wild TV" channel.

As we built each range, we created open areas and planted grass and clover with the deer in mind. We cut walking trails throughout the property that are now used by us, as well as the deer and moose. Each fall we bring in several loads of carrots and feed the deer. This keeps the does and fawns attracted to our sites, and as hunters know, there is no better bait for a buck than a doe.

So now with some careful planning, we have hunting seasons like we wanted them to be, with an opportunity to see lots of game, usually every day and throughout the year, a chance to pick and choose which deer we want to take, and a feeling of achievement having made all of this happen.

"Be first or be dead . . . there is no second place winner in a gun fight."
—Bill Jordan, lawman (1911–1997)

"The person who says that something can't be done, should never interrupt the person who is doing it."
—Author unknown

COMPETITION

Competition Story—What about That Russian?

Lanny Bassham was an Olympic shooter who won gold at the 1976 Olympics in Montreal. He now runs a shooting school where he trains other Olympic hopefuls. He tells of his training regime where he was getting up at 4 AM and training for several hours before he started the rest of his day. As anyone can imagine, there were times when it was extremely difficult to get up and stay motivated to do the work that was required.

On one particular morning, the alarm went off and he was contemplating how easy it would be to just turn it off and go back to sleep. As he allowed sleep to ease back into his mind, his wife rolled over and said to him, "Do you think that Russian shooter that you need to beat to win a gold medal is sleeping in this morning?"

Bassham said that from that time on, he found it easier to get up to train. Competition shooters need to keep their goals in mind and remember that they have to do the training if they want to achieve those goals.

CHAPTER SUMMARY

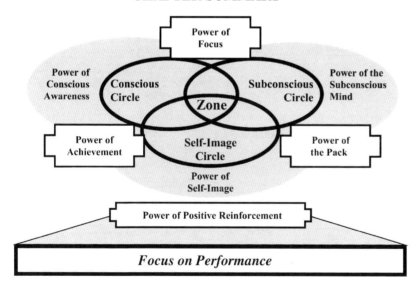

This chapter is about how you operate in the world and how you interact with the people in your life. There are four important powers that, once you acquire them, will help you control the way you function in the world, the way you perceive the world, and, therefore, the way you succeed in the world.

➢ The power of positive reinforcement—The more we think about, talk about, write about, or hear about something

"What you desire is what you can be."
—Author unknown

"Achievers like to be measured."
—Author unknown

"It's a funny thing about life; if you refuse to accept anything but the best, you very often get it."
—W. Somerset Maugham, writer (1874–1965)

"If you think you're going to die, you will. If you think you'll live, you might—and you'll stay in the fight."
—Sgt. Matt Kirkpatrick, soldier

"Victory is not won in miles but in inches. Win a little now, hold your ground, and later win a little more."
—Louis L'Amour, writer (1908–1988)

happening, the more we improve the probability of that thing happening.

➤ The power of focus—Wherever you are, be all there.
➤ The power of the pack—We raise or lower ourselves to the standard we are around. We tend to copy the group; therefore, surround yourself with people who are where you want to go.
➤ The power of achievement—If you want to achieve it, you will work to accomplish it.

These powers can be used to improve your marksmanship. As you work to acquire them, they will make your training a joy. As you succeed in acquiring these powers, they will make your life (whether it's competitions or operations) more satisfying and fulfilling . . . and more successful.

NOTES

1. The solution to crossfiring is to consciously see and recognize your target in your sight—not around or over your sight, but in the sight picture—for every shot.
2. We will cover this subject in more detail in the chapters on tools, and especially in Chapter 7—Tools to Increase the Power of Your Self-Image.
3. The term kph refers to kilometers per hour; 25 kph is approximately 12 mph (miles per hour).
4. Trentham is a range in New Zealand that is notorious for difficult wind conditions.
5. "Can I Give You a Little Honest Feedback" by Linda K. Miller was originally published in the *CoachNet* newsletter (September/October 2001) and has been republished in Favorite Stories for the Competition Coach.

"My mother drew a distinction between achievement and success. She said that 'achievement is the knowledge that you have studied and worked hard and done the best that is in you. Success is being praised by others, and that's nice, too, but not as important or satisfying. Always aim for achievement and forget about success.'"
—Helen Hayes, actress (1900–1993)

"Optimism is the faith that leads to achievement. Nothing can be done without hope and confidence."
—Helen Keller (1880–1968)

— Chapter 4 —

The Zone

SECTION 4-1: DEFINING THE ZONE

Have you ever had one of those shoots that goes just right? Where you make all the right decisions? Shoot nothing but perfect shots? Catch wind changes just because you feel there should be a change? Matches like these are the easiest thing you have ever done.

Keith tells the following story in our mental marksmanship seminars about when he first realized that he was "in the zone" during a match:

> In 1986 I was a member of the Canadian Forces Combat Shooting Team (CFCST) going to Bisley, England. The match was the 300-yard rapid-fire event, where the shooter has 25 seconds to go from standing alert to prone and fire five rounds each at two Figure 11 (charging man) targets.
>
> At that time I was doing a lot of visualization prior to matches. While waiting for the event to begin, I would sit quietly nearby and in great detail visualize the actions I needed to carry out in order to properly shoot the match. I would make my mind see what needed to be seen, feel what needed to be touched, and even smell the smells. I would sometimes get so involved that the range officer would have to specifically get my attention to get onto the firing line. It was intense mental rehearsal. I could see myself standing in the alert position and how I was holding

The Zone

the rifle. I could see the targets appear and how I would get into the prone position, and I could feel the rifle as I settled in behind it. My plan was to focus on centering the front sight in the rear (we were shooting the FN-C1 with iron sights) and to deal with recoil recovery after each shot. I visualized taking a breath after the first five shots as I shifted to the second target. I could feel the rifle run dry and the action stay to the rear, and finally I could see the targets go down, indicating the end of the exposure. It all felt so real.

I suddenly heard the range officer shouting, "Watch and shoot. Watch and shoot." We were into it! The targets came up, and it was as if I was watching myself from a few meters back. I remember saying "center in the rear sight" and the rifle fired as if by someone else's doing. And each time the sight alignment was correct, the rifle fired. I switched to the second target, taking a breath just like I had rehearsed. And again the rifle fired at the moment the sight picture was correct. Then I was finished—I had fired my 10 shots, five at each target, but there were still a lot of people firing. Had I fired too fast? Had I come all this way to blow this match by "spraying and praying"? I thought about how my performance had felt. I didn't remember much about it except that the sight picture had looked very good for each shot—but I had fired it so quickly!

Finally, everyone else on the firing line finished and the targets went down. Everyone waited for them to return with indicators and scores, and eventually they did. Each target had a score-board beside it that indicated the total number of bull's-eyes and the total number of inners (the next scoring ring out; there were only two scoring rings). My target had only one set of numbers. "Oh, no!" I thought as I grabbed my spotting scope to have a better look. As I focused in on my target, I could hear the range officer calling out the official score for my target, "Target number 14, ten, wash," he said.

"Ten wash," I thought. "Ten wash. That's their way of saying, 10 bull's-eyes and no inners. WOW . . . that's a perfect score of 50." Now my mind raced. I had just fired a perfect score in the 300 Rapid. I had never done that before. "I can't believe I just shot a perfect score." My mind was a blur of what had just happened. It hardly registered what the RO meant as he was telling me I had to do a shoot-off. "Oh, yes," it was coming to me. Everyone who shoots a perfect score has to reshoot the match right away, and that score will be the deciding score for all the competitors who shot a perfect score. If there were still a tie, then those tied would come back out later and shoot a shoulder-to-shoulder shoot-off.

Suddenly my mind raced in another direction. Now I was thinking such thoughts as, "What if I blow this shoot? What if I just screw this one up? Everyone will think the first one was a fluke! My, God, what if I blow this shoot?"

And such was the way of my thinking as I prepared to shoot again the very match in which I had just performed so well. I reverted back to the "spray and pray" technique, which had never worked well for me in the past, but I was now in a panic mode. Of the 13 competitors who had to do this shoot-off, I came dead last. But little wonder, given my way of thinking.

Now, flash ahead one year. It's 1987 and I'm again on the army team, in Bisley, on the 300-yard range and getting ready to shoot the 300 Rapid. This is the first time we're using our new C-7 rifles, and I am thinking about last year and how I so nearly had this match but let it go because of the way I handled it mentally. I was determined to be in mental control this year. The visualization had worked so well (when I used it) last year that I would do the same this year. I focused on centering the front sight in the rear aperture and called nine good shots and one slightly right. I scored 49 out of 50.

Forty nines are good scores, but they wouldn't win anything. Still, I was rather pleased with my performance; I had, after all, stayed in mental control. I turned in my scorecard and prepared to leave the range. The range officer stopped me to say that there had been no perfect scores, and since it was the last relay, there wasn't going to be any so they were shooting off 49s. I was to get ready to do a shoot-off.

"Ah, hah," I said to myself. "I have been here before, and I am going to shoot this match just like the match that got me here." I visualized my performance as I loaded my magazine and was still visualizing as I finished my sighting shots and prepared for the warning to start the match. I shot this match just like I had rehearsed it in my mind and called all shots good. I smiled a deep, knowing smile as the range officer read out my "ten, wash" score. I had won this match, and I won it by being in the zone, being in control mentally, and performing just as I had rehearsed.

You're in the zone, the ideal performance state when the conscious, the subconscious, and the self-image are in balance and working together. Everything feels completely natural. You're concentrating on performance. You have trained so well that you're shooting subconsciously. Your attitude is that it's "like me" to win.

Military Story—"In the Bubble"

Gunnery Sergeant Carlos Hathcock (one of the U.S. Marine Corps' top snipers in Vietnam and subject of the book, *Marine Sniper: 93 Confirmed Kills*) tells of how he used a mental picture of "getting in the bubble" when it was time to fire a shot. This allowed him to shut everything else out that might cause a distraction so he could focus on firing the perfect shot. While in the bubble, he saw only sight picture and target. He didn't feel the rain running down his neck, the insects biting him, or even the snakes crawling nearby. It was like a cone of concentration that allowed him to shoot a perfect shot no matter what was happening around him. Once the shot was fired, he was back into the scan mode, making the conscious mind do its job, bringing his situational awareness back on line.

Law-Enforcement Story—Hostage Rescue

There are certainly many stories of police officers who were in the zone, the ideal performance state. The state trooper mentioned in Chapter 2 was certainly in the zone and on autopilot.

One of our local police officers tells a story of when he was in the zone and shooting to defend the life of a hostage. He was called to a domestic and arrived to find a woman being held hostage by her boyfriend. They were out on the front lawn; the boyfriend was holding her around the neck with a knife to her throat. Our cop was trying to talk this guy down when more police officers arrived.

As the conversation continued, the boyfriend started to walk backward, dragging the woman with him toward the house. The police officers followed, trying as hard as they could to talk this guy out of this and knowing they couldn't let him go into the house with the hostage.

Right to the very end they kept talking. As the boyfriend opened the door, he pushed the hostage into the house, and as he closed the door, our cop fired three shots. The first hit the doorknob, the second went through the last crack of the door as it closed, and the third went through the glass panel beside the door. The last two hit

> "One person with a belief is equal to a force of ninety-nine who have only interests."
> —John Stuart Mill, philosopher (1806–1873)

> "There are some people who live in a dream world, and there are some who face reality; and then there are those who turn one into the other."
> —Douglas Everett, Canadian senator (1927~)

the boyfriend, ending the situation at the door. The officer was completely focused on firing perfect shots into the target. For a few seconds, his world was that doorway and the immediate threat. The rest of the situation faded while he zoned in on shooting effective shots.

Hunter Story—Cape Buffalo

How about the hunter? Does he need to be in the zone? He needs to be in the zone if he wants to deal with "buck fever" (i.e., the excitement of the trophy) or, as the hunter in the following story needed it, to save his life.

A friend of ours had always dreamed of hunting Cape buffalo in Africa. He was experienced in all kinds of shooting, having been a cop, a competitor, and now a contract worker in Iran. He was also an avid hunter, always getting his deer and moose each year. He finally got all the permits in place and embarked on his dream hunt of a lifetime. He was booked in to shoot some plains game, do a little sightseeing at a game park, and lastly hunt a Cape buffalo.

All was going according to plan, and he was finally on his Cape buffalo hunt. The guide had scouted out a couple of herds and each had good bulls, ideal for the hunt. The guide had skillfully stalked the biggest of the bulls and now had our friend in place to make his shot. At a range of about 50 meters with the wind in his favor, he decided to take a standing shot without the use of shooting sticks. He had made many of these shots before, and this one was just another one like all of the other ones.

As he raised his rifle, an eddy of wind blew his scent directly at the buffalo. The huge bull suddenly wheeled to face his foe and immediately started to charge. The guide, seeing the charge develop, thought the best tactic would be to first take cover in a nearby clump of trees before shooting the enraged bull. He yelled at our friend to join him as he ran to the relative safety of the cluster of trees, but our friend didn't hear him. He was using a custom-built bolt-action rifle in .416 Rigby, mounted with a 1.5-5 power Leupold scope, with the power on the lowest setting. The buffalo shuddered slightly as he absorbed the big bullet and continued his charge.

Our friend reloaded and fired the second shot. The buffalo stumbled slightly but continued, now with blood running from its nose.

Our friend, still as calm as if he were shooting at a beer can, reloaded and fired his third shot. The buffalo slowed slightly, the shot bouncing off its boss, and continued the charge.

The hunter reloaded and, at a range of about 20 meters, fired his fourth shot. The buffalo stumbled and almost went down, but recovered and resumed his charge.

Our friend, now having fired the last round in his rifle, reloaded a single round from his belt and at a distance of 10 meters fired his fifth shot. The buffalo, now with blood spurting from several wounds about his head, neck, and shoulders, stumbled again and fell, skidding to a halt at our friend's feet. Without taking a single step, the hunter lifted his boot and placed it on the buffalo's horn.

Only now did he turn to look for the guide, who was standing near a tree with his face ashen. Our friend said, with a straight face and meaning every word, "So, is this how these buffalo hunts are supposed to go?"

Now, that's one cool individual who was truly in the zone and focused on what he had to do.

Competition Story—Relaxed and Intense

From "How Good Shooters Think,"[1] Linda says:

It seems to me that when I'm petrified (extreme match pressure), I can't think straight, I am pretty much immobilized by my fears, I cannot deal with very many thoughts or factors at once, and it takes a great deal of mental will to calm myself down.

When I'm very, very calm (no match pressure at all), I am likely thinking only a few thoughts. In fact, the Zen state focuses on only one thing until the meditator is able to empty his mind completely.

The Zone

In between these two extreme states (petrified and meditative), I have varying capacities for entertaining multiple thoughts. The ideal is something I describe as "relaxed and intense." In that state, I can think of many things fluidly and easily, but for excellence in shooting performance, I find it is best to focus on only a few critical things.

Competition Story—The CISM Match in Sweden
The following is excerpted from "The Performance Response . . . That Winning Feeling."[2]
Linda says:

When Keith first told me the story about the deer,[3] a shiver went through me. At that time I had never been deer hunting, but I knew exactly what he was talking about. I had felt that "feeling." I had felt it when I was target shooting; in fact, some of my very best results were achieved while I was feeling that "feeling." I had also felt it when I was coaching.

COMPETITION

Keith's story:

In September 1996 I shot on the Canadian Forces CISM rifle team in Sweden. (CISM stands for Conseil International du Sport Militaire.) It's a military world championship in a number of sports, of which shooting is one. The fullbore rifle shooting part is standard rifle, 300-meter, three-position ISSF (Olympic style) course of fire. It involves 20 shots prone, 20 shots standing, and 20 shots kneeling. The 10-ring is slightly smaller than 4 inches. A couple of days after shooting this course of fire, we shoot another called the rapid-fire event. It's the same course of fire but shot in 10-shot strings, with each string having a specified time limit.

Due to a problem with a very small airline on one of the legs of our travel, only two of the five team members had all of their equipment. Four of the team members shoot left-handed, and one of the two rifles that arrived was left-handed. What all of these statistics mean is that four of us shot the same rifle, and we passed shooting clothes around like folks trying on clothes at a department store sale.

Linda had been asked by the Canadian Forces to come along as a coach. This was of particular good news to me because the team needed help on the mental management side of international competition, and I knew she was very good and successful in this area.

My goal for this match was to shoot a personal best. We don't have this event in Canada, so our team was just getting started, and I felt this was a good interim goal. The competitors are world- and Olympic-class shooters, and although one day I would like to be on the podium with the likes of Glenn Dubis (of the U.S. Army Marksmanship Unit), it will likely take a while to get there.

My confidence and focus weren't good starting the prone event. I was shooting a strange rifle, using shooting clothes that didn't fit properly, and with a frame of mind that wasn't something to write a story about. My prone was dismal, to put it politely. While changing over to the standing position, I had to get away for a moment and used going to the bathroom as the excuse. As I returned, Linda could see that I was frustrated and upset with my performance and at the thought that I had probably missed my goal in the first 20 shots.

She got into my face. She made me talk. She knew that if I went back onto the line, I would carry this mood on to the standing. You can lose this kind of match in the prone, but you win them in the standing. I tried to step around her and return to the line. She stepped in my path. I was now angry with her for not letting me stew in my own juices. I lashed out at her, but what I was saying wasn't an assault against her. The real problem was coming out.

"That's a junk rifle I'm shooting in there. It's an absolute piece of shit. I don't care if other people have shot it well; it's junk to me. And these clothes don't fit; they don't feel right. All I want is my own rifle. Why do you think I paid so much money for it and worked so hard putting it together? So some hick airline can drag their butts at finding it and will probably get it here the day after we're done shooting? And I want my own clothes. They fit me; they feel right. All I want is my own equipment. Is that so much to ask?"

She waited until I was finished. She said, "You know, you are absolutely right. No one should have to compete like this in an international event. You have a fine rifle that shoots well and clothes that are tailor-made for you, and you perform well with it all. But now you have to shoot like a champion with what you have."

She paused to let it sink in. She was right, of course. I had few options except that I could control my attitude toward this situation. What a victory it would be to still shoot a personal best using other shooters' equipment. It was when she said, "Now go in there and shoot the best standing that you have ever shot," that I felt it. The "feeling" came over me like a wave of warm water. I no longer felt angry or frustrated. I felt calm . . . deliberate . . . determined. I formulated a plan in my mind of what I would have to do to shoot the best standing I ever shot. With this plan came confidence and focus. It was going to be all right. I had the "feeling."

By the way, I did meet my goal. My new personal best wasn't as good as it could have been, but it was a personal best, and one accomplished under difficult conditions.

Oh yes, 20 minutes after I fired my last shot and just as Linda was finishing her debrief with me, the team captain strolled up and said, "Hey Keith, your equipment just arrived." That also was a good "feeling."

SECTION 4-2: ASSESSING YOUR "CIRCLES"

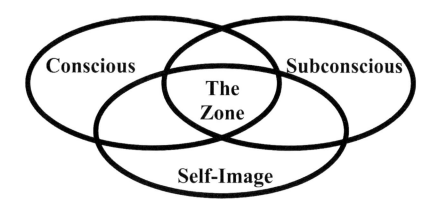

Sometimes your conscious, subconscious, and self-image circles aren't well balanced and working together. Sometimes, one circle dominates and reduces the effectiveness of the other two. Sometimes one circle isn't well developed and it becomes the weakest link.

The main part of this book is about recognizing which of your circles you want to improve and then applying the tools you need to accomplish that. The tools are the subject of Chapter 5, "Tools to Increase Your Conscious Powers," Chapter 6, "Tools to Increase Your Subconscious Powers," and Chapter 7, "Tools to Increase the Power of Your Self-Image." First, you need to be able to recognize circles that are out of balance. Let's look at a few typical situations.

SECTION 4-3: THE BEGINNER

The Beginner

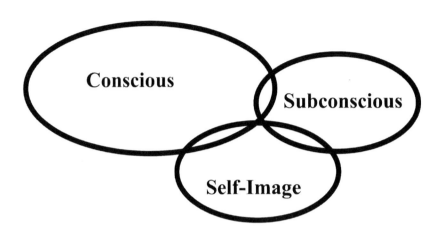

The shooter represented in the diagram above is out of balance. He hasn't developed any subconscious skills and has little self-image. All new shooters look like this when they begin shooting.

When you're learning something new, you have to consciously think through each step. In other words, the beginner has a very large conscious circle. Nothing much can be put on autopilot, so the subconscious cannot yet make a contribution. Your confidence hasn't yet been built, so the self-image circle is still very small. When you're at this point in the learning curve, your circles don't overlap sufficiently to let you get into the zone.

This is the classic beginner profile. It applies whenever you're learning something new. For example, when you learn to drive a car, you have to think through each detail consciously. Learning to play the piano is the same. Learning to type (or "keyboard") also requires the beginner to consciously think each step of the way. In fact, a large part of the learning process involves suffi-

> "The longest journey begins with a single step."
> —Lao Tzu, founder of Daoism (6th century BC)

> "I have good news and bad news. The good news is, it's not magic. The bad news is, it's not magic."
> —Linda K. Miller & Keith A. Cunningham in "Police Sniper: Finding His Own Truth"

cient repetition so that the driver, the pianist, or the typist will be able to let the subconscious take over some of the tasks.

An experienced shooter trying a new position or a new trigger will return to this category. When you're first learning a new skill, each action has to be broken down into practice segments and practiced separately and individually. Once the conscious mind has a clear picture of the skill's characteristics, it takes repetitive practice to commit the new skill to the subconscious. Once this process begins, the development of the self-image can progress.

The tools to help the beginner structure his conscious learning are in Chapter 5, "Tools to Increase Your Conscious Powers." Tools to help increase his subconscious and self-image circles and thereby develop his performance zone include those found in Chapter 6, "Tools to Increase Your Subconscious Powers," and Chapter 7, "Tools to Increase the Power of Your Self-Image," as well as Chapter 8, "Advanced Tools—Your Powers Applied."

"Awareness is good, but without skills and ability tied to that awareness, all you have is anxiety."
—Tony Blauer, close-quarter combat trainer, as quoted by Lt. Col. Dave Grossman's *On Combat*

"Strange as it seems, no amount of learning can cure stupidity, and higher education positively fortifies it."
—Stephen Vizinczey in *An Innocent Millionaire*

"Learning is not compulsory . . . neither is survival."
—W. Edwards Deming (1900–1993)

"Don't look for more honor than your learning merits."
—Jewish proverb

MILITARY

Military Story—Operations Drills

When the army is learning a new operations drill, they break it down like they teach their parade ground drill. They first do a classroom lecture on the drill, or at least where the instructor can make a diagram of what is expected. Then they do a walk-and-talk-through at a slow pace until each member understands what he is expected to do.

Then they pick up the pace and open up the space until the drill is carried out in a realistic way. Once everyone understands the drill, it's practiced until it becomes a reaction.

The conscious mind recognizes the situation and the subconscious mind reacts, goes on autopilot, and carries out the activity as it was practiced.

POLICE

Law-Enforcement Story—New Issue Holster

When a military or police agency changes over to a new weapon, a large part of the cost is the training required to provide sufficient repetitions. We asked a police trainer about his experience in this area. Here's what he said:

It is a loaded question, as I have some differing opinions from the manufacturers and some other experts. In terms of repetitions, most manufacturers will recommend "hours of training" vs. repetitions. One recommended that when we switched from the .38 revolver holster to the 0705 Beretta holster that we do a minimum of eight hours of training. When we switched from the 0705 to the Raptor for the Glock, they recommend four hours. I believe that there should be a significant training component that "hard-wires" the muscle movement of the draw (specific to the holster), and then there MUST be an even more important area that anchors the skill by scenario-based training. You remember the old adage that under stress you revert back to your training? Well, studies have shown that that will only work provided your training was stressful in the first place.

In a nutshell, I would have guys do four to eight hours of fundamentals, drawing, reholstering, scanning, reloads from the draw, one-handed draws, weak-hand-injured draws—everything possible to get them working the holster and becoming intimate with it. I usually tell them the day before to bring some painkiller medicine because they're going to have sore shoulders from the amount of work they're going to do (they usually break a good sweat from the drills). Then when I see a basic level of proficiency, I start to seriously stress them out by trying to activate their sympathetic nervous system (SNS). I do this usually by playing "officer down" audio or videotapes and role-playing WHILE doing the drawing motions.

Our reply to the trainer:

Thanks for the info. We're surprised that it's in number of hours because we thought more elapsed time would be required, and that there would be a number of reps or amount of training time within that total elapsed time (you know, 21 days to change a habit). We're trying to relate it to other semiconditioned response training, but it may be that the advances in neuro-linguistic programming (NLP) have changed how this type of training is viewed and conducted.

And the police trainer's reply was this:

NLP can have a great effect on the training. I have used it many times, but it is only part of the whole picture. Many martial arts advocate that for a movement/skill/technique to be reactive to a given stimulus, that skill must be repeated about 2,500 times. You would probably wear out two to three holsters by that time. The biggest factor when teaching a new holster system is the muscle memory and then performing that same muscle memory under stress, when rational thought goes out the window and higher levels of SNS stress are encountered. I would suggest that the function of the presentation of the gun and shooting are all conditioned vs. semiconditioned.[4] The only thing that would be semiconditioned would be the threat recognition (that's learning "what are threat cues" and responding appropriately).

HUNTING

Hunter Story—Learning about Recoil

In our experience, recoil is the biggest problem to overcome for the beginning hunter. Hunting rifles are light and the calibers are usually big. An average caliber of .308 will deliver enough recoil to cause even the experienced hunter to flinch. Make this light, handy rifle a .30-06 and the recoil is pretty spectacular. When teaching a student on any of our courses, we find that once we overcome the flinch, the student is 80 percent of the way to becoming a good shot.

We start our hunter marksmanship students with a .22-caliber rifle so they can develop the feel for what a good shot should be like. They shoot it in all positions and enough times that this feeling is imprinted on the subconscious mind. We then do a great deal of dry-firing with the hunting rifle and minimal live-firing so the mind can accept the recoil in small doses. We have to convince the mind and body that there is no difference between a dry shot and a live shot. A live shot is fired with the same feeling as a dry shot.

Another thing that helps this recoil problem is a muzzle brake. When Linda got her first hunting rifle (a lightweight .308), she could only fire a couple of shots before it became uncomfortable and she had to stop. Keith built her a custom stock that fit her better and installed a muzzle brake. Her first time on the range with this rifle, she fired 30 shots from various positions at a variety of targets, actually practicing the shooting situations that she might encounter in the field. Just like all hunters should do.

We now have muzzle brakes on all our hunting rifles.

COMPETITION

Competition Story—Twice Your Age and Half Your Size

This is Linda's story about her first competition in the Service Rifle matches (Canadian style). She was already an international award winner in both smallbore and fullbore shooting, but she was new to service conditions shooting. Most of the other competitors are rompin' stompin' soldiers, and Linda took considerable pleasure in being the oldest and most petite beginner on the field.

If I had thought that the transition from Olympic-style smallbore to Bisley-style fullbore had been administratively challenging, it was nothing compared to my transition to Canadian-style Service Rifle competition. First of all, the AR-15 was my first semiautomatic rifle, so it required becoming familiar with gas operations, magazine stoppages, and magazine changes . . . and, oh yes, the little matter of actually using the safety. The matches are fired from four shooting positions. I already knew the Olympic-style version of three of them, but now I had no sling, no shooting jacket, and no kneeling roll. Then, the matches required different types of fire: deliberate, snap, rapid, and fire with movement. This was a big deal; a very big deal. The competition comprised 12 different matches, and you pretty much have to know what's coming next in order to be able to get everything done in time to obey the range commands. It's hard to remember all the little details: Do I get sighters on this one? . . . Do I have to start from the standing alert position? . . . Do I need my safety on? . . . Did I remember to take my safety off? . . . What do I change my elevation to during the run? . . . Which targets are coming up for this one? . . . Do I shoot and then run or run and then shoot? . . . Did I remember to take the windage off as I ran closer to the targets?

Since no one expects a beginner in these matches to be able to challenge the usual winners, and since safety is an utmost priority, beginners are usually paired with a senior shooter who coaches them through their first experience. Keith was my "senior." We each put on our electronic hearing defenders and turned the volume up. Keith stood behind my firing point, just off the mound. For each match, he would coach me through the administration: "Okay, this is match one, the 200-meter deliberate. You have two sighters and then carry on with your two five-round magazines. Make sure you're ready to load your two-round magazine. Make sure your sights are set for 200." Later, he would say, "Now, match eight is coming up. Get your two five-round magazines loaded. You're going to be running from the 300 to the 200, so check your elevation. You'll be starting from prone-prepare-to-move position. When you get the flash, focus on your run. When you get to the 200, cock your rifle . . ."

The point here is that, even with my significant experience in other shooting disciplines, I was an absolute beginner for this style of shooting. I needed to make every little step conscious. The only thing I could trust to my subconscious was the firing of the shot, and then only the deliberate shots where time wasn't an issue.

And so, for every match, Keith was there, making sure I knew what to do next. My goal for my first Service Rifle competition was to get all the procedures right. With Keith's help, I met my goal.

No matter what the type of competition you want to get involved in, it's necessary to break it down into its component parts. For me and Service Rifle, this meant attending to the type of fire, the position required, and the match conditions around these. Ideally, you then practice the parts until you're proficient and then start putting them together. Eventually, you have to put it all together under competition conditions, and that's usually when the fun really begins.

With Keith standing behind me, giving me instruction, it was easy to make sure my attention remained at the firing point. In service conditions, as in other shooting disciplines, you must first get it right at the firing point and, once you have it right, let the gun take care of what happens downrange.

SECTION 4-4: THE PRACTICE CHAMPION

The Practice Champion

The Zone

The practice champion is a shooter who has been training for many years but doesn't have the attitude of a winner. He is a better shooter than his self-image will allow.

He is knowledgeable about marksmanship and he has learned his craft well. He shoots well as long as he doesn't think about how well he is doing, or as long as no one is watching. This shooter shoots good scores in practice but gets nervous in competition. Some practice champions can't handle the thoughts of failure, and some practice champions can't handle the prospect of success. When stressed, his thoughts turn to thoughts of failure or success, and he is consumed by thinking about the outcome of the situation rather than staying focused on his performance.

Just as in our beam example from Chapter 2, he shoots well in practice, where the beam is on the ground; in competition the beam is off the building and he falls apart.

This kind of competitor is a coach's nightmare. If the coach is picking the team from practice scores, this shooter may be at or near the top, but the coach can't depend on him to produce the same results in competition. This is the kind of hunter who shoots well at the zeroing range but panics and shoots badly when presented with game in the field. On operations, this is the kind of partner who is a liability.

In short, this is the kind of shooter you can't rely on. If he sees he doesn't shoot as well in competition or on operations as he does at the practice range, he will likely decide to practice more and thus perpetuate the problem. What he needs to do is work on his self-image.

The tools to help the practice champion increase his self-image circle and thereby develop his performance zone include those found in Chapter 7, "Tools to Increase the Power of Your Self Image," as well as Chapter 8, "Advanced Tools—Your Powers Applied."

MILITARY

Military Story—Gung Ho Goes Fetal

Keith recalls an individual with whom he went through training prior to deployment to Vietnam. This individual was gung ho, hard-nosed, and always ready to "kick ass and take names." He was always loud and was first to complete any of the training. He was the kind of soldier that anyone would want to be with in a combat situation.

Keith and he arrived in Vietnam together, completed the Recondo training, and were assigned to the same Ranger long-range recon team. They completed several missions together without enemy contact. But the first contact was inevitable, and it turned out to be a chance contact with a short firefight against a small enemy element. Contact was quickly broken.

The Ranger team was reorganizing and preparing to pursue in order to locate the larger enemy element. But one team member was missing: our "gung ho" soldier. He was soon found nearby in a fetal position with his hands over his ears. He was medevacked and never seen again.

You never know how you'll react in combat, and each successful time doesn't guarantee the next time. Good

"Well, they sure are pretty, I'll give them that, but can they fight?"
—Author unknown

"Among Canadian Target Rifle shooters, we have a lot of really good marksmen, but not very many good competitors."
—Alain Marion, lawman, competition shooter

"If only I had a little humility, I'd be perfect."
—Ted Turner, businessman (1938~)

"Champions aren't made in the gym. Champions are made from something deep inside them."
—Muhammad Ali, athlete (1942~)

health and fitness (physical and mental) provides a good base, and training hard and smart improves your luck. But in the end, operations isn't training and practice champions don't survive.

POLICE

Law-Enforcement Story—The Whistle Blast

We once heard an interesting story from some of our police students. It was about an agency that used a whistle blast while training their officers on the range. Whenever it was time for the firing line to begin firing, they would blow a whistle, the same kind of whistle that was used by their traffic cops.

So, one day this agency was dealing with an armed subject barricaded in a house. They have the house secured with armed police officers on all sides. The situation was tense and everyone was alert. Nearby, a traffic cop blew his whistle . . . and everyone commenced firing.

What you practice in training is what you do under stress.

HUNTING

Hunter Story—Hunter at the Range

Hunters are notorious for being "practice champions." We have seen them come to our range to sight in their rifles and do very well at this. They often complain about the deer they missed last year and had thought that their rifle had been bumped off its zero. Once again at the range, they find that their zero is on.

So why did they miss their deer? They shoot just fine at the range, so what's the problem? Well, when it's time to shoot the trophy buck, the beam is off the 10-story building. The conscious mind is focused on results instead of performance.

COMPETITION

Competition Story—Match Rehearsals

Recently we coached the Canadian Forces Combat Shooting Team at Bisley, England. The CF hadn't sent a team for several years, and this team was their hope to get back into the combat shooting competition. The team was put together in a hurry, with most of the shooters unproven in local competitions, let alone an international event.

We didn't have much time to assess each shooter, and we wanted to see them perform under competition stress. Specifically, we wanted to weed out those "practice champions" from the group. We decided to do a short-form version of our five-step Service Rifle training program.

On Monday, Tuesday, and Wednesday of the training week, we worked on those things that, when done right, would give us the most return for the time. We didn't keep any record of scores; we only wanted them to shoot small groups, well centered on the target. We did this at close range, working to develop the positions that would be used. We eventually did this at the match distance with match targets.

Then on the Thursday and Friday of the training week, we shot a dress rehearsal of the actual competition. It was well known to everyone that the results of these rehearsals would be kept and used to validate their future employment on the team. This was the only time when scores were recorded and counted. Using this technique, the "practice champions" were quickly noted. We were then able to coach them for this specific problem and get them back onto the team.

The Zone

SECTION 4-5: THE UNAWARE

The Unaware

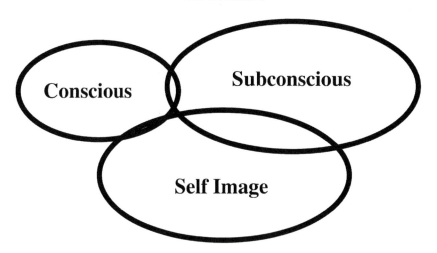

The "unaware" shooter gets in the bubble and never comes out. He is well-trained and has a good self-image, but he isn't alert to what is happening around him. He can shoot perfect shots, but he still loses points and matches.

Often, he will shoot well up to a point, and then he will sabotage his own results. He may arrive at the match without all his equipment so that he starts with a handicap that will give him a solid excuse for performing poorly. This is the shooter who misses a huge wind change or who, having seen the change, moves his sight in the wrong direction. Or he may cross-fire or shoot a no-shoot target. He does these things unintentionally but does them just the same. He won't see any of these things as personal sabotage but as bad luck or lack of training. He needs tools that develop the conscious powers.

The tools to help the unaware shooter develop his performance zone include those found in Chapter 5, "Tools to Increase Your Conscious Powers," as well as Chapter 8, "Advanced Tools—Your Powers Applied."

Military Story—Lee at Gettysburg

Commanding troops in battle has to be one of the most difficult jobs there is. No matter what decision you make it will likely cost lives, and there is always that element of luck that can go either way. That's why Napoleon said, "Let my good generals be lucky." But being aware of all the little details will improve the luck.

General Robert E. Lee at the Battle of Gettysburg made some major decisions without taking all the details into account. Initially, he decided to attack the Union's right flank. This was a logical tactic. He was thinking

> "You see, but you do not observe."
> —Sir Arthur Conan Doyle, writer (1859–1930)

> "Chance favors only the prepared mind."
> —Louis Pasteur, chemist (1822–1895)

> "Reality is that which, when you stop believing in it, doesn't go away."
> —Philip K. Dick, writer (1928–1982)

that the end of a defensive line would have minimum support and if he could turn the flank, he could "roll up" the Union line, attacking a small frontage. However, one of his commanders hesitated, giving the Union time to prepare defenses. Now, with the ground against them—having to attack uphill and through woods—this Confederate attack was defeated.

General Lee then decided to attack the Union left flank, thinking that if the Union had strength on its right, it may not have had time to strengthen its left. He was almost correct with this decision; there were troops in place but not in strength. Again, the ground wasn't in favor of the Confederates. The commander in charge originally wanted the attack to start from a position further to the Union's left, where the ground was more in his favor and where it would have been unexpected. General Lee insisted that it go according to his plan.

This attack went against a very determined Lt. Col. Joshua L. Chamberlain, who was put in a desperate do-or-die situation by his superiors. Lieutenant Colonel Chamberlain used the ground to his advantage and, almost out of ammo and outnumbered, he broke the Confederate's last attack by means of a bayonet charge.

General Lee now decided that if the Union had strength on its right and left flanks, it must be weak in the center. This set up what became known as Pickett's Charge. First, the Confederates used cannon fire to soften the target, not knowing that their bombardment was falling long, behind the Union line, and not producing the casualties they imagined. The infantry advance crossed a mile of open ground under direct fire of Union artillery and then met devastating Union rifle fire. The final battle for Gettysburg was lost.

General Lee seemed to be unaware that the two flank engagements were lost not because he went against superior strength but because he went against unfavorable ground. He then made decisions based on these incorrect assumptions. Had he been aware of the details, the battle—and the war—may well have ended differently.

The final irony at Gettysburg was that the Union forces, having found success, failed to pursue it. As the Confederate troops faltered, Union General George Meade hesitated to finish the battle and thus allowed them to withdraw to fight another day. Had General Meade been more aggressive in the moment, the Civil War may well have ended at Gettysburg, saving another two years of casualties. If only he had been aware.

Law-Enforcement Story—Waco

In law enforcement, there is a real and present danger for any officer if he loses situational awareness by getting mesmerized on a single suspect. The problem, of course, is that there may be other perpetrators nearby who are also dangerous. To counter this, law-enforcement training requires the officer to scan all around after each engagement. This breaks them out of their tunnel vision and "unaware" state and brings them to a situationally aware state.

In Waco, Texas, where officers were moving in on a suspected cult, they were sneaking and peaking around the buildings and eventually moved up onto the roof of the main building. Suddenly, shots ripped through the roof and the officers, after a moment's hesitation while they realized they were under fire from below, scrambled to safety. This was, perhaps, a moment of being in an "unaware" state. While these officers had most certainly been taught to scan, they probably didn't think of scanning all around, including up and down. Broad scan doesn't mean just in front of you. And of course, officers need to be aware that bullets can go through things and then hit you.

Hunter Story—The Buttonhook

In Africa it's a well-known fact that a wounded Cape buffalo will run to the thickest bush he can find. Once inside, he will do a buttonhook[5] back onto his trail and wait. It's also a well-known fact that professional hunters (PHs) don't allow their clients to track after a wounded buffalo. This is one of the most dangerous jobs that the professional guide must take on. With the client in a safe place, the PH picks up the trail, following tracks and blood in the dirt.

The Zone

It's as if the buffalo has the power of reason. Stopped just beside his own trail, he waits until the hunter comes by and attacks from an unexpected direction and almost always, because of the thick bush, from very close range. If our hunter, who is at times forced to crawl on his knees to get through the bush, becomes distracted or mesmerized by the trail he is following, he can find himself very quickly in a life-and-death situation with a one-ton enraged and determined beast. Professional hunters have been trampled and gored as a result of becoming unaware at just the wrong moment.

COMPETITION

Competition Story—The 300 Snap and the 500 Rapid

One of our closest and dearest friends is Capt. Steve Tibbetts. Steve and Keith served together as infantry officers in the same regiment. Steve is one of the best subconscious shots there are. We once saw him in the 300-meter snap match miss both of his sighters— not surprising since he had taken possession of the rifle just that day and this was the first he had ever fired it. So, he was on the verge of a disaster, having missed both sighters and not knowing where the rifle was shooting. On the first of 10 three-second exposures, he fired his shot at a spot in the backstop. By doing this, he could see from the splash that the rifle was shooting about 2 feet low. With just this information, he fired the next nine exposures holding off accordingly, hoping to put his shots on score. He ended up shooting nine bull's-eyes, ripping success from the jaws of disaster, and he scored a respectable 45 out of 50.

Because Steve is such a good shot, we use another one of his experiences as an example of why it's always important to stay aware. Steve was competing in the Canadian Forces Small Arms Competition and was in contention for the Queen's Medal. The Queen's Medal is awarded each year to the top shot in the Canadian Forces, and a couple years later Steve did win one. But this particular year he had just fired the 500-meter rapid-fire match and had a target irregularity. Since the target had acted not in accordance with the rules for this match, he was granted a reshoot. All reshoots were shot in accordance with match conditions, which included sighters. Steve would fire his reshoot on the left-most target. In those days the end target was normally not assigned to a shooter but was put up to receive any cross-fires from other shooting lanes. When Steve shot his sighters, the butt staff didn't put the cross-fire target up and Steve imprinted on shooting at the end target. When he fired his shots for score, the butts put all targets up, even though he was the only one firing. Unfortunately, Steve was so focused on firing his shots that he fired at the end target, which was the cross-fire target and consequently scored zero for his match.

In competition, just like combat, you need to be continually aware of what is going on around you.

SECTION 4-6: THE KNOW-IT-ALL

The Know-It-All

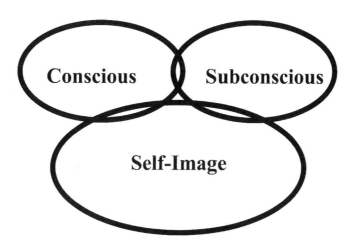

The "know-it-all" shooter has too much self-image for his capability. His self-image isn't supported by his skills. Large self-image is good as long as it's balanced by equal levels of concentration and subconscious skills.

This shooter can "talk the talk" but he hasn't yet done the work to be able to "walk the walk." Overconfidence is a trait we must avoid. Not only are know-it-alls not very pleasant to be around, their delusions prevent them from fixing their shortcomings. They don't think they need to learn anything, but actually they need both conscious and subconscious skill development.

The tools to help the know-it-all increase his conscious and subconscious circles and thereby develop his performance zone include those found in Chapter 5, "Tools to Increase Your Conscious Powers," and Chapter 6, "Tools to Increase Your Subconscious Powers," as well as Chapter 8, Advanced Tools—Your Powers Applied."

Military Story—Coaching the Elite

Shortly after we started our business of teaching marksmanship, we were hired by one of the Canadian Forces elite groups to put on a three-day course. We were to focus on the marksmanship needs of their snipers.

In and of itself, this was a straightforward course: an easy topic for us, and one we had done many times before. However, this time we had to admit that we were a little intimidated. While we had trained many top shots, most of them were top shots in world competition. These guys were experienced operations people and had "been there and done that." It had been a lot of years since we had "been there, done that." We wondered what we could possibly

"Real knowledge is to know the extent of one's ignorance."
—Confucius, philosopher (551 BC–479 BC)

"Egotism is the anesthetic that dulls the pain of stupidity."
—Frank Leahy, coach (1908–1973)

"Criticism comes easier than craftsmanship."
—Zeuxis, artist (c. 464 BC–?)

teach them that they didn't already know.

The first morning we spent in the classroom teaching our version of the marksmanship principles. We knew these guys would have heard about marksmanship principles before, but perhaps they would get a little something more from the way we presented them.

During the morning, the topic somehow got onto how tactical officers often have a "we're better than everyone else" attitude. We mentioned that we had often seen this among the police tactical officers that we had worked with and that we understood it. When you spend so much of your training time doing things that others only dream about doing and you're getting good at these skills, you're bound to feel a lot lucky and a little superior. We were somewhat taken aback when the senior person on the course replied, "Yeah, well there's one difference between us and them—they just think they're good while we are good." We looked at each other and smiled. We had heard this before, and from what turned out to be "mere mortals."

Later, we were on the range waiting for our class to arrive for the practical part of the day's training. We were very impressed with what the class did when they arrived. The senior member got everyone to gather around him and give him an opinion of the wind speed. He then got out a handheld wind meter and confirmed what the wind was really doing. We mentioned to them

"Better to be ignorant of a matter than half know it."
—Publilius Syrus, writer (1st century BC)

"It is what we learn after we think we know it all that counts."
—John Wooden, coach (1910~)

"Education is a progressive discovery of our own ignorance."
—Will Durant, writer (1885–1981)

"The greatest obstacle to discovery is not ignorance—it is the illusion of knowledge."
—Daniel J. Boorstin, writer (1914–2004)

"The greater the ignorance the greater the dogmatism."
—Sir William Osler (1849–1919), physician

what outstanding training this was and to certainly keep doing it.

We then got everyone on the firing mound and explained the first training drill. It was to be a simple "shoot a group" exercise so we could get an idea what they, their rifle system, and the ammo were doing. We were using our own grouping targets, which had the simple aiming point of a 1-inch black square. Everyone was told to hold center of visible mass on the black square, and we talked them through the principles we had covered in class that morning.

After everyone shot, we went downrange to the targets to analyze the results. Most groups weren't acceptable to our standard, and none were the little "knot holes" that we expected. Some of the groups weren't centered on the point of aim, and we made suggestions as to the sight adjustments needed to get properly zeroed. We then went back to the firing line to coach them through another grouping exercise.

We noticed that some of the class members made the suggested zero adjustments while others didn't. Some muttered that their groups were "good enough" or were "close enough" to do the job and that there was no reason to do this again. We pointed out that a simple zeroing error at 100 meters would be exaggerated as the range increased and that "close enough" should never be "good enough" at 100 meters. It should be as exact as the equipment will allow. We pointed out that the rifles and ammo they were using were both capable of better groups.

Secrets of Mental Marksmanship

But the one thing that we really noticed was that these guys were no better than the folks they were criticizing. We had seen groups of this size with all of our previous sniper courses and had seen them improve with our coaching.

On the next group, we could see an improvement in those who were ready to accept the fact that they could do better. Some zeros were better centered, while one in particular didn't respond as expected. Again we suggested sight adjustments for a proper zero.

By the third group, most were improving and getting zeroed. Still, a couple of groups were quite large, and one was still not moving in accordance with the sight adjustments. Having watched the shooters on the firing line, we decided that the large groups were a result of flinching, and the best exercise to fix this would be our trademark "live and dry" exercise. The senior member laughed out loud and scoffed at the thought that any of them were flinching. We suggested that if that were so, then this exercise would show it, and if it weren't so, then this was the best exercise to fix it.

In this exercise the students are paired. One fires while the other loads the rifle for each shot. The guy loading the rifle selects either a live round or a dummy round and does so in such a manner that the shooter doesn't know whether he is shooting live or dry. Then the shooter fires the shot. If he isn't a flincher, he gets lots of good practice proving that is so. If he is a flincher and he thinks his rifle is loaded, he will flinch. If it isn't loaded, his sins won't be covered up with recoil. Once we know the shooter has a problem, his partner tries to trick him into thinking every shot is dry, until he finally gets him to fire a live shot without flinching. The idea for all shooters is to fire every shot as they would if they knew it was a dry shot.

We got all the students to gather around to watch a demonstration of this exercise. The senior member was selected to be the shooter for the demonstration. We talked the class through the procedure, step by step, as it was important that everyone understood it in order the get the most from the exercise. The senior member got into a prone position with his rifle resting on a bipod. We suggested that he dry-fire a few shots before the start of the exercise. We weren't surprised to see that he was flinching even on the dry shots, and it only got worse when he didn't know if the rifle was loaded. We tried to coach him on ways to improve this and be a better shot but gave up after he kept insisting that he wasn't flinching.

Since we weren't going to be able to help the senior member with his group size, we decided to have a look at the individual who had a rifle system that wasn't adjusting as expected. We shot through several groups trying to solve this problem. He was shooting reasonably sized groups but always someplace other than where we expected them to be. We analyzed our hearts out, but the solution came only after we confirmed that he was holding center of visible mass on the little black square. He told us that he always shot better groups when he held on a corner of the black square and that he was holding on a different corner for each group. So now that we knew which corner he was holding on, it was easy to get his rifle to zero.

The senior member complained that he could shoot a better group if he had a better trigger. Several other members mentioned that they didn't like the trigger either. We asked what the problem was with the trigger, and they stated that there was too much travel before the rifle fired. We mentioned that these were fine European rifles and had a reputation of always working well. It was the look on everyone's face that answered our suspicion when we asked if they had two-stage triggers. We explained that a two-stage trigger has travel before it gets firm and stops. Then with just a bit more pressure it fires. It's designed this way to let the shooter take up most of the trigger weight on the first stage, then settle on the detailed sight picture and fire the shot with what now feels like a light trigger pull. It seems that everyone was pulling the trigger in one long sweep, pulling through both stages as if they were one.

We did some additional dry training on the proper trigger manipulation and clearly saw an improvement in the size of the next group. All except the senior member, who wouldn't enjoy a better group until he admitted to and fixed his flinch.

So now we aren't intimidated by any of our students. They all learn something from us, some more than others. The irony is that the ones who learn the least are the ones who really need to learn the most.

The Zone

POLICE

Law-Enforcement Story—The Booby Traps

This is a sad story for us to tell, but it's one that needs telling if for no other reason than so others can benefit from its awful cost.

On our Police Sniper 5 course, we have a final exercise that has our students navigating across country, making a shot, and then navigating back to the command post. This is a simple exercise that involves many of the skills that were taught during the course. There are many trails and rough roads throughout the 1,000-acre exercise area, and to keep the students from using them, we set up simple tripwire booby traps. These are made with a rat trap and tripwire, and they give off a loud noise when tripped. We use the scenario that the roads are booby-trapped because there are marijuana growing operations in the area, but the point is to discourage the students from using the trails for all of the reasons you should not use trails. This point was clearly made to all students.

The exercise went very well, with each of the students arriving in the target area, making a successful shot, and leaving, all without being seen and without setting off any traps. The last student was a bit late, but not to the point where it would create a problem. He had arrived on target and made his shot and was now navigating out of the area. It was then that it became a problem . . .

We heard one of the booby traps go off. It was our plan to be the last ones to arrive at the command post, traveling by means of the booby-trapped road so we could deactivate them. And then we heard the next booby trap go off . . . and then the next one . . . and so on all the way back to the command post.

We gathered all the students in the classroom for a debriefing of their operation. We asked the usual intelligence questions: Did you see anyone in the area? Did you get a description? Did you come across any roads or trails not marked on your map? Did you see any signs of the grow ops within your area of operation? Did anyone follow a road or trail? Did anyone trip a booby trap?

It was, of course, after these last two questions that we expected a particular officer to admit to his actions. But he didn't. He just looked away and said nothing. In fact, when asked specifically, he lied and said he hadn't been on any trails and didn't set off any booby traps. Only after he was challenged with the evidence did he finally admit to his potentially deadly transgression.

Keith put on his sergeant major voice and became, in most certain terms, the chief instructor. He had seen firsthand the effects of booby traps in Vietnam, and his experience wouldn't be lost on these young tactical officers.

But, we knew it was all lost as far as this particular officer was concerned when he responded with the remark, "This was a stupid exercise for police. We'll never be expected to deal with booby traps! What's the point of traveling through the bush when there are perfectly good trails to walk on?"

Well, the saddest part of this whole story was the irony of its conclusion. This young officer was killed by a booby trap when he approached a grow ops using a trail. 'Nuff said . . .

HUNTING

Hunter Story—I Always Get My Deer

One of the strangest comments we have ever heard from hunters is this one: "I can't hit a target, but I sure can hit a deer." This is the hunter who scoffs at others who want to confirm their zeroes before the hunt, saying, "I don't never zero my gun 'cause I can't never hit one of those paper targets, but I always get my deer."

As a kid growing up, Keith heard this many times at the hunt camps and, not really understanding what it meant, was in awe of the hunter who had honed his survival and marksmanship skills to the point where he could only hit game.

It was only after Keith had more experience as a hunter and marksman that he noticed that, although these kinds of hunters did almost always get their deer, they seldom got it cleanly. They almost never had a story of shooting their deer where "it fell right there where I shot it" or "it went only 30 yards and then piled up."

No, their stories were generally more drawn out and included descriptions like, "Toughest damn deer I ever shot. I hit him solid with my first shot and then had to track him for four hours. Hit him several more times before he finally fell." It would be several days later, during the skinning of the animal, that Keith would notice that there was only one wound channel, and it would be in the leg where an artery had been nicked, or there was a hit somewhere in the gut.

Sometimes the deer would get away, never to be seen again, and the deer he finally got to justify his comment "but I always get my deer" was the second, third, or fourth deer he shot at during the season.

The reason these hunters never shot at a paper target was because these kinds of targets were usually smaller than the kill zone on a deer. They were such bad shots that they just simply couldn't hit it. A deer was very much bigger, and if the deer eventually bled to death from a wound in its leg, well, he got his deer, didn't he? And it just goes to show you that he was right—he didn't need to zero his rifle, and he did always get his deer.

COMPETITION

Competition Story—The Van Doo Cradle

A couple of years ago we were the coaches for the Canadian Forces Combat Shooting team competing in Bisley, England. We always enjoy the opportunity to work with the soldiers, sailors, and airmen, hoping that what we teach will stand by them one day. It's also an outstanding opportunity to meet with coaches from other countries and a chance to pick up new ideas and techniques.

One of the many things we teach is the variety of positions shooters can use. We're always watching for modifications to the basic positions, giving the new variant a name and then teaching it as an option so that we have a position to accommodate any body type.

One of these is a modified sitting position that we got from a shooter with Canada's French-speaking regiment, the Royal 22nd Regiment. They have a nickname: "Van Doos." This, of course, is a literal pronunciation for "22" in French, which is *vingt deux*. Thus the position became known as the "Van Doo Cradle."

This is a very unorthodox position, and it's very effective. The shooter sits cross-legged at 90 degrees to the line of fire. He then cradles the rifle by putting the crook of the elbow of the forward arm around the magazine and the butt in the crook of the elbow of the rear arm. He then rests everything on his knees and relaxes forward into the position. Now, he must look through the sight from above.

As we said, it's unorthodox, but it is effective. It's the steadiest of all the sitting positions. Many of our students use this position in the sitting match at the National Service Conditions Championship. From 200 meters, the shooter has 30 seconds to go from standing alert to sitting, fire five rounds at one target, change magazines, and fire five rounds at another target. All of the competitors who use this position can, with ease, get into it and aim the rifle by looking through the scope from the top. They marvel at how steady the position is, how forgiving it is, and how many good hits they get with it.

So, this particular year we're in Bisley, and most of the team is using the Van Doo Cradle. One of the coaching staff of the Australian army rifle team sees our guys using this position and comes straight over to speak with us. He starts the conversation, as the Australians are famous for, by getting right to the point: "That's the silliest position I have ever seen, and it can't possibly work. You have to look through the sight from above, and it will certainly screw up your zero. It just can't work."

We were both taken aback a bit by such a challenge to something that was so proven by experience to us. We explained this and assured the Aussie coach that we wouldn't teach a position unless we had first tried it and were satisfied it had enough history to be proven effective. We also suggested that he simply look at the scores the guys were getting when using this position.

None of our points or reasoning were getting through, and our Australian colleague was clearly becoming upset at our insistence of something that was just "wrong" to him. We tried yet again to give examples of its effectiveness, citing the fact that we use the position ourselves when we compete in these matches.

That was all our friend could handle. He became very agitated, veins sticking out and eyes popping. We decided that it was all right if he felt this position couldn't possibly work. It meant that our team didn't have to go against his team using this most effective position. They're tough enough to beat as it is.

SECTION 4-7: BIGGER CIRCLES

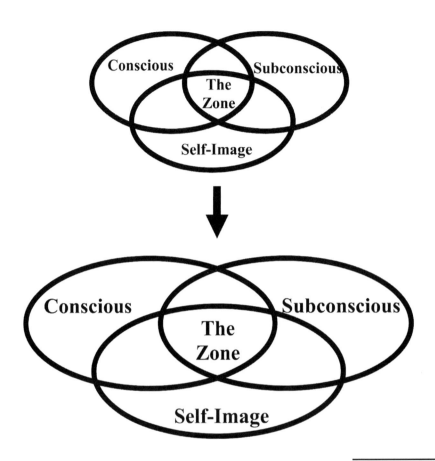

How do we beat someone who is performing well in the zone? Make your circles bigger! Work on all three elements (conscious, subconscious, and self-image) and make your zone bigger and more powerful.

The tools to help you develop your performance zone include those found in Chapter 5, "Tools to Increase Your Conscious Powers," Chapter 6, "Tools to Increase Your Subconscious Powers," and Chapter 7, "Tools to Increase the Power of Your Self-Image," as well as Chapter 8, "Advanced Tools—Your Powers Applied."

Military Story—Training for a Gunfight
The following is an excerpt from Keith's story, "Only Hits Count."[6]

I believe there are two training areas that lead up to a gunfight. First we're taught the desired skills and given the opportunity to practice under a coached environment. Once the skills are learned and embedded in our subconscious mind as a reactive impulse, we must learn to conduct the skills under stress, again in a coached environment. No matter the type of

"The number of things the shooter must be consciously aware of when he fires a shot are an indication of the state of his training. Performance is generally best when active concentration is needed on only one phase of the shooting act."
—Gary Anderson, Olympic gold medalist (1939~)

pressure we put on ourselves during training, it isn't the same as we feel in competition. In competition, we take our skills out and expose them to strangers, with our honor and reputation at stake. We place it on the line against others who have trained their own way and who want to beat you as much as you want to beat them. In the end the trophy is secondary. What the competitor wants is for everyone there to know that he is the top gun, the one who beat everyone there today. If he can successfully handle this stress and the training has proven to be effective and the equipment performed reliably, then he is better prepared for the next level—the gunfight. While it's true that what you feel in competition won't be the same as you feel in a gunfight, if you're afraid to take your skills to a competition, I can hardly imagine that you're ready to take them to a gunfight.

In a competition, as in a gunfight, the focus must always be on performance and not on the end results. If you're thinking about dying going into a gunfight, then your mind won't be clear to picture the right thoughts to which the subconscious mind will react. As well, your ability to flow and react to a changing situation will be dulled. Survival in a gunfight is doing the right things a certain way to put the odds in your favor.

When referring to competition, we must be very specific. The precision required for an Olympic-style competition may not give you much in return

"A lot of these things you can't really teach. All you can do is create a situation where if people want to learn they can. The best teachers I ever met were the horses themselves. You find a lot of folk have opinions, but if it's facts you want you're better off going to the horse."
—Nicholas Evans in
The Horse Whisperer

"Only the mediocre are always at their best."
—Jean Giraudoux,
writer (1882–1944)

"Excellence can be obtained if you care more than others think is wise; risk more than others think is safe; dream more than others think is practical; expect more than others think is possible."
—Author unknown

toward a gunfight, but many of the practical type of matches could. If they don't, then find a competition that does, or invent one that will test your skills against others with something at stake.

There seem to be three areas of shooting being discussed: the long-range battle, the assault, and fighting through the objective, or close-quarter combat. Certainly all of these types of shooting must be looked at separately, as they each call for specific skills. One shouldn't scoff at a competition that provides effective training just because it doesn't relate to the style of shooting that one holds holy. The military should be training and practicing their infantry units in all three.

The Canadian military conducts its Canadian Forces Small Arms Competition (CFSAC) each year, but only with great difficulty. Many senior officers scoff at it as "belly shooting" and not relevant to combat shooting. Many others and myself have fought a holding battle trying to point out its value. Our current [in 1999, when this story was originally written] Chief of Defense Staff is a shooter who understands the benefits of these competitions, and this does much to bolster our cause. These matches practice many excellent battle-shooting skills. We shoot at all ranges from 100 to 500 meters, which covers the long-range battle. We shoot rapid and snap shooting, which relates well to defensive situations as well as some advances. We must run and then engage targets from several positions, which relates to the assault. In one match we must run 100 meters and, from the standing position at a range of 100 meters, engage head-sized snap targets that are exposed for three seconds. This one is a good start to the close-quarter battle, although I would like to see more of Pat Rogers' techniques worked into the match conditions.[7] These matches practice some basic battle-shooting skills that are common to all elements of the military but do require the units to carry out operation-specific training.

I shoot in every kind of shooting competition that I can. In conventional rifle matches, I learn and practice wind-reading skills, apply marksmanship principles under stress, test my training techniques, test the equipment I will be using in combat, test my ability to perform on demand, test my physical and mental stamina, establish and confirm zeros at known ranges, etc. You cannot practice too much, provided it's the right practice, in preparation for the gunfight.

Law-Enforcement Story—The Look in His Eyes
Many of our stories come from our students, and this one is no exception. It illustrates the need for situational awareness, attention to detail, and the ability to fire effective shots under stress.

Jeff is a retired police officer and an outstanding IPSC competition shot. He came on one of our police sniper courses to refine his marksmanship skills in the area of precision sniper shooting. He was honing his skills since he had already applied for a contract in "the sandbox" and felt sure he would likely get the chance to use these skills in an operational environment.

As it turns out he had many exciting stories to tell, but there is one that is most interesting. It needed more than just marksmanship skills to live through this one.

Because of his sniper skills, on this day he was tasked to provide "watch over" at a checkpoint that was manned and under the control of the Iraqi police. They weren't doing a very good job at controlling the traffic, and many vehicles and pedestrians simply bypassed the checkpoint without being properly searched.

Jeff was positioned behind a large, armored Ford pickup truck and noticed a black car carefully making its way through the checkpoint without being stopped. It very slowly turned toward Jeff's position and continued its approach.

Jeff said his police training kicked in, and he was immediately suspicious. At first he was unable to see the driver clearly because of a glare on the windshield. But his suspicion was confirmed when he eventually got to see the face of the driver. He said the driver had a look that he had seen before. Years ago he had confronted a criminal who was intent on killing a cop, and now he saw that same look on the face of this driver. Jeff opened fire on the driver and the car blew up.

The explosion was close enough that Jeff received minor injuries, but

"Next to excellence is the appreciation of it."
—William Makepeace Thackeray, writer (1811–1863)

"It takes a long time to bring excellence to maturity."
—Publilius Syrus, writer (1st century BC)

"The Master [urges him] to go further than he himself has done, and 'climb on the shoulders of his teacher.'"
—Eugen Herrigel in *Zen in the Art of Archery*

"Of that ecstatic moment in sport, Yuri Vlasov, world-champion Russian weightlifter, said, 'There is no more precious moment in life than this, the white moment, and you will work very hard for years just to taste it again.'"
—Charles A. Garfield in *Peak Performance*

it could have been much worse had he not had the situational awareness to notice the car in the first place. Or had he not had the attention to detail to see and recognize the intent of the driver. Or had he not had his extensive competition experience, firing many thousands of shots under pressure and making every one count. All these skills and abilities were rolled into one smooth and effective reaction that ultimately saved the lives of himself and his colleagues.

HUNTING

Hunter Story—The Rock Hunt

One of the points that we try to get across on our hunter marksmanship course is that the firing of the shot should be the easiest part of the whole hunt. Getting packed into camp, surviving the conditions, and packing the game out can all be hard work. But the firing of the shot should be the easiest part.

To make it this way, you need to work on each of your circles, making each one bigger and more developed. You need to analyze each of these areas and see which one needs the work and then develop a training plan to move you in that direction.

When it comes to making the shot, the conscious mind has to be aware of many things. Is this the animal I want to take—is it the right size, does it have the right rack, is it an ethical shot? Is it a safe shot—are there any other hunters, buildings, or vehicles behind the game? Is the range within my point blank zero—do I have to hold a bit higher or lower? What is the wind doing—is it a factor?

One of the best ways to train this is to go out on a "rock hunt." First you must find a safe place to do this. There must be enough space both to shoot shots and deal with any ricochet that might come off the rock. (We generally find that with modern high-velocity cartridges, once a bullet hits a solid rock, there is very little of it left to ricochet. Still, it must be considered when choosing an area.) Then you walk around the area and look for targets. As soon as you see a target rock, you must start to make decisions. Make a decision as to whether it's a suitable target and within your capability range, what position to use, and how much time you have to make these decisions.

The "self-image circle" comes with confidence. You need to shoot your rifle enough to have absolute faith in its reliability. You know the zero is always on. You know the ammo shoots within standard in this rifle. The rifle feels good and you like to carry it. Spend time at the range shooting targets so that it's "just like you" to hit anything that you can see. Then further develop this by going on rock hunts.

And then there is the subconscious mind. Here is where the actual firing of the shot takes place. You must focus on establishing and holding the correct sight picture, and when it's correct, the rifle will fire. This is best trained by using the rifle. Fire lots of shots both dry and live, and develop the ability to fire shots subconsciously. Dry-fire at home in your basement and live-fire when you get a chance to go to the range. Then further develop this by going on rock hunts.

"The less effort, the faster and more powerful you will be."
—Bruce Lee, martial artist (1940–1973)

"Competition . . . tests, demands, and develops all your capacities; physical skill is only one part of the game."
—Dan Millman in *Body Mind Mastery*

"The psychology of competing is not that we train to win . . . we train to perform well, and we compete to show that we can."
—Linda K. Miller & Keith A. Cunningham in *How to Build a Training Plan . . . That Works!*

The Zone

Make the firing of the shot the easiest thing about your hunt. If you think you get buck fever when shooting at game that is eating grass and will run away as soon as it sees you, you might want to take a second thought about hunting truly dangerous game. Do yourself a favor and train for it. Make the firing of the shot the easiest part.

COMPETITION

Competition Story—Becoming a Champion
The following is an excerpt from Linda's story called "Snatch the Pebble."[8]

On the morning of the third day, I finally won a match outright. I had a good shoot. The young cadet I was shooting with had a very good shoot for his capability, but all I really remember was the increasing disbelief in his voice as he called, "V-bull, your fifth shot is a V-bull." By the time we had finished, I had a 75 (a possible) with 13 V-bulls. The cadet shook his head and shook my hand. I smiled and thanked him for a good match. A very good match indeed.

After lunch, Keith had a shoot-off with Jamie Feehan to determine the winner of the Brassey Match. We walked with Jamie up the range road to the 500-yard firing line. Jamie was clearly excited, talking in bursts, striding rather than strolling, and remembering a previous occasion that Keith had bested him in a shoot-off. I thought at the time that Jamie was developing a self-fulfilling prophecy. And so it was, for Keith won the shoot-off and the match.

After the shoot-off, we walked back down the range road together. Jamie shared some of his personal thoughts on his own behavior. "I'm a high-strung person. When I have to shoot a match, I get wound up. I'm always this way, and especially in shoot-offs." We challenged him to change his thinking. We asked him to consider saying, "When I shoot, sometimes I am excitable. Sometimes I am not. It's my choice, and right now I choose to get down to business."

Finally, after two-and-a-half days, nine matches, and 95 record shots, it was time for the Lieutenant Governor's finals. I still had that soft, warm calmness about me. I looked for my squadded position, and it was on the second firing point. "What the heck am I doing way up there?" I said to myself.

"Well, you're in second place, you know," one of my fellow competitors said. I was surprised, first because I didn't realize I had asked my question out loud, and then because I didn't realize that I was anywhere near the top of the heap.

As I walked along behind the firing points, I looked to see who else had made the finals. I was delighted to see a couple of the young female cadets who I'd enjoyed shooting and talking with during the matches. I wished them well and carried on down the line. As I approached the top end of the line, where the match contenders were, I could feel the tension in the air. Like electricity, it zapped me and my heart jumped. "Okay," I thought, "I always have a little stage fright before a good performance. That's normal for me."

I have always had a moment of panic before I have to perform. When I was a kid, it was the piano recitals and the public speaking. In my line of business (management consulting), it still happens often. Just before I deliver that final presentation to the client, my heart feels like someone has reached inside my chest and is squeezing it to death. Even in my avocation (speaking about, and teaching courses in, marksmanship), I will get at least a fluttery feeling in my heart just before I start.

Over the years, with a lot of practice, I have learned that it's okay. I always recover. The moment I start into my performance, the butterflies are gone and there is only one thing on my mind: the performance itself. I now look on the butterflies as a technique my body uses to inform me that I care a great deal about how this event goes, and that it's with me all the way to stay engaged and energized and focused.

As luck would have it, Jamie Feehan (the one who was in the shoot-off for the Brassey) was paired with me. If there was a match that he could get excited about, this was it! During the course of the match, Jamie's ammunition jammed in his rifle and he had to remove spent casings with the aid of a cleaning rod. After the first jam, he was starting to lose his cool, and he lost a point on the next shot. This continued for three shots in a row. Then Jamie did something extraordinary. He decided not to let the ammo jams get to him. He decided to take full responsibility for all of his shots. He took control of himself and the situation. He finished the match like a champion.

My first sighter was a bull with 4 minutes of wind, and my second sighter was a bull with 5 minutes of wind. I played the next shot for a V-bull, and lost the call . . . I lost the point. I played the next several, trying to get V-bulls, and shot only bulls. Somewhere during that sequence, I realized that we had only 1-minute variation in the wind. I thought about the odds of calling the changes correctly—can I really perceive a half-minute of wind at 1,000 yards correctly to get the shot centered nicely in the V-bull, or should I just set the sights for the mean of the wind settings and shoot perfect shots until something changes?

I decided that I could stand to have fewer V-bulls, as long as I got the points. I set my sights for the mean wind condition and settled in to shoot perfect shots. The mirage wasn't reliable, so I was watching flags to make sure nothing changed in the conditions that would require a change in strategy.

I was particularly interested in one of the flags that wasn't quite halfway down range. It was quite sensitive, it seemed; possibly because it was one of the few flags that didn't have any trees or berms protecting it from the wind conditions. It would dance around quite a bit, but the angle didn't really change much unless there was a real condition change. And the best indicator for what the condition changes were (when there were any) was the red safety flag on the top of the backstop—a little hard to see accurately at 1,000 yards, but it seemed very truthful. There were several times when I would have changed my sight setting if it had been my turn to shoot. But by the time it was my turn again, my key flag was back to its flippant little dance, and the condition was back to "my" condition.

I'm not sure whether it takes more courage to change your sights or to leave them alone. When I first started in this long-range game, I used to challenge myself to make the changes. The first few bold changes really took courage. But I had gotten over it in South Africa, where all the changes had to be bold. This match was a different story. It took a great deal of self-discipline to leave the sights alone.

I finished the match without dropping another point, and while I picked up only three V-bulls, I was well satisfied with a score of 74 out of 75 at 1,000 yards.

My mound partner, Jamie, had dropped only one point after he made his courageous decision to shoot like a champion no matter the adversity. And he finished with a 71 (and five V-bulls), moving him up from seventh to sixth overall.

When I got off the mound, Keith was still shooting. I watched his last few shots, confident that he would win the match. I didn't know any of the point spreads; I just knew that (going into the finals) he had been first, I had been second, and the rest came after that.

Keith finished and immediately came over to me. "What did you shoot?" he said. I was surprised at his question. Usually he would ask me, "How did it go?" or "How did you shoot?"

I thought for a minute and then realized that he wanted to know my score! I stammered, "Seventy-four and something. Well, seventy-four, anyway."

He looked at me and said, "Well, I think you've got the match." I said, "Well, it's possible; 74 is a good score at 1,000 yards. But there are a lot of good shooters here, and the conditions could have given up a 75." (As it turned out, I had the second highest score in the field, having been edged by Peter Westlake with a 74—and seven V-bulls—which moved him up from eighth to third overall.)

"No," he said, "I think you may have won the match."

"The whole thing?" I couldn't quite process the information.

I had no idea what the point spreads were of the competitors who were trying to catch me, but I didn't really know whether my 74 was a good score or a great score for the conditions. "Well, what did you shoot?" I asked, thinking that Keith's score would give me a good idea of what a "good score" would be off that line. He said, "A 71."

We spent a couple of minutes doing the math. I had come ahead of him, by a point. Keith congratulated me warmly, and I remember feeling very strange about having pulled ahead of him. I had won a few lesser matches, even a couple of aggregates ahead of him. But this was the Provincials! The prized Lieutenant Governor's medal!

This was the championship I had helped *him* win in that first year I had known him.

Keith had encouraged me to start into Target Rifle.

Keith had built me a .223/556 rifle first so that I wouldn't be blown away by recoil. Then he had built me a .308/762 so that I could compete to go to Bisley. When we realized that I couldn't use hot enough loads in the old Remington 788 action, Keith had built me a whole new rifle based on a MacLennan action. Keith had built me the best rifle in the world.

Keith had taught me everything about Target Rifle. He taught me to take advantage of my smallbore skills. He taught me about shooting long-range. He taught me about reading the wind. He taught me about using graphs and the Canadian "Plot-o-Matic." He taught me to have confidence in my observations, courage in my sight settings, and conviction in my decisions.

Together we had refined the use of performance-oriented goals. We developed an outstanding method for doing performance analysis. We worked together on understanding self-talk and changing our own habits and behaviors. Keith had done everything he could to keep me interested, to help me progress, and to focus my attention on the skills and behaviors of a master.

He had given me everything that he had to offer. He never held back. He had never reserved information or encouragement. He had competed

"One machine can do the work of fifty ordinary men. No machine can do the work of one extraordinary man."
—Elbert Hubbard, writer and philosopher (1856–1915)

"Train half for yourself and half for your partner."
—Jigoro Kano, founder of Judo (1860–1938)

"Maximum efficiency with minimum effort."
—Jigoro Kano, founder of Judo (1860–1938)

fairly and squarely with me on the line, but he had never been competitive off the range.

I felt two strong feelings as I realized I had come in ahead of him at this championship. The first was that I was proud of myself for being able to apply all that I had been given, all that I had learned, and rise to the top of the list. The second was that I was awed by just how completely generous Keith had been in sharing all he could with someone who could ultimately beat him. I felt that I had snatched the pebble from the master's hand, and that was proof that he was indeed a fine master.

Just as he and I realized I had squeaked in ahead of him, the rest of the competitors figured out that they hadn't caught up with me. If the official stats version agreed with us, I had indeed won the match.

I wasn't sure whether I should celebrate or wait for the official version. I decided that I would kill some time by packing my kit. I heard a lot of excited conversation down the range around the scoreboard. I wondered if I would be seen as ungracious if I didn't go down to investigate; just in case I really had won, it would look better if I showed some interest. And of course, if I hadn't won, I certainly wanted to know who to congratulate.

By the time I had walked down to the scoreboard, the official stats version was in. I had won. The coveted ride in the sedan chair was mine! I realized at that moment that I had had a dream about riding in the sedan chair and had felt the hard wood against my back. I was swarmed with congratulations, and I remember Wordy Price saying, "My Lord, you've won the whole thing!"

The weather had cooled, and I had thrown on a

jacket. As I was about to get into the sedan chair, Jim Bullock whispered to me, "Do you really want all the pictures to record you in history wearing a camouflage jacket?" What an incredibly thoughtful thing to say! I realized then that this was a moment in history, the history of the Ontario Rifle Association. I had joined a venerable group of shooters. And I was very proud to be counted among them.

Keith commandeered the leading position on the sedan chair rail, at my right-hand side. It seemed entirely fitting to me. Later, the pictures would show that my other carriers changed often, but Keith was always there. I remember feeling like I was floating across the range and down the road to the prize presentation area, smiling like the Queen of England and looking down occasionally to make sure Keith was still there.

Finally, I truly understood the honor of being chaired off the range on the shoulders of your fellow competitors. Honestly, when I was first introduced to fullbore shooting, I thought it a somewhat quaint custom. But I had failed to appreciate the recognition implied by having those who have won before, and those who will win in the future, pay respect to today's champion.

When we arrived at the presentation area, I was told that I was the first female ever to win the championship. I thought to myself, "What a difference between 'top female' and 'first woman.'"

I overheard one of the female cadets say, "I shot with her!" and it was at that moment that I realized the importance of this win. While it's a little strange to think of myself as a symbol, for those young ladies, I symbolized an achievement they could aspire to. When I was later asked whether it would be alright to engrave "First Lady" alongside my name on the bronze plaque that would be attached to the sedan chair, I was quick to assure the match organizers that it would please me enormously.

Many people asked me how Keith felt about me winning this match. My answer is simple: "Keith is a champion. He always shoots to win. He wanted to win this match, like any other he competes in. But, if he is destined to come second, there is no other person he would choose to come first than me." In fact, Keith won just about every match during these Provincial Championships, and I took First Expert in almost as many.

But that coveted Lieutenant Governor's medal was mine.

And now the game has changed. I'll continue to enjoy every match, every shot, I shoot . . . but now that I have tasted the pleasure of being a champion, I thirst for more.

Out of all of this, the big winner is Keith. Now, when Keith wins he is the champion, and when I win he is the master.

And I can take pleasure in having snatched the pebble until the next contest.

The Zone

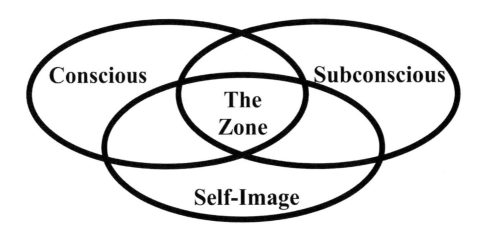

In some people's terminology, the "zone" or the "ideal performance state" is described as "success." Anthony Robbins, author of *Unlimited Power*, has spent considerable effort in modeling successful people. He says that:

➢ Successful people know what they want (have a clear picture).
➢ They take action.
➢ They assess the results of those actions.
➢ If necessary, they change their actions until they produce the desired result.

It's easy to picture these steps as the framework for a successful training session. The shooter has a clear picture of the quality of holding pattern he wants and the elegance of the subconscious shot release. The shooter changes his position and balance and focus and timing . . . and keeps trying until all of the elements of firing a perfect shot are produced simultaneously.

The basis of Robbins' approach is that we control what we think. He cites the science of neuro-linguistic programming as both the proof and explanation that this is so. NLP has mainly been used in therapy to help people change destructive thinking patterns. However, it's the same NLP that shooters use to model positive images and positive behaviors to fire a perfect shot, regardless of the conditions (internal emotions or external challenges). Most shooters would agree that they weren't born with the image of the perfect sight picture; they planted the image in their own brains, and they consciously project it every time they shoot. This is NLP applied.

Robbins asks the reader if he's ever been in that magical state where he could do no wrong . . . and then asks if the reader has ever been in that state where everything he touches turns to mud.

He says that the difference is the neuro-psychological state that you're in. And he says that you can control what state you're in. He says that successful people can put themselves into a state that supports them in their achievements. This is also known as an "ideal performance state."

So how do they do it? Robbins suggests that there are two components that they control: the first is their internal representation of the situation, and the second is their physiology. So, a successful shooter sees the competition situation as an opportunity to be the best he can be (internal representation), and his body language projects confidence, ease, and intensity (physiology).

The important thing to remember is that your internal representation (how you see things) is only a guideline to reality. It's your way of representing reality, much as a map represents a physical reality of roads and towns. The key point is that you choose your own representation, and if you're going to be a successful person, you need to choose one that supports your ability to achieve. Successful people are consistently able to access an empowering inner state.

The importance of state isn't just how you feel about the world and your current situation in it. The importance of state is that when you're in one, you access behaviors that you have modeled with that particular state. For example, some people believe that if they feel "butterflies" before a shooting match or any other event in their lives, they are nervous, scared, and panicky, and so believing it, they become those things. Linda decided years ago, when piano recitals and public speaking were her challenges, that butterflies simply meant that her body was marshalling forces and that every part of her was prepared to focus and deliver. For her, the butterflies state became an empowering one, because from it, she was now able to access behaviors that would help her achieve her aim.

Robbins says that if we can take control of our own communication within ourselves, we can produce outstanding results. He says that the most effective managers, coaches, and parents are people who can represent and project successful models, even in the face of challenging (even hopeless) situations.

Your beliefs can limit you or they can empower you. Some of the most memorable people of all time are people who changed our beliefs, whether they were religious leaders or explorers or scientists.

The first step to excellence is the realization that we choose our beliefs. And you can choose beliefs that limit you or you can choose beliefs that empower you. Our beliefs originate with external sources such as our environment, the events we witness, and the knowledge we gain from direct experience or indirectly from a book or another person. We can also create (and certainly reinforce) our beliefs by our results. Accomplishment begets confidence. Many shooters use this tool: "If I can shoot one perfect shot, I know I can shoot another . . . and another . . . and another . . ." And we can create a belief just by imagining it's so. And that's the purpose of the mental imagery that shooters use. We picture ourselves shooting the perfect shot, and then shot after shot, until we have pictured a perfect match.

Robbins emphasizes that if your beliefs aren't working for you, you need to change them. If your beliefs set you up for sadness, anger, and failure, then change your beliefs! He says that there are seven "lies" that successful people believe—not that they're really lies, but that no one really knows for sure whether they're true.

➢ Successful people believe that everything that happens can serve our purpose. They see possibilities in every situation.
➢ Successful people believe that there are no failures, only results. This one is particularly important for shooters. A shot that lands in the eight-ring isn't a failure; it's an outcome. It's data; it will inform the shooter's decision making for the next shot.
➢ Successful people take responsibility for their world. Again, this one is very important for shooters. The shooter who says that the wind is trickiest on his lane and it's the wind's fault that his score is low isn't addressing the situation as a learning situation. The successful shooter says, "What wind indicator did I not see? Where should I be looking before the next shot to ensure I understand what the wind is doing?"
➢ Successful people focus more on using things than on understanding things. It isn't as important to be able to answer "why?" as it is to be able to answer "so what?" We all know very clever people who can explain the why of things and cannot do anything with them. Shooters who do this are very knowledgeable in the technical or the physiological or the mental aspects of shooting, but they cannot fire well.
➢ Successful people believe in people. They usually admire and respect the abilities of others. Shooters who ask the match winner what he was using to read the wind, or what he was thinking when he shot so well, are exhibiting this belief. They assume that the match winner got on the podium by doing things well, and they're keen to understand and model his achievement.

The Zone

➤ Successful people love their work; in fact, they approach their work as if it were their play. Shooters who think that training is drudgery will likely not get the most they can out of their time on the range. Champion shooters enjoy shooting.

➤ Successful people are committed. Successful people know what they want to accomplish, and they keep trying until they achieve it. They're willing to sacrifice things that don't lead to their goals, and they don't see it as sacrifice. The athlete who wants to achieve great success sees going to the range as an opportunity to find the path to success (not as an interruption to his social life, for example).

But if you don't "naturally" believe in these secrets to success, what can you do to become successful? The answer that Robbins provides is this: change your beliefs.

All champion shooting takes place when the shooter is "in the zone." Making your zone robust and reliable improves the chances that you will be able to call it up when you need it most: in a championship match, when hunting big or dangerous game, in an operational confrontation, and in a firefight. The rest of this book is devoted to giving you the tools you need to make your zone bigger, increasing the odds that you'll be the winner when winning matters most.

NOTES

1. "How Good Shooters Think" by Linda K. Miller was originally published in the *CoachNet* newsletter (July/August 1999) and has been republished in *Favorite Stories on Attitude*.
2. "The Performance Response . . . that Winning Feeling" by Linda K. Miller and Keith A. Cunningham was originally published in *Precision Shooting* (March 1997) and has been republished in *Favorite Stories on Winning*.
3. Keith's deer story is recounted in Chapter 1.
4. It is hard to find clarity on the specific differences of conditioned versus semiconditioned responses, but the traditional Pavlovian conditioned response is what most shooters believe they have achieved when they fire a "subconscious shot," where the trigger squeeze is a reaction to the correct sight picture. This phenomenon is so broadly accepted that all trained shooters now know that they must keep their finger off the trigger to prevent an unintentional subconscious reaction to the correct sight picture.
5. A buttonhook is a tool used to assist in doing up button boots. It's a hook that turns back almost to the main stem.
6. "Only Hits Count" by Linda K. Miller and Keith A. Cunningham was originally published in *Tactical Shooter* (April 1999) and has been republished in *Favorite Stories from a Professional Perspective*.
7. By 2006, we had introduced a CQB (close-quarter battle) match to both CFSAC and the National Service Conditions Championship. It starts at 100 meters and moves forward, with a total of 60 rounds fired in a fast-paced course of fire.
8. "Snatch the Pebble" by Linda K. Miller was originally published in *Precision Shooting* (July 2000) and has been republished in *Favorite Stories on Winning*.

— Chapter 5 —

Tools to Increase Your Conscious Powers

SECTION 5-1: THE KEY IS THE MENTAL PROGRAM

You can see by the mental marksmanship map that we have covered all the powers, and we're now ready to discuss the tools that can help you develop strength in each area.

In this chapter, we're going to focus on the power of conscious awareness. The purpose of the conscious mind during the firing of a shot is to be picturing the right thoughts so that the subconscious can fire the perfect shot.

Conscious Powers—The Key is the Mental Program

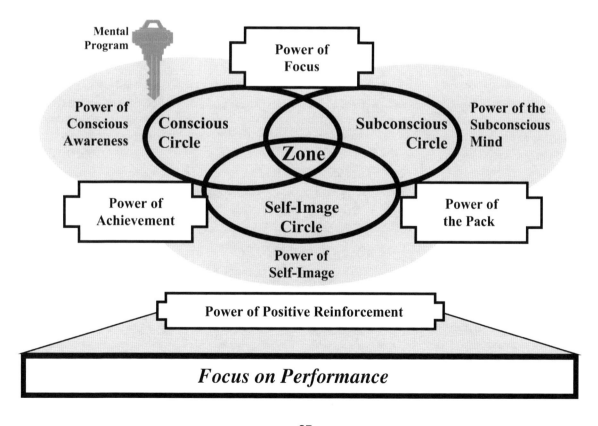

You already know that you shouldn't change your physical position during the shot; you should be completely consistent in all the details of your contact with your firearm. Similarly, you should think the same thoughts each and every time leading up to the firing of a perfect shot. You must stay focused on these thoughts, and these thoughts must drive to one irresistible conclusion: a perfect shot. You must not have the conscious mind thinking about technical things (like trigger control, for example), or else firing becomes a conscious act. You must not allow thoughts of unrelated things (like that new scope you saw on the firing line) to interfere with the process. You must stay focused, and you must have the same thoughts each and every time you fire. To do this, you use a mental program.

The mental program is a series of thoughts that are individually tailored to what you need to do to consistently carry out the procedure of firing a perfect shot. These thoughts must always be positive. That is to say, they must outline what you need to do, and not something that you need to avoid.

The mental program starts a few seconds prior to firing the shot. It's short: four or five steps, each described by only two or three key words. Each step causes you to carry out an important procedure or set of procedures that you need to do consistently for each shot.

You must develop your own mental program, tailored to your needs, and modify it as new

> "Float like a butterfly, sting like a bee."
> —Muhammad Ali, athlete (1942~)

> "Sidestep, scan, breathe."
> —Police mental program, antidote for tunnel vision

> "Draw, fire, scan, assess."
> —Police mental program, antidote for premature reholstering

> "The mental program is such a magical thing that we wrote about it in *Precision Shooting* (May 1996) . . . it is an essential part of self-talk. It is the easiest place to start."
> —Linda K. Miller & Keith A. Cunningham in *The Power of Self-Talk*

requirements are found. An example (and a very good starting place) is as follows:

> ➢ Breathe and relax
> ➢ Correct target
> ➢ Level
> ➢ Sight picture, sight picture . . .

You must not include anything to do with the actual manipulation of the trigger, because trigger control must be a subconscious act that automatically happens during the last step of the mental program (sight picture, sight picture . . .). You remain focused on the perfect sight picture while you subconsciously squeeze the trigger until the rifle fires.

Having said this, you might initially require a step in the mental program to remind you about trigger manipulation (for example, finger placement on the trigger), but it shouldn't replace the "sight picture" step, and it should be removed as soon as you're able to perform correct trigger manipulation without prompting, thereby keeping it subconscious.

You may start with a mental program that has more steps and, as your abilities improve, you remove the steps you no longer need until you're left with only the bare bones of the perfect shot.

You must write down your mental program, saying it as often as you can and picturing it at every opportunity. You must then apply your mental program with each and every shot you fire.

The mental program must have a start point that leads you to the last step when it's time to fire the shot. For example, in rifle, many shooters use the closing of the bolt as the start point. Some shooters use the settling into position, and often they use a specific touchstone, like settling the cheek on the cheekpiece. In pistol, you might use the raise to start the mental program, and you might use "front sight" instead of "sight picture" to finish the mental program. In snap shooting, you would run your mental program up to "sight picture" and then wait until the target appears to finish it. In any series of shots, you would run your mental program (or a portion of it) for each and every shot. For double-taps and rapids, you would likely repeat only the last step for each subsequent shot, so the mental program for a five-shot rapid might sound like this:

- ➣ Breathe
- ➣ Target
- ➣ Sight picture [gun goes off]
- ➣ Target, sight [gun goes off]
- ➣ Target, sight [gun goes off]
- ➣ Target, sight [gun goes off]
- ➣ Target, sight [gun goes off]

Running your mental program gives you a plan, which eliminates pressure and keeps the mind occupied with performance.

MILITARY

Military Story—Up . . . He Sees Me . . . Down

As do most militaries in the world, the Canadian Army has, within its training systems, many little sayings that have been invented to help the soldier remember what he is supposed to do under stress. Most of these are simple little mental programs that get the conscious mind to picture the right thing so that the subconscious mind can carry out the skill action.

When training soldiers in the attack, it's very difficult to get them to move forward under fire, and once they're up and moving, they tend to stay up too long, giving the enemy a better chance to bring them under effective fire. The basic drill is for some members of a subunit to dash forward in a short bound, zigging and zagging, while receiving covering fire from others. They then take up a fire position and provide covering fire while others advance in a short bound. And so they alternate, providing covering fire and bounding forward until they have closed with the enemy.

The problem is that if the distance over which they must do this leapfrogging is very great, it becomes very tiring. So the soldiers tend to take longer bounds. It's these longer bounds that get them into trouble.

In some long-ago army, an NCO came up with a little mental program to motivate the soldier to keep his bounds short. It was, "Up, he sees me, down, crawl, return fire." As soon as it's the soldier's turn to bound, he starts the mental program with "Up." After taking the first step,

"Coach the mind; the rest will follow."
—Keith A. Cunningham, soldier (1950~)

"Mental control is self-control."
—Linda K. Miller, coach (1952~)

"You and I have the conscious ability to choose the images that we are going to hold in our mind . . . we choose our thoughts . . . and when I think something I control what I attract into my life."
—Bob Proctor, philosopher

"Your wish is my command."
—The Genie

"Some things have to be believed to be seen."
—Ralph Hodgson, poet (1871–1962)

he pictures in his mind the second part of the mental program, "He sees me." This then leads to an interesting and important picture starting to form in the soldier's mind, and the third part, "Down," becomes easier to do. Once on the ground, the fourth part of the mental program gets the soldier to "crawl" a short distance from where he went to ground before he establishes a firing position and "returns fire" onto the enemy position. The whole procedure takes from three to five seconds to carry out and minimizes the enemy's opportunity to establish effective fire onto any single soldier.

POLICE

Law-Enforcement Story—Tap, Tap . . . Scan . . . Advance

Law-enforcement personnel have told us of a mental program they use. It's exactly like a mental program should be: simple and to the point.

They're trained that when they engage a bad guy, they are to fire two shots (commonly called "double tap"), scan for any other threats, and then advance to cover or disarm and take control of the situation. When reduced to its simplest form, the mental program becomes, "Tap, tap, scan, advance."

As with all mental programs, it gives the officer a plan, and it reminds him of his training and exactly what he must do right now.

HUNTING

Hunter Story—Make it Right . . . NOW

This mental program idea can be used anywhere it's important to carry out a particular drill, especially when there will be other thoughts wanting to creep into your mind. It's these other thoughts that can get you killed.

We were once told by a professional hunter from Namibia about a mental program he used, and it has, in fact, saved his life several times. At the time we were talking with him, he didn't realize he was using it or what it was. We asked him about the times he had to track after wounded dangerous game or had been charged and had to kill the animal before he was trampled or gored to death.

He told us of having to kill Cape buffaloes on three separate occasions, and elephants on two others, that were in a full-out charge. He told us how a wave of panic would come over him when he first realized that the animal was going to try to kill him. He controlled the panic by recognizing that there was no way out but to face the charge and shoot the best shot he had ever fired. At this moment a wave of calmness came over him—he had a plan, he knew what he had to do, and he knew he could do it.

We asked him what he was thinking as the animal came nearer, and it was here that he told us his mental program. He said he kept repeating in his mind, "Make it right . . . make it right . . . make it right . . . NOW!" The "make it right" referred to the sight picture. He knew he would likely not get too many chances to stop this charge, so he wanted to make every shot count. He wanted to make sure the sight was on the most vulnerable part of the animal, that part that would most likely stop it in its tracks. The "NOW" was when he could see the sight picture was as good as it was going to get, and the animal was as close as he dare let it get so as to guarantee a hit and yet have enough room to get a second shot if it was required. The "NOW" triggered the shot. He said only once had he ever needed a second shot; although the animal was down, it was by no means out. He told us that the look of pure murderous hatred in its eyes was the primary reason for the follow-up shot. (He also told us that the look haunts him yet, and that after these charges, he often needs two hands to light a cigarette.)

Tools to Increase Your Conscious Powers

COMPETITION

Competition Story—Breathe and Relax
The following is from a story called "The Ontario Lt. Governor's Match 1995—Keith's Story."[1]

I'm not sure when I decided that I was going to win the Ontario Lieutenant Governor's,[2] but it certainly wasn't on the drive to the range that first morning of the ORA[3] annual Target Rifle matches. I hadn't been shooting much Target Rifle that summer, focusing more on fun times by taking Linda and my son Jesse to Service Rifle and Precision Rifle matches. Neither of them had shot either one before, so my hands were full, making sure things went well for them. These ORA events were the first Target Rifle matches Linda had seen, so my thoughts that morning were on shooting as well as I could and getting Linda hooked on another shooting discipline.

With the Commonwealth Game trials in 1993, I had actually decided that I would win the trials the year before. Throughout that year, every shot I fired was a practice shot oriented toward winning those trials. Every day, whenever I had a free moment to think about something other than daily routine, I would lie back, rest my mind, and imagine the things I would have to do to win those trials. I knew that I would probably not be in the lead right away but would maintain focus, shoot each shot individually, carefully watch the wind, and religiously follow my mental program for every shot. Then, when it was over, I would go and look at the scoreboard.

However with the ORA annual matches, I had no such previous thoughts. I did once think that it would sure be nice to win something big to sort of help Linda's introduction to fullbore matches. But I really wasn't taking things very seriously, at least until after that first match at 400 yards. Linda had said that she was happy to watch the proceedings of a fullbore match and would act as my coach. I had smiled to myself and thought that she would probably get bored coaching me; after all, what was there to coach? She knew nothing about fullbore shooting, and I was an experienced shooter in this game. At least that is what I thought until after that first shoot at 400 yards.

That shoot was my wake-up call. My mind was a jumble of thoughts, my shooting techniques were rusty, and I had no focus even for short periods. I cross-fired once and shot a very tall group costing me two high inners. You can figure out the score from there, but the real score I had to face was the look on Linda's face when I came off the firing mound. She was truly disappointed in my efforts. Linda knew, as I did, that I was capable of better. I also knew that she would have a better introduction to this sport if I shot to my potential.

And then she started doing it. Linda started acting like a coach. She didn't have to know much about fullbore shooting; she just knew that it was important to fire perfect shots each time, focus throughout the match, and use a mental program for each shot. Linda began to ask me questions that, when answered correctly, would cause me to figure out what I had to do. She asked about my equipment. The other day during a practice, the rifle and ammunition had shot well into the V ring. It was the same rifle and ammo. She asked about the wind. It had been a light, steady breeze. I had lost nothing to the wind. She asked how I felt physically. I was feeling fine, glad to be back at it after such a light summer. So now when we had eliminated all the easy stuff, Linda finally got around to the point she was heading for all along.

"What were you thinking?" she asked.

"Nothing in particular," I responded, wanting to appear cool and aloof about the whole thing.

It was that knowing smile on her face that caused me to wake up. She summed it up in one of her famous, quite-to-the-point comments: "Perhaps when you're trying to fire a perfect shot, you *should* be thinking about something very specific."

"I've got it," I said. "I've got to reestablish my mental program so that I have a consistent thought process for each shot, and in there I have to make sure I include seeing my target number in my sight picture to prevent cross-fires."

She cut me off with her next question. "And how are you going to do that?"

I replied that as soon as I could get back to my truck, I would sit my gear down and write out a simple shot sequence, put it in my shooting book, and follow it without deviation in the next match. My head was so full of thoughts about just what I would include in this mental program that I hardly heard her say, in her usual soft tone, "You know, that just might work."

It didn't take long. I had, of course, used this uniform thinking process before. Everyone who has ever won must do this for consistent performance. I had been away from it for a while and needed to be reminded of its importance. I sat down quietly and thought out exactly what I had to do to fire each perfect shot. This mental program would start when it was my turn to shoot and I had closed the bolt. I wrote down the following steps:

- ➢ Breathe deeply and relax.
- ➢ See my target number in my front sight.
- ➢ Level the front sight.
- ➢ Center in the rear sight.
- ➢ Center in the front sight.
- ➢ Center . . . center . . . center . . .

It wasn't long before I had an opportunity to put this to the test. The very next match, I scored a 50 with lots of Vs. And so it went throughout the matches. I did lose the odd point here and there for not getting the group centered quickly enough or missing a wind change, but I was shooting at a level to which I had grown accustomed and having a lot more fun. Linda continued to do her coaching thing: keeping me focused and making sure I was on time to the match and didn't talk too long with friends and become distracted with someone's rifle problem. She would stay with me right to the firing mound and at the very last remind me of the thoughts I needed, point out which flag I needed to watch, and that I was doing good—to just keep doing what I was doing. (I found out later just how good smallbore shooters are at watching wind and recognizing uniform conditions.)

There were a couple of times when this thought process was really put to the test. Once, as I was about to go up onto the mound after Linda's usual coaching talk, I was intercepted by my good friend Craig Bawden. He was a new range officer for this day, having just arrived back from the Canadian Forces Small Arms Competitions (CFSAC). I hadn't shot at CFSAC that year, as I was on retirement leave from the CF and the "powers that be" thought I couldn't be on leave and run the LFCA (Land Forces Central Area) Reserve Small Arms Team at the same time.

I had spent many years training this team, and this was the first year they were without me. Craig knew this and was as eager to update me as I was to listen to him. We spent several moments of my preparation time finding out that, although one of the team members had won the Queen's Medal, the team on a whole didn't do well. I was glad in a way. The "powers that be" had tried to reinvent a wheel that had already gone through many years of success. But at the same time, I knew that Capt. Conrad Schubert, my second-in-command and now team captain, had tried to do his best with what he was given to work with, and he and the team members would be disappointed. We had all won so much in the past . . .

I looked back at Linda just as I was hurriedly getting into place and just before the "commence fire" was given. She looked concerned that perhaps I might have become distracted and it might affect my performance. Although my beloved shooting team was very much on my mind throughout this match, I was able to focus for the short periods needed to fire a perfect shot because of my mental program. I did, however, shoot a slightly larger group and scored a rather ragged 50-6V.

The next time this mental program came to my rescue, there was no one else involved but myself. It was always my prematch procedure to set my sight and in all ways prepare my equipment for the next match. Having done his, I settled in on the firing mound fully expecting to convert both sighters and score a perfect score. I had noticed that the targets hadn't been cleared from the last relay and that whoever had been shooting here had a real nice V-bull for their last on score. Just then the message was sent to the butts to clear all targets and get ready to start.

Tools to Increase Your Conscious Powers

I fired the first shot, and the target came up with a nicely centered V-bull, very similar to what had just been cleared. This V-bull was what I had expected to shoot, and therefore I settled in for the good performance to follow. My second sighter was whatever you get when you just touch the bottom of the target frame. I was now not so settled. I checked my sights for tightness. They were tight. No need to check for sight setting; I always do that before the match. I came up a little in elevation, but not so much as to put me out of the bull if my first sighter was the right one. I fired my first shot on record and scored a magpie beside my second sighter. I tried to figure out what else could be wrong—my sights were tight, and I had checked the setting before the match. I thought how glad I was to have done that and not have to worry about it now. With two shots on the bottom of the board, I came up half as much as was needed to put me in the bull and fired my second on score. It was an inner exactly halfway to the bull.

And then it hit me like recoil on the chin. The same thing had happened to me in the Commonwealth Games[4] Trials (but there I was able to recover after the first sighter). I had set my sights before the match—had looked at them but hadn't actually read them. I now read my sight setting . . . damn . . . reset it to what I thought I had it on to begin with . . . shot a bull followed by 13 straight Vs for a 72-13V. (I think my first V-bull sighter was the shot on the target when it was cleared at the start of the match. The old shot hole hadn't been patched out and was signaled as my first

> "The more obstinately you try to learn how to shoot the arrow for the sake of hitting the goal, the less you will succeed."
> —Eugen Herrigel in *Zen in the Art of Archery*

> "Whatever the mind of man can conceive, it can achieve."
> —W. Clement Stone, writer (1902–2002)

> "Man becomes what he thinks about."
> —Morris E. Goodman in *The Secret*

> "The real hero is the man who fights even though he's scared."
> —Gen. George S. Patton, soldier (1885–1945)

sighter.) There is no way that I could have recovered as well as I did without a consistent mental thought process to keep the waves of disappointment and frustration at bay.

It must have been just before this match that I thought I had a chance at the Lieutenant Governor's, because coming off the mound I was thinking that I had just misfired on any further chance at winning any of the big ones. I was in a horrible state of mind, and although Linda was trying her best, there was no way my spirits could be lifted after this one. I was in this state of mind for some time before I slowly came around to realize that the Des Burke Match wasn't part of the Lieutenant Governor's aggregate. I was certainly out of the running for the Grand Aggregate but not the Lieutenant Governor's.

I now had to bring myself out of this horrible state of mind and get back into the winning one. Linda coached her heart out. She reminded me of all the good performances I had put in over the last couple of days, how I had recovered from shaky shoots and scored well. We looked over my shooting diary and studied all the good matches. I was able to nap and woke refreshed and ready to shoot. In fact, it was at this point that I knew I would win. I would follow my mental program, focus hard on the wind, and keep my group centered. I knew I was going to win but would have to work hard and smart to do it.

As I was being chaired off the range and riding the high of this incredible recognition, I truly felt that I didn't deserve it all. I looked back to see if I could at least telepath my feeling to my coach in a

— 89 —

glance, a look, a mouthed thank-you. But Linda, ever the coach to the end, while I was basking in the moment of my glory, was tidying up my shooting gear, getting it ready to be removed from the range. Linda Miller, an accomplished shooter in her own right, knows (more than I can appreciate) the efforts she put into this win, for without her knowledge, understanding, tenacity, and drive, this particular Lieutenant Governor's would have had a different outcome. She now wears the coach's version of the Lieutenant Governor's gold medal. You must ask her about it sometime.

SECTION 5-2: MORE TOOLS—THE LOGBOOK

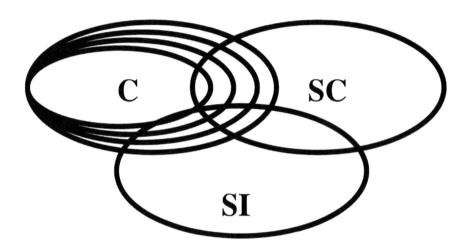

While the mental program is the key for keeping the conscious mind picturing the right pictures for the actual firing of a perfect shot, there are other areas that will need our conscious attention. One of the best ways to take care of these is through the use of a logbook.

The logbook is the place where important and relevant information is kept for easy reference. It's both a fact base and a historical record. It's used to help you make better decisions in the future.

One of the main components of the logbook are organization lists. Prior to the start of an operation (whether it's police, military, field, or competition), the conscious mind has a lot of things to think about in order to get ready for and through the event successfully.

Equipment lists are required to ensure that you have taken everything you will need while on an operation. We use a series of equipment lists that are specific to the type of competition or event we're going to. For competition, we have separate lists for Target Rifle, Service Rifle, Sniper Rifle, Pistol, etc. We have separate travel lists for local and international events. We have hunting lists. We have lists for each of the courses we run.

All complex missions are run with lists—equipment lists and checklists. The pilot runs a comprehensive preflight checklist. The hospital operating room staff ensures that all the equipment is in place before the surgeon arrives.[5] Military operations centers have notebooks full of various lists that they need to continually check to ensure the planning is complete.

We also use charts and tables for quick reference. Elevation settings and/or points of aim are particularly important for long-range shooters (military snipers, police snipers, big-game hunters, competition shooters). We keep a separate table of settings for each rifle (rifle, scope, and ammo combination) and for each location (i.e., each shooting range) at which we train or compete. Each table starts with a computer-generated setting, and we keep a separate table for each range that we shoot on (to account for differences in "known distances" and alti-

Tools to Increase Your Conscious Powers

Sample Wind Chart

Windage Chart for .308 Match in MOA

168-gr Sierra MK; MV 2600 fps; BC .462; Temp 70F; Elev 600 ft

Wind Value	Range in Meters								
	100	**200**	**300**	**400**	**500**	**600**	**700**	**800**	**900**
1	0.09	0.18	0.27	0.40	0.52	0.66	0.81	0.97	1.15
2	0.18	0.36	0.57	0.79	1.05	1.31	1.62	1.95	2.29
3	0.27	0.54	0.84	1.20	1.58	1.98	2.44	2.93	3.44
4	0.36	0.72	1.15	1.61	2.10	2.65	3.24	3.90	4.58
5	**0.45**	**0.90**	**1.42**	**2.00**	**2.61**	**3.30**	**4.06**	**4.88**	**5.73**
6	0.54	1.09	1.72	2.40	3.14	3.96	4.88	5.86	6.88
7	0.63	1.27	2.00	2.79	3.67	4.63	5.68	6.84	8.03
8	0.72	1.45	2.30	3.20	4.20	5.28	6.50	7.81	9.18
9	0.81	1.63	2.57	3.61	4.72	5.95	7.31	8.78	10.33
10	**0.90**	**1.81**	**2.87**	**4.00**	**5.25**	**6.62**	**8.12**	**9.76**	**11.47**

Sample Communications List (Target Rifle competition)

Code	Short Form	Explanation
1		Firing is about to commence
2		No spotting disc visible
3	Value/shot disagree	Spotting disc unmistakably disagrees with signaled value. Check that spotting disc shows LAST hit, and signal its correct value.
4	Check for a hit	A shot has been fired but no signal has been made. Examine target carefully and signal the hit, if found, or a miss.
5	Challenge for a higher value	The firer has challenged for a high value for his hit. Check the value of the shot signaled, and examine the target for any other hit. Signal the correct value of the highest scoring hit found.
7	Challenge for a hit	A miss has been signaled but firer has challenged for a hit. Re-examine the target and the spotting disc carefully and signal the results. Confirm by radio.
9	Hurry up	Marking/Shooting appears to be unduly slow. Butt/Firing Point Officer, check and correct as necessary. (Note: this message may be passed in either direction.)
10	We're done	Stand easy. (The shooters are finished firing.) If marking has been particularly good, the shooters may send "Message 10 with compliments".

Secrets of Mental Marksmanship

Sample Field Firing Aid

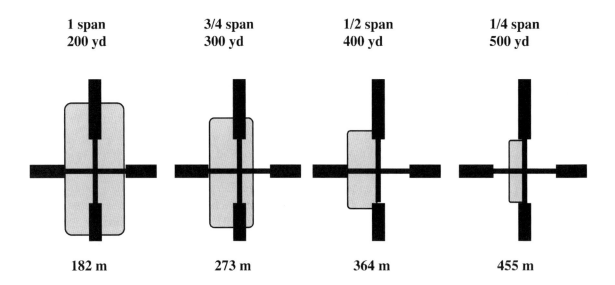

| 1 span | 3/4 span | 1/2 span | 1/4 span |
| 200 yd | 300 yd | 400 yd | 500 yd |

| 182 m | 273 m | 364 m | 455 m |

Weaver Scope: Crosshairs span 2.5 mils   **Target width 4.5 mils**

tudes). The sight settings we used will help get our first shots closer to the center. This reduces reliance on our memories in stressful situations and improves the chances that we will use the correct data.

The wind charts or diagrams (or other aids that you find the easiest to use) are kept in the logbook for easy access. This would apply to competition shooters and snipers as well as hunters shooting game at long range.

We keep other *aides-mémoire* in our logbooks, such as communication codes for operations, for hunting, and for competition. (When we hunt, we have a series of radio messages we use to communicate among the hunters in our party, and we each keep a little card with the message code and meaning.)

Other reference data pertinent to the operation needs to be kept handy. For competition shooters, this would include match conditions and rules. For operational shooters, this could include panoramic sketches, judging distance aids, field firing aids, or street maps. For hunters, this would be a map with trails and stands, for example.

All of these logbook items are only as good as you make them. You need to be able to easily add to your maps, diagrams, and lists. As soon as you identify a needed change, make it immediately. The lists are only useful if you actually use them. They must be handy, and you must be in the habit of using them.

Military Story—World War II Sniper

In our research, we chatted with a World War II sniper who brought out the use of a logbook very nicely.

This sniper had been assigned to set up an observation post overlooking a group of farm buildings. These buildings were well preserved and had somehow missed the shelling that had been taking place all around them. The buildings were now in a bit of a "no-man's land" and had changed possession several times over the past week. Neither the Germans nor the Allies wanted to set up a headquarters in them, as they were such obvious targets for artillery on both sides. Each just wanted to know whether the other side used them so they could respond appropriately.

So our sniper was assigned the job of watching the buildings and reporting any enemy activity. He could also engage quality targets if they presented themselves. A couple of soldiers were assigned to him, and they worked out a shift routine so they each could get some downtime when not watching the buildings.

Our sniper found himself in position for several days with nothing happening and was becoming bored, at least as bored as anyone can get in such a situation. He remembered his training, where they taught him about the use and benefit of making up range cards and panoramic sketches. Most of his sniper situations had been fast moving and he never had time to do a sniper position "by the book."

They had no idea how long they were going to stay at their post, but all appearances were that they would be there for at least a couple more days. Our sniper decided to make up a panoramic sketch of the buildings. He got his sniper logbook out of his pack and found lots of open spaces among its pages. He also found he had a bit of an artistic streak in him as he sketched with considerable detail. He got the other two soldiers with him involved, and they started looking for details he could include in his sketch. They noted the number of bricks high in the little decorative wall around the house, the number of bullet holes in the various buildings, which windows were still intact, doors and windows open or closed, curtains that could be seen, shrubs and flower gardens, and so on. In general, he found it entertaining and a good way to pass the time.

They finally got word to fall back quickly to the main positions; the Germans were launching a local offensive to gain some high ground that the Allies held. The fighting lasted for a couple days and was fierce at times. The Allies were pushed back a short ways but eventually regained the ground and were in their original positions, with some forward elements near the previously mentioned farm buildings. However, they were taking deadly sniper fire from these buildings, which resulted in several casualties.

> "History is . . . a dialogue between the present and the past."
> —Edward Hallet Carr, historian (1892–1982)

> "A generation which ignores history has no past and no future."
> —Robert Heinlein, writer (1907–1988)

> "Keep a diary, and some day it'll keep you."
> —Mae West, actress and writer (1893–1980)

They had called for the artillery to simply blow the buildings away, but they couldn't get it. It seemed the artillery was low on ammunition, and they weren't going to expend what they had on just one sniper. So our friend received the call "sniper up." His job was to locate the enemy sniper and deal with him.

He moved forward cautiously, not knowing where the enemy was hiding and himself expecting to be shot dead at any moment. One of the forward elements was located near his old sniper hide, and he reoccupied it. He watched the buildings carefully for several hours and saw nothing. While studying one of the outbuildings, he heard a shot ring out, and soon there was a shout for a medic. He needed to find this guy, and soon.

He remembered his panoramic sketch and wondered if it would help. The last shot seemed to have come from the house. He carefully studied his sketch and compared it to the house. Eventually he noticed that a window that had been closed was now open, and the curtain that was visible before now was not. He focused his attention there and, using his binos and scope, finally noticed movement. He continued to watch throughout the day, and as the light changed he began to recognize the shape of a man's head and a scoped rifle. He fired his shot, and the head and rifle disappeared.

That night he joined a patrol to investigate the situation in the house and found his handiwork sprawled on the floor with a bullet hole through the left eye. He was able to accomplish this and saved Allied lives as a result of the information in his sniper logbook.

Secrets of Mental Marksmanship

POLICE

Law-Enforcement Story—PS1 Logbook

We issue a logbook to each of the students who attend our Police Sniper 1 course. It's a small three-ring binder with a waterproof cover. The cover has places to keep pencils and pens. There are a couple of bulldog clamps to keep the pages open at specific places. The book is divided into sections, each covering a specific area of interest. These sections include (among others) the following topics:

- ➤ To do list—Anything that needs to be done for the next time, and a general area to make notes or jot down reminders.
- ➤ Equipment list—A list of all the equipment that might be needed for an operation.
- ➤ Rifle information—Serial number of rifle and scope, and any other information about the rifle deemed important.
- ➤ Elevation chart—Elevation chart for all known distances (in 25-meter increments) and computer print-out for those distances not yet confirmed with live fire. A small diagram of what your elevation and windage dials look like when properly set on base zero, as well as the number of minutes up from bottom to zero.
- ➤ Windage charts—Favorite windage charts (for your specific rifle/ammo combination) to help with the wind calls.
- ➤ Panoramic sketch—A place with appropriate paper onto which can be drawn panoramic sketches.
- ➤ Range card—A predrawn range card that can be filled in as required.
- ➤ First aid—A brief description of immediate first aid.
- ➤ Navigation—A reminder on how to use map, compass, and GPS, just in case you're the one who has to lead everyone in on that grow-op mission and it's been awhile since you last navigated in the woods.
- ➤ Observation log—A fill-in-the-blanks form to help the user acquire and record the pertinent information as he watches a location.
- ➤ Judging distance—In the event your laser stops working, some reminders of how to do it by eye and other means.
- ➤ Performance analyses—These are fill-in-the-blank forms to be used after a training day to help you analyze what went well for you.
- ➤ Operation notes—These are pages made of card stock, onto which any notes concerning the operation can be made and kept for future reference.

These sniper logbooks are considered important because they contain information, charts, and knowledge that will help you successfully complete your mission. By way of importance they come third, right after rifle and ammo.

An interesting use of a logbook was told to us by one of our students. He and his partner went around to every bank within their jurisdiction and located a good hide overlooking the front of each bank. They drew up panoramic sketches and range cards and noted any bits of information that would be important to them later if they were ever called out to that bank. They noted the best way to get to the hide without being seen and listed names, phone numbers, and e-mail addresses of key individuals in the bank. They also provided their own contact numbers to the key bank personnel. They drew out a floorplan of the inside of the bank, including all the ways in and out.

All of this information took up only a few pages in their logbook and was with them all the time.

HUNTING

Hunter Story—"Deer Diary" and Technical Log

Keith has kept a hunter's logbook every since he shot his first deer in 1966. At the time, he didn't know that this was the right thing to do. He was only thinking that it might be fun to one day have a story about the deer that he has hunted. That also turned out to be true.

Now, he keeps a more detailed hunter's logbook, primarily because of his sniper training and background. The pages of this book include a story about the hunt, details about shot placement and bullet performance, the distance to the deer, details about the ammunition used, and any other information that might be of use.

He also keeps a second book to record technical information about all of his hunting rifles. It's a small three-ring binder with a waterproof cover, exactly as is issued to each of the sniper students who attend the MilCun sniper courses. It's divided into sections, one per rifle, with detailed information about each gun: a recipe for the hand-loaded ammunition being used, the number of clicks up from bottom of both elevation and windage to zero the scope, hand-drawn pictures of the correct hold-over for different ranges (out to what he considers to be the maximum range he can be effective with this rifle), and any other information that might be useful.

COMPETITION

Competition Story—Where's That Baseline Zero?

A logbook for competition shooters is just as important as for operational snipers. We were at a long-range match one time when a friend of ours came over and told us a very sad story.

He had just finished the last match and had to retire because he couldn't get on target. He was frustrated, nervous, and ready to go home.

We asked him if he had a base zero. He said he did—it was at 100 meters—but he had no idea where that was. He had applied elevation for the last range—what he thought was the right elevation—but because he wasn't on with his first shot, he had moved the elevation and windage all over the place and now had no idea where he was.

We asked him if he had a logbook with base zero information noted for just this kind of situation. He said he didn't. He said he had zeroed at 100, slipped his elevation and windage dials to zero, and came to the match, and now he was lost and had no idea where his zero was. We asked him if he would stay if we could get him on in time for the next match. Reluctantly, he said he would.

Keith set up his rifle on some gear so it would point at an object downrange and removed the bolt. He did a field-expedient bore sighting, finding both elevation and windage off by a great deal, and, when he thought it was very close, he finished it off by turning the dials to the closest zero. Since Keith was shooting a similar cartridge, he then applied his own elevation setting for the next range.

After the next match, our friend was almost giddy. He was on target for his first shot and, with some minor elevation adjustment and getting the wind right, he had an excellent shoot. We reminded him of the need to keep this kind of information in a logbook, and he vowed he would keep one. The very next year he won a long-range championship, and he now always keeps his logbook with him.

SECTION 5-3: MORE TOOLS—ORGANIZATION LISTS

Lists are used by lots of people every day. And the people who use lists are the ones who are the best organized, get the most done with their time, and arrive at their destination with all their gear and equipment. Sure, there are lots of people who get through life without using lists, but aren't we all particularly glad that airline pilots use lists for their preflight check? So, what we're saying here is that the more important it is to be organized, to get the most done with your time, and to arrive at your destination with the gear and equipment you need to do the job, then the more important it is to use lists.

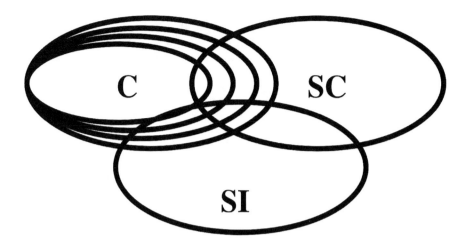

One thing to remember about lists: they only work when you read and use them. If you're on operations and realize that there was something left off the list, then add it to the list right away. Keep doing this and eventually the list will be complete and one of the most valuable items in your possession.

Military Story—Aide-Mémoire

Every military in the world provides lists to help their soldiers follow the Roger's Rangers creed, "Don't never forget nothing." They're much more formalized now than they were in the Roger's Rangers day and have the fancy French name of *aide-mémoire*.

When Keith was the second in command of an infantry company, he was responsible for the administration of that company. This involved absolutely everything the company might need to function either in garrison or in the field. And every single item of that administration required its own form or procedure in order to acquire it, manage it, and expend it. And then there were all the reports that had to be submitted daily to higher HQ. It was impossible to keep all these things in mind; it was enough just to remember where to find the information. Keith developed his own *aide-mémoire* built from all the others provided by the military that were relevant to his specific needs. He also added some of his own lists as well. He ended up with a three-ring binder that was 2 inches thick. This binder was always within arm's reach. In fact, he might better forget his rifle than this binder.

Law-Enforcement Story—Police Sniper Equipment List

As we do in our personal and professional lives, we promote the use of lists in all of our police sniper courses. In fact, one of the lectures we do is specifically on equipment lists.

In this lecture, we show a list of equipment that a police sniper might want to consider if preparing for a call or operation. The list is very extensive and includes items that you might not want for a specific call. The list started fairly small but has grown over the years as students suggested equipment that worked well for them.

One item that was on our original list was the screw-in or tie-on type steps that are used by hunters to get into a tree stand. They have so many uses, you're limited only by your imagination. The screw type can be installed in a tree, post, or any kind of wooden surface in just seconds. It can give you an instant tie down, a step to see over a wall, or a rifle rest. The tie-on type has some limitations but is best used on steel posts when the screw-in type cannot be used.

After seeing this item on the list, one of our students said to us, "That's the greatest thing I have ever seen. I'm going to add it to my equipment list."

Hunter Story—Hunting List

We bet every hunt camp has a story about someone who arrived there for the hunt and forgot his rifle or some important piece of it, like the bolt. Well, it kind of goes back to how important it is to arrive at your destination with all of the gear and equipment you need to do the job. If you left your rifle only a few kilometers from your camp, then it's really just a bother to retrieve it. But if you're on a safari and now you're an ocean away from the favorite rifle that you had been dreaming about using on this expensive hunt. . . well, your PH will be able to lend you one, but now you're one of the stories he will tell about the hunter who forgot his rifle.

These problems can be avoided with the use of a simple list. Start the list well in advance of your hunt, and keep adding to it as things come to mind. Ask your guide for input. Keep your developing list with you, and add things to it the moment you think of it (otherwise you will surely be distracted, and it will only get on the list if you happen to think of it a second time). And most important: use the list. Get in the habit of checking off each item on your list as you physically pack it in your bag or on your person.

Competition Story—Competition Lists

We have spent a great deal of time involved in competition shooting of all kinds. Our biggest fear is that we show up for the match having forgotten some important piece of equipment. We have certainly seen other competitors go through this. Rifles, bolts, ammunition, spotting scopes, and anything you could possibly need to compete have been left behind. They will run around trying to find someone with extra equipment to borrow or try to use the equipment of someone who is on a different relay. Of course, some equipment simply cannot be lent, like a bolt or hand-loaded ammo, but they will generally make a nuisance of themselves trying to use the equipment you brought.

We try to set these people right by pointing out that there is a solution to forgetting their equipment. They will slow down just enough, in their frantic search for something to shoot, to look at you with glazed eyes and say, "My God, what is it?"

You say, "A list of all the equipment you need to bring to a match; then use it to lay out that equipment and then pack it so you will have it all. It works for us every time."

The reply is, "Oh, I don't use lists. Have you got a spare rifle I could borrow?"

It's hard to feel sorry for people like this.

We have lists for every type of competition we shoot in. Each one outlines the equipment we will need for that competition. We have travel lists for clothing and items that we want to have with us. These will vary depending on where we're traveling. These lists have always worked for us as long as we read them and use them.

"To be prepared is half the victory."
—Miguel de Cervantes, writer (1547–1616)

"Before anything else, preparation is the key to success."
—Alexander Graham Bell, inventor (1847–1922)

"There is no such thing as luck. There is only adequate or inadequate preparation to cope with a statistical universe."
—Robert Heinlein in *Time Enough for Love*

"Luck is what happens when preparation meets opportunity."
—Lucius Annaeus Seneca, writer (54 BC–AD 39)

A good friend of ours once spent a few days with us. He noticed how often we used lists and how well they kept us organized. He vowed to start using lists because he could see how much more we got done because of them.

SECTION 5-4: MORE TOOLS—PERFORMANCE ANALYSIS

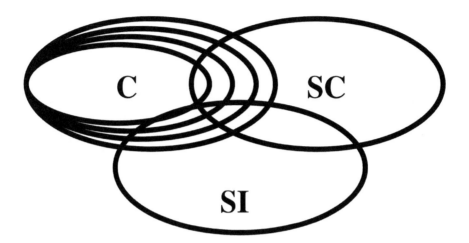

Performance analysis is a very powerful tool. This approach to assessing what you are doing will give you a whole new perspective on your ability to develop your shooting skills AND your operational or competition skills. For those of you who are producing better scores during low-key practices and training than in scenario-based training or matches, this is an easy-to-learn way to produce your best performances on demand.

The first skill you need is to be able to control your thoughts. And your thoughts need to be positive images of *what you need to do* to fire perfect shots. The important thing is that you must be able to identify and picture what you need to do at your end of the range . . . and let the rifle take care of what happens at the other end of the range.

This requirement is fundamental. You can only control what happens at the firing line. What happens at the other end of the range is a consequence of what happens at the firing line. You can influence the consequences, the outcomes, the results—but the only thing you can control is your own performance at your end of the range.

During a training, matches or operations, you keep the conscious mind picturing the right pictures with positive reinforcement. Think of every shot you fire as purely information to improve the performance of the next shot. Where the shot lands is data, just pure data. Use it to confirm your performance or to guide you in changing your performance. (If you have trouble staying cool about it, pretend you're coaching someone else, and imagine what you'd say to them to improve the odds of the next shot going in the center.) Focus only on performance and think of nothing else but performance.

After the match or training session, continue with the positive reinforcement by doing a "performance analysis." This is where the logbook pages come into play.

"An ounce of performance is worth pounds of promises."
—Mae West, actress and writer (1893–1980)

"The score never interested me, only the game."
—Mae West, actress and writer (1893–1980)

Tools to Increase Your Conscious Powers

Sample Performance Analysis Statements

Performance Analysis

- ❖ I always make my position as solid as it can be.
- ❖ I always correct my position until it is completely right.
- ❖ I always check my holding pattern is smooth, slow and small.
- ❖ I always adjust my position until my holding pattern is smaller than my target area.
- ❖ I always check that my natural body alignment is oriented directly towards my target.
- ❖ I always correct my natural alignment from the ground up.
- ❖ I always set my sight correctly and focus on my sight picture.
- ❖ I always run my mental program: Breathe & Relax, Correct target, Level, Sight picture…
- ❖ I always have a slow, smooth, steady, subconscious squeeze.
- ❖ I always call my shot.
- ❖ I always analyze my recoil.

Performance analysis calls for a different way of looking at what you're doing. So often we analyze what we do wrong and stop there. The definition of a coach in the Canadian Army is one who finds faults. What is really needed is someone who provides solutions.

We believe that coaches should be analyzing what you're doing right, and while you are focusing on what you're doing right, what you're doing wrong will just be pushed out of the way. If you have an "oops," regard it as data, data that will guide you for the next shot. Immediately figure out what you need to do better—this is solution analysis. If you don't know what went wrong, phrase it this way: "I need a solution to . . ." That way, you don't get "stuck"—you have a plan, you're going to find a solution, and you're on your way to solving things and making things work.

Whenever we are coaching, we start with the premise: "Great advice, Coach, but how?" A coach's job is to always answer the question "how" before it's asked. Coaches that sit around with their eye in a scope watching the group form aren't looking at the right place to identify solutions. The coach should be watching the shooter, making sure the shooter is doing everything right . . . that's how the shooter gets the pretty group down range. Coaches who are constantly watching the targets down range are doing so because they don't know what to look for at the shooter end of the range.

We think that if you have shot a five-shot group and one shot is out of the group, you should ignore that one shot and focus on what you did right for the four shots in the group. Figure out what you did right for these shots, do it the next time for all five shots, and the one shot out will just go away. Analyze what you do right, and what you do wrong will just go away.

MILITARY

Military Story—"You's Flinchin'"

Keith likes to tell the story of the first time he got to shoot the M16 rifle during his basic training in the U.S. Army at Fort Knox, Kentucky. The exercise was a preliminary grouping and zeroing at 25 meters. They would shoot a five-shot group and then go downrange to examine the results, adjust zeroes, and be yelled at by the drill instructor (DI).

Keith was disappointed with his first group, as it was somewhat scattered. The DI came by and yelled, "Hell, boy, you's flinchin'. All you gotta do is stop flinchin'."

Great advice, coach, but how?

With this kind of advice, the young trainee is returning to the firing line trying to figure out what flinching is and how to stop doing it. The coach is feeling good that he did his job and sorted out another one. But what advice did he really give the student? What picture has he left in the student's mind toward fixing the problem and becoming a better shot?

— 99 —

Now we fully appreciate that DIs don't have much time to spend with each trainee, but he could have answered the question "how" with only a few more words: "Hell, boy, you's flinchin'. What you gotta do is keep the upper body relaxed, focus totally on the front sight and your sight alignment, and press the trigger with a steady increase of pressure until the rifle fires. Focus on the front sight and alignment from front to rear."

Okay, so it's more than a few more words. But you can see the picture that has now been established in the student's mind. And it's this picture that will influence his next group of shots.

Law-Enforcement Story—Bragging Rights

Since we have been working with police officers on our tactical rifle and police sniper courses, we have noticed one place where they focus particularly on mistakes made. We understand that they use critical debriefs to modify and develop policy, tactics, and training, but there's a difference between finding fault and finding solutions. Just listen to the way typical cops kid with each other.

If a police officer makes a mistake in tactics somewhere on a training day, he will hear about that mistake hourly for the next six months or until some other officer makes another mistake that gets someone's attention. With each joke from each member, they emphasize the mistake and improve the chances that someone will repeat it the next time they use that tactic.

Can you imagine the training value if everyone heard or thought about the *right* way of doing that tactic every hour for the next six months? Want to place a bet on the odds of this team doing that tactic right the next time they use it?

In Lt. Col. Dave Grossman's outstanding book *On Combat*, he makes the same point about leaders (although we think it applies to everyone). He says the following:

> *Friends tease each other. SWAT teams tease each other; it comes with the territory. If you are a leader, however, you are not permitted to play the teasing game. You never joke about your trainees' failures, but you do brag about their achievements. Your entire repertoire is to talk about what went right, and when you say these things over a beer with your peers, they will want you to brag about them next time. When word gets out that this is the type of trainer you are, people will no longer avoid training but will want to be there because of the environment you have created.*

This is exactly what happens on our courses. We build on what the student does right, we set the student up for success, and we create an environment where it's fun to learn. We don't have our students long enough to teach them everything we would like to. We don't have time for the "frus-

"When people start focusing on what they want, what they don't want falls away. And that part [what they want] expands and the other part disappears."
—Jack Canfield, writer (1944~)

"Whether you think you can or you think you can't, you're probably right."
—Henry Ford, businessman (1863–1947)

"Focus on performance."
—MilCun instructors

"Whom fortune wishes to destroy, she first makes mad."
—Publilius Syrus, writer (1st century BC)

trated drill sergeant" or "the less the instructor knows about it the louder the instructor yells about it" approach to teaching. Students learn best when treated like adults and when it's obvious that the student and instructor have a common goal: to pass on or absorb as much of that skills-developing, life-saving information as possible.

Hunter Story—Picture This!

Each year we conduct a hunter marksmanship course. This is a simple weekend course where we teach hunters to shoot more accurately with their hunting rifles. Almost all our students are there because they're "afraid they might miss the deer." This could be because they don't want to put the animal through unnecessary suffering by firing a bad shot and wounding it. Or it could be because of the horror stories they have heard from hunting camps as to what someone goes through if they miss a shot. Either way, you can see that their heads are full of pictures of failure. You can imagine it like the children's game of "King of the Mountain" where the big bad thought of failure stands on top of the mountain and keeps pushing any good thought of success off the top. We have to change that image so that good thoughts of success become the "King of the Mountain."

We start with them shooting .22 LR rifles, first teaching them what a perfect shot should feel like. We fill their minds with successful thoughts and the tools to perform well.

We usually have to defeat the flinch they have developed by shooting their hunting rifles. We use the same positive reinforcement along with live and dry techniques that we use for all marksmanship training.

We then show them how to use a variety of field-expedient shooting positions in order to better steady the rifle so they can hold inside the kill zone of their target. We encourage them to look at the holding pattern that the position can produce and decide whether it's sufficiently small to hit the desired target area. If the hold isn't small enough, we help them improve their position or find another that will produce the desired holding pattern.

Finally we let them shoot a few shots from their hunting rifle, mixed with live and dry practices until they can shoot their major caliber while keeping the upper body relaxed. Eventually we take them out on a "hunter's trail," and they get to shoot at some realistic-sized targets under field conditions.

With a positive image of the desired performance firmly planted in their minds, and with a realistic assessment of their own current skill level, all leave the course better field shots than when they arrived.

Competition Story—Performance Analysis

The following is an excerpt from "The Power of Self-Talk"[6] combined with an excerpt from "How to Build a Training Plan . . . that Works!"[7]

It's easy for us to get into a bad habit of saying negative things. It's also easy to be positive when things are going right, but what happens to our attitude when things go

> "Performance is your reality. Forget everything else."
> —Harold Geneen, businessman (1910–1997)

> "You can influence the outcome; you can control the performance."
> —Linda K. Miller, coach (1952~)

> "I have no control over the shot once it leaves the gun. I can accept that."
> —Police sniper, a MilCun student

> "What you resist persists."
> —Carl Gustav Jung, psychologist (1875–1961)

wrong? It's important that we learn from every situation and that this learning be as positive as possible so we'll remember it as a good experience.

One of the best ways we have found to do this is by means of "performance analysis." After each match or practice session, we find a quiet spot and relive the shoot, focusing on the things we have done right and solutions to the other things.

The coach should plan for and allow time for the shooter to write this performance analysis. The coach should review the analysis to ensure that the shooter is making positive corrective comments, and that the comments are specific enough to picture the right way to do it next time. If your coach has spent his time on the line with his face in a spotting scope, he may not be able to see the benefit of performance analysis. All the coach will see through a spotting scope is bullet holes. What needs careful study is you, the shooter, not your bullet holes. When you're doing it right at your end of the range, the rifle takes care of the other end.

The first thing we do in performance analysis is review our goal. This goal should be established and written down before we start the match or practice session. Here we must be careful—the goal must be performance-oriented and must not be results-oriented. We're responsible for our performance: we cannot control the outcome. Instead of having a goal "to score a perfect possible," it would be better to have a goal "to follow my mental program for every shot." There are many reasons why you might not score a perfect possible (e.g., bad round, broken sight, gust of wind), but there is no reason why you couldn't meet a goal of following your mental program for every shot.

The next paragraph in our performance analysis is called "solution analysis." Here we recognize all the things that were missing from our perfect performance. But we must turn them around from a negative overtone to a positive one. If, for example, we missed a wind shot, we wouldn't write down, "I missed a wind shot." This causes you to mentally list all the ways you accomplished this mistake. Instead, you should write down the solution for this in the present tense, first person, as if you're already doing it correctly. For example, "I always memorize the wind flags and the mirage, I relate this to the results of my last shot, and I use this information to apply the correct setting to my next shot."

The next thing we do is list all the things we did right. This paragraph is called "success analysis." Here we analyze and reinforce all the things that went right. This should be a pleasant experience, and it's important to say as much as possible. It's also written in the first person, present tense, as if you always do this, because that is exactly what you want to do. Such a statement might sound like, "I always make my wind decision and move my sight aggressively," "I always follow my mental program for every shot," or "I always apply the six Ss of trigger manipulation: slow, smooth, steady, subconscious squeeze, straight to the rear." Remember when writing these paragraphs that the more we talk about, think about, or write about something happening, the more we improve the probability of that thing happening.

The purpose of success analysis is to put focus and attention on those things that we already do well, and the purpose of solution analysis is to put focus and attention on those things that we need to do well.

Some people find it very difficult to do a performance analysis. First, they can't let go of analyzing faults. Our world is a pretty negative place, and most of the opinions people give are critical. It's relatively easy to be a critic; it's considerably harder to be a constructive problem solver. We ask all our students to give up the critic role and instead focus their efforts on finding solutions (and then acting on them). Second, they think that writing something down as if it were already happening is "lying" when what it really represents is projecting their own desires into the real world.

If the shooter reports that he feels "jittery" 80 percent of the time, he reinforces feeling jittery. What we want him to think about is a solution for feeling jittery. What we want him to focus on is the 20 percent of the time he feels calm, relaxed, and in control and he sees only a soft, straight, small recoil during his follow-through. If the shooter feels jittery 80 percent of the time, he writes in his solution analysis: "I am always calm, relaxed, and in control. I always see a soft, straight, small recoil during my follow through." For the 20 percent of the time that he succeeds in the desired behavior, he writes in his success analysis: "I am always calm, relaxed, and in control. I always see a soft, straight, small recoil during my follow-through."

Similarly, if he chokes 50 percent of the time and can't get a clean shot away without either yanking the trigger or resetting, we want him to focus on the 50 percent of the time that he delivers the clean, smooth, rhythmic shot. The way performance analysis works is this: if the shooter shoots half of his shots without choking, he writes in his success analysis: "I always deliver a clean, smooth, rhythmic shot." If the other half of his shots require resetting, the shooter writes in his solution analysis: "I always deliver a clean, smooth, rhythmic shot."

In this way the subconscious mind is reinforced to produce the desired behavior all the time. Importantly, this means that the subconscious is never reinforced to produce the undesirable behavior. Eventually, the shooter can produce only the desired behavior because that's all he is programmed to do.

He may write these statements in both places for weeks or months or years . . . but one day, he will write it onlyin one place: his success analysis."

Competition Story—The Coaching Effect
From "The Dream Team":

As everyone who reads our stories in *Precision Shooting* and *The Accurate Rifle* knows, Linda loves to coach. One of her favorite stories about "the coaching effect" is the time that Canadian shooter Jim Bullock came over to her and said, "I'm having a little difficulty. Things aren't going well. I'm not sure what I'm doing wrong. Could you watch me and tell me what you think?"

Linda watched Jim shoot the next relay. The way she watches when she is coaching is that she throws the spotting scope aside and watches the shooter, not the shot fall. When Jim finished shooting, she said, "Jim, I don't think I can help you. I didn't see you do anything wrong. Everything looked very, very good from here."

Jim laughed and said, "Well, with you watching me, I focused on doing every little thing right . . . and I shot a possible. Can you watch me all the time?"

SECTION 5-5: MORE TOOLS—PERSONAL MOTTOES

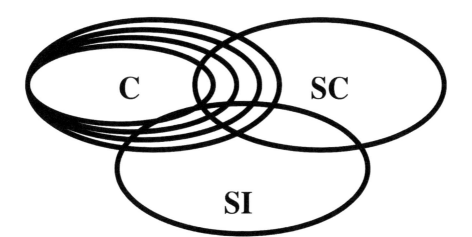

Have you ever heard a motto or a saying that puts a shiver down your spine? Those special few words that make you feel warm all over and make you ready to do what has to be done? It's seldom something that you made up but usually something you heard or read that just sticks with you. When you need it, you think it and it makes a difference.

Secrets of Mental Marksmanship

A friend of ours was a sniper with the British army during World War II. He jumped into Arnhem (Operation Market Garden) with what he figured was the best shooting Lee-Enfield sniper rifle he ever shot. He eventually tossed that rifle into the Rhine River so he wouldn't be captured with it. He said it was a hard thing to do but necessary to stay alive. He was captured and eventually escaped back to friendly lines.

When it was time to use that fine shooting rifle, he said that the phrase that motivated him and made him focus was, "Time to get down to business." When he said that phrase, a shiver went down his spine. He turned into the hunter, the predator, the wolf, the marksman, the sniper. It was his business—sniping wasn't something that he did; it was something that he was.

All that is old is new again. In 1503, Erasmus created 22 principles as a "Guide to the Righteous Protector." The tenth rule says, "SPIT, AS IT WERE, IN THE FACE OF DANGER. Keep a stirring quotation with you for encouragement."

MILITARY

Military Story—Tuskegee Airmen

One of the most interesting military stories is that of the Tuskegee Airmen. They were an all-black American fighter squadron of World War II. As you can imagine, they had an incredibly hard time to prove to their country that they were as good as anybody at defending it. They flew bomber escort and never lost a bomber. They were highly decorated and asked for by name when bomber pilots wanted the best escort. They were all heroes.

They took their motto from a song of the day, "Straighten up and fly right." Whenever anyone saw an enemy aircraft, they would announce it to the others by saying into the microphone, "Straighten up." The rest of the pilots would acknowledge with the remainder of the motto, "and fly right."

One can easily imagine what kind of picture might come to mind as you wing over to set an intercept course with enemy fighters that are most capable of shooting you out of the sky in flames.

But instead, with the words "Straighten up and fly right" foremost in your mind, you can see the mental picture that is being developed. "Straighten up" means get your mind back into the war; it's time to get down to business. And the "fly right" part simply means have confidence in your skills: you're a good fighter pilot, and we will stop this enemy from getting at our bombers.

The subconscious mind will move you toward what the conscious mind is picturing. As we move toward a life-and-death situation, we need to make sure the conscious mind is picturing the right thing. It needs to be on "wide scan" as we make the approach, alert to everything around us. When we need to fire the shots, we need to go "narrow attention control" just long enough to fire effective shots and then immediately back on wide scan. Put the conscious mind on situational awareness and let the subconscious mind deliver the skills.

> "I am the greatest."
> —Muhammad Ali,
> athlete (1942~)

> "Straighten up
> and fly right."
> —Tuskegee Airmen
> credo

> "I am the thin blue line."
> —Cops everywhere

> "Kick ass, take names."
> —Soldiers everywhere

> "If not me, who?"
> —Russian Special
> Forces credo

Tools to Increase Your Conscious Powers

POLICE

Law-Enforcement Story—Stacy Lim

In Lt. Col. Dave Grossman's book *On Combat*, he tells the story of Officer Stacy Lim of the Los Angeles Police Department. She was confronted by a carjacker and was shot through the chest with a .357 Magnum pistol. The bullet penetrated her heart and created a tennis-ball-size exit wound out her back. Stacy stayed in the fight and, in fact, became the aggressor and pursued her assailant, shooting him several times and killing him.

Stacy died twice on the operating table, requiring 101 pints of blood, but she did survive, and she eventually returned to duty. Although she was the victim of a surprise attack by deadly predators, she not only stayed in the fight, she took the fight to them. She won this fight because she was both physically and mentally prepared. She had a competitive attitude that refused to let her lose. She had a plan; it was a visualized determination to win, to always win.

> "You need to prepare your mind for where your body may have to go."
> —Stacy Lim, police officer

> "The mind leads the body."
> —Koichi Tohei, founder of Ki-Aikido (1920~)

HUNTING

Hunter Story—Be the Wind

Neville Watson, our professional hunter friend from Namibia of whom we spoke earlier, related a most interesting story about how he got started in his profession. On several wonderful evenings while sitting around an open fire, with darkness and the sounds of Africa in the background, we listened with great interest. We do need to admit here that those "sounds of Africa in the background" did cause an element of distraction.

He told us of an old professional hunter whom he met many years earlier. Neville had shown great interest in hunting, and the old man had taken a liking to him and decided to teach him what he knew about hunting the mysterious and dangerous game of Africa.

The old man had grown up in Africa during the early 1900s and had hunted elephants for the ivory trade. He also spent some of his time guiding the rich English clients who came over for the excitement of an African safari. He was frequently called upon to help hunt down rogue elephants that had decided to even the score against man, or marauding lions that had developed a taste for the easy-to-catch villagers. He had told Neville how he particularly enjoyed hunting these rogues and marauders. It had become personal for him when he played the game of life and death with a huge animal that had killed men. He needed to use all of his wits and knowledge to keep from being another statistic in the history of that elephant or lion. He had read about such statistics: how this elephant had gored or trampled 28 people before finally being hunted down and killed, or how that lion had mauled and eaten 56 natives before it was stopped.

The old PH said that he often woke up at night from a recurring dream and would need a half bottle of whiskey to allow him to go back to sleep. He would be stalking some man-killing animal when suddenly it would appear from nowhere and attack. He could feel teeth tearing at his body and feel life being smothered from him as the lion bit through his throat. In the next scene he would see a wanted poster with a mug shot photo of a lion. Below the picture was the number of humans this beast had killed. The lion would turn to him and smile and the tally below would click over to show one more victim.

The old man was no longer the handsome and rugged man of his youth. He had spent too many days on the trails of something that could kill him and too many nights on the cold, damp ground waking up from a bad dream, and too many half bottles of whiskey had taken their toll. His face was weathered and showed scars from the lion attack that almost made his dream come true.

Secrets of Mental Marksmanship

The old man always carried a pistol with him, a 1911 Colt .45 ACP. He was never seen without it. As a young man he had won the pistol in a poker game with an American client. The American gave it up only reluctantly, as he thought surely his two pair would take the pot. He did eventually concede that the three kings the old man laid down were indeed enough.

His friends laughed at him for carrying such a little pistol as a backup weapon. He would laugh back and reply that the pistol wasn't a backup against animals; it was a backup for himself, as he had no intention of being eaten alive.

Just as in his dream, the lion attacked from nowhere. It was on him in a flash, looking forward to another easy meal. The force of the charge sent him and his rifle flying in different directions. He was stunned and disoriented. He felt horrific pressure on his head and could smell a most foul odor. Suddenly his mind cleared and he realized that the lion was on top of him, gripping his head in its jaws. He tried to move his arm to draw his pistol but he couldn't; a giant paw had him pinned to the ground. Damn it . . . after all his precautions . . . he hoped the lion would bite down quick and end it.

The lion shifted his hold, releasing his grip on the old man's head in an attempt to get a better hold on his neck. It took only a second for the man to stuff his left arm into the lion's mouth as far as he could reach. When the lion had moved, his right arm was suddenly freed. He grabbed for his pistol. He carried it loaded with the hammer at half cock. He tried desperately to get the hammer cocked all the way back, but he couldn't get his thumb to work properly. He gripped the pistol in a shooting hold and rubbed the hammer hard against his chest. Over the noise of the lion choking on his arm and growling, he actually heard or felt the hammer cock. But now he didn't think about shooting himself. He jammed the pistol into the fur behind the lion's front leg and pulled the trigger five times. The lion startled and released the grip on the old man's arm. He looked at the man as if surprised. He coughed or sneezed and covered the man with blood from his nose. The old man put the pistol to the lion's ear and pulled the trigger three more times. He was glad he carried an extra round in the chamber.

The old man lay still while the lion convulsed and writhed. He had seen big cats in their death throes before, and he was certain this one was done for it. He slowly began to move his own body parts to see which of them still worked. His face and chest were covered in blood. He wasn't sure if it was his or the lion's—maybe a bit of both. His left forearm was broken and the left elbow wouldn't bend. His shoulder was very painful, but everything else seemed to work. He found his rifle and started the five-kilometer walk back to his car. On the way he noticed that some of the blood that covered him was drying up and some wasn't. He found the sources of the fresh blood and was able to stem the flow. Once in his car, he drove himself to the nearest missionary doctor, about 50 kilometers away. There he spent two weeks healing and fighting off infection.

During his first night in the hospital, the dream came back to him. His temperature was very high and his body was full of the drugs he needed to fight off the infection caused by the lion bites. In his dream, the beast attacked in the usual manner, but this time it was the old man's own face on the wanted poster. And this time he turned and smiled as the counter below clicked over one more casualty.

Neville visited the old man at the missionary hospital and, when he was well enough to go home, stayed with him for a few days. They talked for many hours about hunting and the animals they both loved.

The old man talked about the way he hunted the rogue ones. These he stalked. He preferred this way to other hunting techniques that were safer. He said it was more personal. Neville pursued the old man on this, knowing he had killed many animals this way and wanting to know how he did it. The old man told him that once he found the track of the animal he was after, he would follow it very quickly until he could see the tracks were very fresh. He would then turn on his stalking attitude. He did this by saying over and over to himself, "Be the wind . . . be the wind." With this phrase in mind, he would see himself moving easily from one step to the next, slipping around and through the underbrush as a gentle wind does, making no sound or giving away his presence. This also reminded him to always be aware of the wind direction and keep it to his favor. The old man had his own personal motto that kept him focused and on task when it was most important to do so.

Tools to Increase Your Conscious Powers

COMPETITION

Competition Story—Calm Blue Ocean

During each running of our marksmanship courses, we require each of the students to come up with a personal motto—a short phrase that creates the right mindset to help them perform at their best. The motto needs to be performance-oriented, causing the student to focus on doing it right at his end of the range. Some resist coming up with a motto, but with regular encouragement they eventually do.

Sometimes the motto can be very aggressive, especially among the police and military students, but that's appropriate because theirs is an aggressive world, and besides, it's their own personal motto. However, we did have to correct the one motto: "All I want to see is bone chips and red mist." This motto is results-oriented, as it draws the focus downrange. This student needed to come up with a motto that would get him to focus on the performance required at his end of the range in order to get him the downrange results he needed. You have to do it right at your end before it can be right at the other end.

These mottoes can often be a surprise to the instructors. One military student resisted telling us his personal motto for several days. He kept telling the instructor that he didn't have one. The student kept hearing the mottoes of the other students every day and still he kept telling us he didn't have one. The instructor thought that perhaps the student's motto was so bloodthirsty that he was embarrassed to tell it. But eventually all was revealed. After several days of gentle but consistent pressure, the student blurted out, "Look, I don't have one. Whenever I am about to fire a shot I think, 'calm blue ocean' and I just can't come up with a personal motto." The instructor had to smile at this one as he explained to the student that he had an outstanding personal motto. Thinking "calm blue ocean" would keep him calm and relaxed at exactly the right time to fire a perfect shot.

CHAPTER SUMMARY

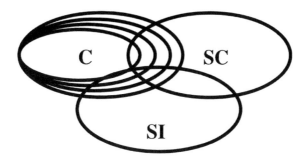

In this chapter, we focused on the power of conscious mind, or awareness. The purpose of the conscious mind during the firing of a shot is to be picturing the right thoughts so that the subconscious can fire the perfect shot. Just as you must have the same physical position during the shot, you should think the same thoughts for each and every shot. You must stay focused on these thoughts, and these thoughts must drive to one irresistible conclusion: a perfect shot.

The mental program is the key for keeping the conscious mind picturing the right pictures for the actual firing of a perfect shot.

There are other areas that need our conscious attention. One of the best ways to take care of these is through the use of a logbook. The logbook is the place where important and relevant information is kept for easy reference. It's both a fact base and a historical record. It's used to help you make better decisions in the future.

One of the main components of the logbook is organization lists, both "to do" and equipment checklists. Prior to the start of an operation (whether it's police, military, field, or competition), the conscious mind has a lot of things to think about in order to get ready for and through the event successfully. The more important it is to be organized, to get the most done with your time, and to arrive at your destination with the gear and equipment you need to do the job, then the more important it is to use lists.

During a match or a training session, keep the conscious mind picturing the right pictures with positive reinforcement. After the match or training session, continue with the positive reinforcement by doing a "performance analysis." Performance analysis calls for a different way of looking at what you're doing. Analyze what you do right, and what you do wrong will just go away. If you're having a problem, look for solutions. Record, enjoy, and repeat what you need do right. Write the "success" statements and write the "solution" statements. You may write these statements in both places for weeks or months or years . . . but one day, you will write it only in one place: your success analysis.

Have a personal motto that keeps you focused, that pulls you up from any setbacks, and that keeps you on track when things are going well. Remember Erasmus, who said, "SPIT, AS IT WERE, IN THE FACE OF DANGER. Keep a stirring quotation with you for encouragement."

NOTES

1. "The Ontario Lt. Governor's Match 1995—Keith's Story" by Keith A. Cunningham was originally published in *Precision Shooting* (May 1996) and has been republished in *Favorite Stories on Winning*.
2. There is a lieutenant governor as the head of state in each province of Canada, so the lieutenant governor's prize would be similar to a U.S. state's governor's award. The national head of state for Canada is the governor general, and the governor general's award is contested at the national matches; it would be similar to a U.S. president's award.
3. The ORA is the Ontario Rifle Association, a provincial sports organization for military-oriented shooting disciplines and for Target Rifle.
4. The Commonwealth Games is a multicountry, multisport event, much like the Pan-American Games, but with current and former British Commonwealth countries included. The Commonwealth Games Trials for all sports are typically held by the national sport governing body about a year ahead of the games.
5. In fact, we recently read that the implementation of a presurgery checklist has reduced postoperative casualty rates by over 40 percent.
6. "The Power of Self-Talk" by Linda K. Miller and Keith A. Cunningham was originally published in *Precision Shooting* (April 1998) and has been republished in *Favorite Stories on Attitude*.
7. "How to Build a Training Plan . . . that Works!" by Linda K. Miller was originally published in the *CoachNet* newsletter (July/August 2001) and has been republished in *Favorite Stories for the Competition Coach*.

— Chapter 6 —

Tools to Increase
Your Subconscious Powers

SECTION 6-1: THE KEY IS PERFECT PRACTICE

The purpose of the subconscious mind is to fire the perfect shot. The basic concept here is that only perfect practice makes your subconscious power increase perfectly. In sports, this is often called muscle memory. In psychology, it's called a semiconditioned response. In all cases, the conscious mind pictures the desired behavior, and the subconscious orchestrates the muscles to perform it. The subconscious mind learns this through repeti-

Subconscious Powers—The Key is Perfect Practice

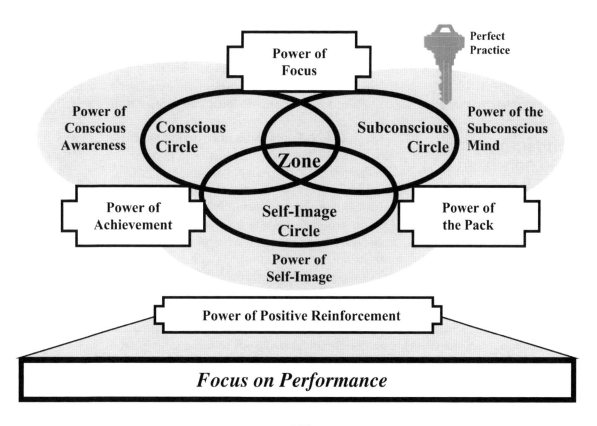

tion. Every complex skill requires practice to ensure that the muscles learn their parts and that they can perform flawlessly with no conscious intervention.

People who practice martial arts learn through a series of repeated practices. People who play a musical instrument learn through a series of scales, exercises, and many hours of practice. People who learn marksmanship do so through effective drills and hours of structured training and practices.

MILITARY

Military Story—Drill Details

From drill movements to full battle scenarios, the primary peacetime competency of the military is training. And one of the things that the military knows how to train is drill.

As we said in the "I Love a Parade" story in an earlier section of this book, if there is one thing that any serious military organization can do, it's put on a spectacular parade. It stands to reason that if they can train their soldiers to march properly and perform the drill movements while under the watchful eye of some general or other such dignitary, then there is likely a good chance they can train the soldiers for battle. Drill teaches the soldiers to have discipline, to feel like they're part of a bigger organization, and to respond immediately to orders. It, of course, has its roots in the formations that were required on the battlefield.

You can appreciate that they don't just toss the young soldier into a parade without proper training. (There are some stories where the young soldier has been tossed into battle without proper training, but we parents of young soldiers like to believe that those situations are held to a minimum.)

To start with, the parade is broken down into drill movements. And then each of the drill movements is further broken down into segments, or "squads." How to teach a drill period is one of the first things taught to soon-to-be NCOs. In such a lesson, the instructor first demonstrates the drill movement. Then he explains to the class exactly where and why such a movement is used. He then explains that for instructional reasons, this movement will be broken down into squads. He demonstrates what he will call "squad 1." He then explains what happened in squad 1. He then has the students carry out squad 1 on his command while he corrects. Once he thinks the students have it, he has them practice it on their own while he goes from one to the next and coaches them in the details.

Once he is satisfied that the students have accomplished squad 1, he then demonstrates squad 2, picking up where squad 1 left off. This procedure continues for as many squads as are necessary, and once all have been learned to his satisfaction, he then combines all the squads into a single movement. This movement is then practiced individually and in the group, under the continual coaching of the instructor, until it can be accomplished perfectly, every time and on demand.

All of the drill movements are taught in this manner, and eventually several drill movements are combined.

> "Correct repetition is the mother of skill."
> —Lt. Col. Dave Grossman

> "Whatever we plant in our subconscious mind and nourish with repetition and emotion will one day become a reality."
> —Earl Nightingale, motivational speaker (1921–1989)

> "There is nothing noble in being superior to some other man. The true nobility is in being superior to your previous self."
> —Hindu proverb

> "For this is what the art of archery means: a profound and far-reaching contest of the archer with himself."
> —Eugen Herrigel in *Zen in the Art of Archery*

Tools to Increase Your Subconscious Powers

As more drill movements are learned, more of them are combined, and eventually the soldiers are ready to parade.

We think this is the exact right way to learn a skill, and it applies directly to learning marksmanship. Break the firing of the perfect shot into segments, and learn each segment before you put them all together.

Law-Enforcement Story—Holsters and Other Drills

A good friend of ours was the training officer for a local police agency when it decided to go from a level two to a level three holster. This meant there was one more thing that had to be accomplished during a draw. Our friend felt there had to be a minimum of 2,000 correct repetitions[1] with the new holster before it was properly imprinted on the subconscious and the officer could be relied on to draw correctly.

Remember the story we told earlier about the state trooper who, after taking a blast of buckshot in his vest, drew his sidearm and successfully engaged his attacker. He had learned to do this as a competitor in IPSC matches. In these matches, you're required to draw and engage targets; to win, you must do it quickly. He practiced doing this dry in his basement, which resulted in thousands of repetitions and a firm and clear imprint on his subconscious mind. He could draw and fire effectively because he knew of no other way to do it.

On the other side of this coin is what happens if you practice the wrong thing—you get good at doing it wrong. We told you earlier about an agency that was teaching its officers to draw and fire two shots. In order to speed up the drill, they taught the officers to automatically holster after they fired the two shots in order to be ready for the next repetition. But under the stress of real-life incidents, this was exactly what the officers did—they drew, fired two shots, and immediately holstered. This, of course, isn't always the right thing to do if there is still a threat. Training must always have a logical and operationally oriented conclusion.

Hunter Story—The Shot Not Taken

The people who come on our hunter marksmanship course are often experienced hunters who have had a bad experience in the field. Their minds are full of negative images: an injured animal, a badly placed shot, an uncontrolled rise of buck fever, endless negative reinforcement every night at the hunt camp. They come to the course looking to find the solution to the unconstructive videos that keep playing over and over in their minds. They're victims of practicing the wrong thing, and they know it. We tell them they have come to the right place to solve this problem.

One fellow had taken a wild shot at his first whitetail deer, hit it in the leg, and injured it. Matt knew that the animal was hurt, so he spent the rest of the day tracking it, hoping to find it and put it out of its misery. He never found it, but he had no doubt that the wolves did. He needed images of perfect shots in his mind to replace this tragic first experience. He needed to erase the old videos and record some new ones to reset his standard for practice, perfect practice.

"Trifles make perfection, but perfection is no trifle."
—Michelangelo, artist (1475–1564)

"Train hard and train smart."
—Keith A. Cunningham, soldier (1950~)

"The Japanese method of instruction . . . demonstration, example, imitation . . . practice, repetition, and repetition of the repeated with ever increasing intensity."
—Eugen Herrigel in *Zen in the Art of Archery*

On the course he learned about the firing of the perfect shot, then firing the perfect shot from field positions, then firing the perfect shot from field positions on a realistic target. Then we took him out on a little hunting scenario, where he would have to identify the game, select his fire position, assess whether he had a good-enough hold for a humane kill at that distance, and then fire a live shot. That fall, Matt e-mailed us to say that he hadn't fired on a moving deer from the standing (unsupported) position because he knew that his marksmanship skill wasn't yet sufficiently practiced to guarantee a good hit. He did, however, successfully engage his first whitetail trophy from the kneeling position at about 75 yards. We were proud of him on both accounts, and especially on the shot not taken.

COMPETITION

Competition Story—Dry-Firing for Two Years

Lanny Basham is a renowned, gold-medal-winning Olympic smallbore shooter from the United States. He won his gold medal at the 1976 Olympics in Montreal. He now runs a shooting school where he trains potential Olympians. He also conducts seminars, of which we have taken two.

At his seminars, Lanny tells the story of when he was trying to get some training time to compete in an international match. However, his army job wouldn't give him an opportunity to train. He had two years to prepare for this important match, and he had to do it without range time or matches to shoot in.

He and his wife were living in military-provided married quarters, and there was a spare room. Here he set up a place where he could dry-fire. He made the lighting right. He put small dots on the wall that were sized to be relatively the same size as the targets he would be shooting at in the match. He set up the representational targets for the three positions he would be shooting from: one at each height for prone, kneeling, and standing. He spent every moment he could dry-firing the various positions, but he focused on kneeling, as he knew it was his weakest position.

His training followed the principle that "if you get it right at your end of the range, the rifle will take care of the other end." The most interesting point about this training is because it was all dry-firing, he didn't have shot holes or scores to distract him from focusing on firing the perfect shot each and every time. He called every shot when it went "click" and knew when it was perfect. His goal was to be able to call every shot perfect.

In the two years leading up to his major match, he was able to get to two lesser matches. These events confirmed for him that his training was working. He later went on to win the international match, with his kneeling performance making the difference.

SECTION 6-2: MORE TOOLS—PRACTICE TIME, PRACTICE QUALITY, PRACTICE INTENSITY

If you practice only once a week on a complex skill like marksmanship, you tend to lose ability. If you practice two or three times a week, you can usually maintain your current level of skill. When you practice four or five times a week, you can improve your skill. If you practice six or seven days a week, you tend to start getting stale and you start to burn out, and you will likely lose skill. Therefore, you usually need to train about four or five days a week for best results.

The quality of this practice is critical. As we say when we're training marksmen of all types, "When you're shooting good, shoot lots." Too often, when people are training they think the opposite. When they're shooting well, they think, "I've got that part; I'll just move on to something else." In fact, what they need to do is repeat the practice over and over in order to reinforce the correct performance.

"Correct repetition is the mother of skill." Once you have figured out how to do something correctly, you need to repeat it, over and over, until the body and mind know only one way to perform the task.

And the converse is also true: when you're shooting badly, stop. Too often, when people are training they think

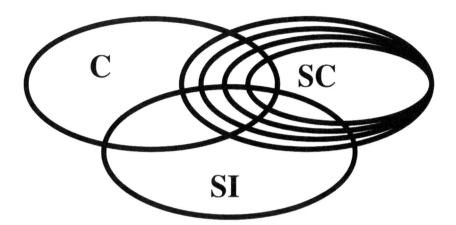

the opposite. When they're shooting badly, they think, "Oh, I'm not doing well. I'd better keep hammering at this until I get better." In fact, what they're doing is reinforcing poor performance. They should stop training and go to a different drill they can do well, a lower intensity drill, or a "back to basics" training session. In some cases, they need to do something completely different for a while.

Get lots of good practice. Take every opportunity. As Lt. Col. Dave Grossman says, "Piss on golf. Real men go to the range."

Rob Leatham is one of the best action pistol shooters in the world. Like us, he trains law-enforcement and military special operations personnel on how to shoot fast and accurate under pressure. Some time ago, he made some comments (on the forum at www.brianenos.com) on the debate between competition shooting and combat gunfighting. He noted that his students often got more nervous in competition than they did in combat, mostly because they had time to think. He thought that, on the battlefield, warriors do things that aren't "practical or tactical" by training or competition

"There are no secrets to success. It is the result of preparation, hard work, learning from failure."
—Gen. Colin Powell, soldier and statesman (1937~)

"Ambition by itself never gets anywhere until it forms a partnership with hard work."
—James Garfield, 20th U.S. president (1831–1881)

"Train like you fight, because you will fight like you train."
—Linda K. Miller, coach (1952~)

standards, but they survive because whatever they do, they do quickly, accurately, and decisively. However, he has concluded that those who master a shooting skill in match conditions are "more likely to do well in a pressure situation." If you "train hard and test yourself in the arena of competition," you will find out what you know and what you can do.

Train with the best shooters. Your practice time will be well leveraged if you can spend time with good shooters. This is an application of the "power of the pack": we raise or lower ourselves to the standard we're around. We tend to copy the group; therefore, surround yourself with people who are where you want to go. In order to see yourself as a good shot, you need to hang out with good shots. You become part of the group, and you may learn something from each other as well.

One of the aims of your practice that will improve your shooting is to minimize the time between shots: learn to shoot quickly. Ironically, you don't learn to shoot quickly by focusing on "quickly." You learn to shoot quickly by:

> Minimizing the number of things you do that don't lead directly to firing the shot.
> Doing all the remaining things as smoothly as possible.
> Staying "in the bubble," completely focused on the process, with no time spent on distractions or irrelevant things and no time lost reacquiring the required focus.

All of these things support the development of subconscious shooting, which is by far the most accurate and most pleasurable type of shooting there is.

One aspect of training that often gets overlooked is practice intensity. It's critical that the intensity be matched to the training level of the shooter. Just as you wouldn't put a soldier in a parade before he has learned the drill movements, you wouldn't put a police sniper on a call before he has learned to shoot a perfect shot on demand under stress.

We distinguish low-intensity training from high-intensity training. For example, firing groups is at the low-intensity end of the spectrum, while scenarios with live fire are at the high-intensity end. Many shooters (and many marksmanship courses) start at the wrong end of the spectrum, throwing the student into high-intensity situations before they have learned the underlying skills in a low-intensity training environment.

Low intensity should be used whenever you're learning something new. Break the skill into squads—short, simple activities that can be practiced over and over until they're habitual. The focus during low-intensity training is to be as smooth as possible and then to work on getting smoother. Doing it right is the most important thing; doing it on demand and doing it fast will come later. Low-intensity training has no stress in it. The student takes the time to learn the skill and imprint it on the subconscious. This training provides the strong foundation that the student will draw on when the intensity increases.

In marksmanship, low-intensity training includes practices like holding and aiming, the safety-on drill, dry-firing, trigger tapping, and hot and cold exercis-

es.[2] These drills can be mixed for variety and are an effective way to ensure the fundamentals are being learned. As the student requires progression in intensity, the types of fire can be added: deliberate fire, snap fire (on demand), rapid follow-up (two shots timed fire, on demand), rapid fire (multiple shots timed fire, on demand), multiple targets, moving targets, fire with movement, and so on.

High-intensity training gradually introduces stress—a little at first until the marksman is able to deal with the stress and still fire a perfect shot. The key is to add the stress in progressive increments and to teach the student how to deal with each type and amount of stress. Some ways to add intensity include:

> Change targets to include moving, turning, reactive, and/or realistic targets.
> Push timings for planning, reacting, and shooting.
> Add distractions, including spectators, noise, or concurrent activities.
> Add challenges, such as problem solving, unknowns, unexpected changes, surprises, longer ranges, and field firing.
> Introduce competition. Whether it's a small bet between friends or an international match, competition adds spice to your training and gives purpose to your drills.

The training should return to low intensity whenever a new skill or tactic is being added, new equipment is introduced, problems arise and solutions are required, and for warm-ups and cool-downs. This benefits all types of shooters, but we're truly impressed with just how important it is for tactical team members, who often train only scenarios and equally often lose sight of the foundational skills and, with that, lose confidence in their equipment and themselves.

Warm-ups and cool-downs should focus on a simple drill like the police sniper's "Cold Clean Barrel and Group," where a single shot is fired at one aiming mark and a follow-up group is fired at a second aiming mark.

> "Correct repetition is the mother of skill."
> —Lt. Col. Dave Grossman

Tools to Increase Your Subconscious Powers

Cold Clean Barrel and Group

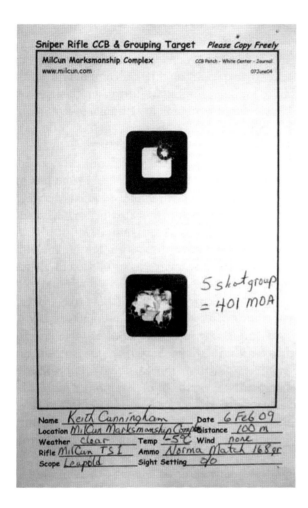

Military Story—More Sweat

One of the basic principles that any of the serious militaries follow is this one: more sweat in training, less blood in battle.

This is an easy concept to follow, and one doesn't have to be a member of the military to grasp its meaning. In order to be prepared for a life and death struggle, you need to be very good at the required skills. In order to get good at them, you need practice time, you need to be practicing the right thing, and you need to think it's important for you to know these skills. In other words, there is some pay value in it for you.

You may recall, in an earlier story, the young Marine sergeant who was teaching his squad three basic unarmed combat moves. His theory was to select the three most important moves and practice those over and over. He believed it was best to be really good at these three than to be so-so with 10 moves. His idea was to be really smooth with these moves because "smooth is fast."

**Law-Enforcement Story—
Low and High Intensity**

Although adequate training time is required (and accepted as such) in many areas of skill development, we often find it necessary to emphasize the same need for marksmanship skill.

Many police officers involved with our training have said to us that they're never given enough training time to practice the basic skills. They arrive for training and are immediately thrown into the high-intensity practices. This is partly due to the chronic shortage of training time, but it is also a result of senior trainers with the attitude that "this is how they will have to do it on a call."

This is certainly true, but before we launch into the high-intensity work, we need to have mastered the underlying skills through low-intensity training. To do it any other way is to send officers into harm's way without being properly trained. (Recall our story on how the military teaches drill.)

An interesting point came out during one of our recent tactical rifle courses. We were instructing a number of agency trainers in some basic marksmanship with tactical rifles. Twice each day (first thing in the morning and first thing after lunch) we shot a zeroing confirmation group. We have found that most tactical scopes won't hold a zero, and the scopes on this course were no exception, with about half needing some kind of an adjustment each time, and some needing an alarming amount of adjustment to bring them back on zero.

It was interesting to see the reaction of these trainers when they realized this, and they began to talk about the number of failures they got during the qualification course of fire. They were wondering if they could change this if they just did a zeroing exercise prior to the test. Then they wondered about the number of officers who were now out on the street with rifles that weren't zeroed. We suggested that they keep records on every scope in their agency every time it passed through the qualifications tests so they would know which ones always needed some kind of zeroing adjustment. Scopes with a history of this needed to be returned to the manufacturer or exchanged. If there were very many with this problem, then a different model of scope needed to be put into service.

This very important point was made only because we did a short bit of low-intensity training before we moved on with the day's high-intensity work. It's very much in line with the idea that when you go to the gym to do some high-intensity weightlifting, you always do some kind of low-intensity warm-up training first.

Marksmanship training must be conducted in the same manner. Always start the day's training with some low-intensity warm-up drills. A drill that confirms that your rifle is still zeroed is a good one.

HUNTING

Hunter Story—Linda's Quality Time

You may recall that we previously mentioned that Linda uses a lightweight hunting rifle in .308 caliber. This rifle produces a noticeable amount of recoil because of its light weight, but the light weight is necessary for her to have a rifle she can handle easily, carry all day, and shoot well.

The factory rifle was light enough, but the problem with it was that the recoil was amplified by the shape of the stock. She could only shoot a couple of shots and then it wasn't fun to shoot anymore and she would stop. She could barely shoot enough to get it properly zeroed.

Hoping to fix this problem, Keith installed a muzzle brake and made her a custom stock that fit her properly. What a difference! Her first time at the range with her new rifle was a wonderful experience, exactly the kind a hunter should enjoy. After she zeroed it, she then proceeded to shoot at a variety of targets from a variety of positions and from a variety of distances, exactly what a hunter should do to practice for a hunting trip. She finally stopped only because she was concerned about the amount of ammo she was using.

She has since made some impressive shots with this rifle on both game and targets. Last year she hit a deer at 80 meters from a standing position. She also used it to make some solid hits on a target at 600 meters. All this is possible because the rifle is comfortable and therefore fun to shoot, and she shoots it often and well.

COMPETITION

Competition Story—Jack Was Still Shooting Standing!

Here's another great story told by Lanny Bassham at his seminars. He tells the story of a day he was training with a teammate, Jack Ryder. They had agreed to spend the morning working on standing and then doing some kneeling. Lanny finished his standing training and looked over to see where Jack was with his training. Jack was still shooting standing.

Lanny carried on with his kneeling training and finished at noon. He checked to see what Jack was doing and was surprised to see Jack still shooting standing. Lanny went off for lunch and when he came back, Jack was still shooting standing.

Lanny was at a loss to understand what Jack was doing—he had shot standing all morning and was still shooting standing. Just then, Jack finally appeared to be stopping, and Lanny was keen to ask him what he had been doing.

Jack's answer was simple. It was based on the principle that when you're shooting well, shoot lots. Jack said that he was shooting the best standing he had ever shot, and he just kept doing it until he stopped shooting so well. It's absolutely the very best practice that you can get. The subconscious mind becomes saturated with firing the perfect shot.

Tools to Increase Your Subconscious Powers

COMPETITION

Competition Story—From Tyro to QM

One of the jobs we particularly like is coaching the Canadian Forces Combat Shooting Team for the army competition in Bisley, England. We enjoy working with the soldiers, and we hope some of the skills we teach might someday save a life. The one problem we have to endure is that the CF never gives us enough time to train the team properly. To overcome this, it's necessary for us to decide what training would give us the most return for the time we have.

The time we're given in Bisley is at a premium. It's hard to get range time, and therefore any time we can get has to be used to the maximum, which results in some very intense training. Some of the team members cannot keep up with this pace and may not be selected for the various team events. Most of them rise to the challenge, thrive on the intensity, and produce superior results. In fact, when they return from this training, the best of them will be contenders for the Queen's Medal, and one will invariably win it. The QM is the highest award given to the top shot at the Canadian Forces Small Arms Competition (CFSAC). The records show that we have trained 12 individuals to a QM, and a couple of them have won it more than once.

And none better to demonstrate this than 2008's QM winner. He was a Tyro in 2007 and shot well enough to win a spot on the 2008 Bisley Team. As a member of this team, he was subjected to the intense training that our lack of training time required. He immediately accepted this with a matter of fact and "get down to business" attitude. He followed our coaching without hesitation and was soon being selected for all the team events and became the backbone of the team. Once back in Canada and with his unit team, he came to CFSAC and won the QM. In our recollection, there is no one else who has gone from Tyro to Queen's Medalist in 12 months.

SECTION 6-3: MORE TOOLS—TYPES OF TRAINING AND TRAINING PHASES

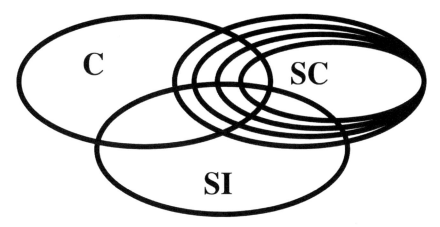

There are two sets of related tools to increase your subconscious powers: types of training and training phases. The various types of training are used to control the intensity of the training and to provide variety to the repetitive nature of repeated practice. The training phases are used to give shape to the purpose of your training periods, with the objective of producing enhanced performance levels when you peak for competition or operations.

The types of training may be, in general terms, described as follows:

➣ Dry (holding and aiming, walk- and talk-through, dry-firing)
➣ Controlled (mixed live and dry, shooting groups, shooting on command, match workups, operational workups)

➤ Rehearsals (simulations of competitions or operations scenarios)
➤ Operational (hunting, competition, police/military operations)

The trick to working through the types of training is to build skill progressively and make sure each foundational piece is solid before moving on to the next building block. Anytime the shooter adds something new (equipment, position changes, types of fire, etc.), he needs to start back at the dry type of training.

For example, Linda recently added a laser sight to her pistol. When she first turned it on, all she tried to do was aim the pistol with the iron sights and see where the laser pointed. Then she tried to aim the laser sight and hold it on the target. Next she did a little dry-firing. Then she went to the range and worked with live and dry to get the laser "sighted in" so that both the irons and the laser would produce the same point of impact. Then she worked through some group shooting before she started on match workups. This progressive training regimen ensures that the new equipment is used successfully and that no time is wasted having to backtrack.

The training phases are:

➤ Experimental phase—This phase focuses on figuring out what you need for training (equipment, drills, techniques/tactics, practices).
➤ Training phase—This phase focuses on getting the training done and includes the competitions/operations.
➤ Recovery phase—This phase focuses on rest and relaxation, with a healthy dose of active physical sport or hobby.

The main idea here is to allow yourself an opportunity to discover new and improved tools and methods, to repeat the ones that work until you are truly proficient, and to provide a formal rest and recovery period. You need to understand which phase you're in and ensure that you stay in the phase (without dabbling in the others inappropriately). For example, Linda wouldn't have added a laser sight to her pistol except in the experimental phase. It is also important to ensure you include the experimental and recovery phases in your plan. If you see your training as one unending training phase, you will be susceptible to burnout. Having an experimental phase adds some variety to your training and perks up your interest in going to the range. Having a recovery phase allows you to recharge your batteries and develop new interest to return to the range.

MILITARY

Military Story—Special Forces Burnout

Some time ago we were hired by a special operations unit to see if we could provide some ideas about their training. The focus was specifically on sniper marksmanship, but in conversation an interesting point came out. A couple of the students commented to us that, with the continuous training, sometimes they felt burned out. If there was any word that could be used to describe the training that these guys did, it was "intense." They had the time, money, and approval to conduct an unlimited amount of training. And that was what they did: day in and day out, they trained and shot and shot and trained. They were certainly the envy of all the regular infantry units.

So what could these high-intensity soldiers do to minimize burnout? To start with, we suggested that they get the individuals involved with the experimental stage. Let them do some of the trials on the equipment and have them write up their opinions on it. Let them come up with some different tactics and see if they will work. Let them come up with new training ideas and scenarios.

As well, they needed some time off from the particular training that was causing the burnout. If actual time off wasn't possible, then at least they could do some cross-training with a different weapon. The old saying that "a change is as good as a rest" would apply here and, of course, still be good training.

Tools to Increase Your Subconscious Powers

POLICE

Law-Enforcement Story—Three-Phase Training for Police

The training procedures that we use in our police sniper and tactical courses very much follow the three-phase training cycle.

The first stage is the experimental stage. During this stage, we educate the student on the principles behind the skill we're about to teach. We then demonstrate how we expect that skill to be carried out, and then we provide lots of coached practice. We set up the sniper rifle to fit properly. We adjust the scope for proper eye relief. We make sure the trigger is right. We experiment with different adaptations of the basic positions to find the one that is right for that individual. We set the student up for success. This is all low-intensity training. Our philosophy is, "Get good before you get fast, and smooth is fast."

The next stage is live rehearsals and scenarios, which extends into operations. This is high-intensity training, and while it starts off slowly, it gains momentum as the skill levels develop. Because the emphasis is on being smooth, the student will get fast without trying. It's during this stage that the student becomes ready for operations.

Then there is the recovery phase. It's widely known and well documented that tactical police officers need some downtime, some time away from the stresses of their job.

> **"Practice is the best of all instructors."**
> **—Publilius Syrus, writer (1st century BC)**

HUNTING

Hunter Story—Three Phases for the PH

We approached our friend Neville, the professional hunter in Namibia, to ask whether he follows this concept of three-phase training. Although he doesn't look on it specifically as "training," he did say that he follows a yearly cycle in preparing for his clients.

Prior to the hunting season, he said, he spends time experimenting. He checks out what is new on the market in the way of equipment that might work better for him and his clients. Some of these pieces of equipment are wonderful ideas, while others are just gadgets. He spends the time to work through it all and field tests some of it to make sure it's rugged and works as advertised.

Also during this period, he spends considerable time getting back into physical shape. He needs to be in better shape than his clients, and he is expected to lead by example. He must not allow a hunt to be cut short just because he can't keep up with it. It's one thing to allow his client to lag behind, but it's quite another if he cannot keep up. He must also be fit enough to take care of any dangerous situation that could occur with a rogue animal or careless client.

It's during this experimental stage that he is breaking in his own new equipment. This is especially true of a new pair of boots. Because of the amount of walking he must do during the hunting season, he must have dependable and comfortable boots. They must be proven to be so, and the only way to know this is to wear them for a substantial period of time before they're needed.

He spends considerable time in the bush looking for the trophy animals that he needs to have a successful hunt. He patterns the game and seeks out their bedding, watering, and traveling routes. He also spends time making sure his own marksmanship skills are honed into form, because lives could depend on them.

Neville sends out "joining instructions" during this time to advise all his clients to be doing the same preparation. Some pay no attention and suffer the consequences on their expensive once-in-a-lifetime hunt. Others follow his advice to the letter and have a much more enjoyable experience.

During the hunt, Neville is very busy and under considerable stress to make sure each client gets a trophy, not to mention having the responsibility to keep them alive and out of harm's way. He must make sure each client is catered to in every way and that they have a successful and memorable experience.

After the hunting season is over, Neville says he needs some recovery time. He must get away from the stresses and simply slow the pace he has been maintaining. He will take his family on a trip to some part of the country they have wanted to see. He is also an accomplished competition shooter and finds going to matches relaxing. And sometimes he just hangs around doing odd jobs he has been meaning to finish. Essentially, he does whatever it takes to come down from the high of intense activity, to replenish his energy levels, and to restore his enthusiasm for the hunt.

COMPETITION

Competition Story—Gadgets at the Match

We have been shooting smallbore rifle and fullbore Target Rifle for a number of years and have often been members of the Canadian national team in international matches. Always at these matches there are vendors selling the latest bit of equipment designed to make you a better shooter. We're always left in awe at the number of team members who will buy these gadgets, install them on their rifles, and shoot them in the next day's team matches. The "big match" isn't the place to be experimenting with new equipment.

We have been at World Cup matches and seen rifles that wouldn't make the required weight. We watched the competitor on the verge of panic trying to figure out what to cut off the stock to make weight. This should have been corrected back in the experimental stage. The shooter should get the rifle right near the beginning of the training cycle and then spend the training/competition stage working with it.

Many of the matches we have competed in require the pull weight of the trigger to be heavier than a specific weight. This weight limit will have been in the rules and can easily be set long before the match. Many competitors will try to set the weight as close as they can get it to the legal weight. They then travel halfway around the world to compete and, after shooting a possible score in a match, which will automatically require a trigger test, find that because of the environmental conditions or because the weight being used in this match is a little heavier, their trigger doesn't pass. They're penalized and now must make the trigger pull heavier. In addition to all the mental turmoil this can cause, they now must shoot with a trigger that is different than the one they used in training. All this upheaval for the sake of an ounce or two is unnecessary; if the trigger had been set correctly in the first place (with some margin for the discrepancies caused by travel), the shooter would have trained with it for months and by now would have been completely at ease with it.

Any change that is made late in the training season, and especially changes made at a match, are likely to cause problems. Sometimes they simply draw the shooter's attention and distract him from the correct firing of the shot. At other times, the change causes some chain of unanticipated consequences, and what seemed like a simple thing makes a huge difference. Changes should be made during the experimental phase and tested at lesser competitions. The only changes that should be considered during an important match are ones based on contingency plans—contingency plans that have been tested.

SECTION 6-4: MORE TOOLS—AEROBIC FITNESS

There are several physical skills required for marksmen, especially for operational marksmen, but the one that contributes the most to the subconscious skills is aerobic fitness.

Aerobic fitness is all about being able to deliver oxygen to the blood, and oxygen to the blood results in clear vision, clear thinking, and controlled performance.

Without aerobic fitness, the shooter is struggling for oxygen before his subconscious can get the shot off. The shooter's conscious is already screaming, "We need air in here," and the shooter is no longer able to shoot subconsciously.

The requirement for aerobic fitness increases as shooting intensity increases. When we're dry-firing in a safe location with no stress, our aerobic needs are at their lowest. When we up the ante by adding any stressors (heat, running, fear), two things happen: we need more oxygen, and we're less able to breathe properly. Aerobic fitness

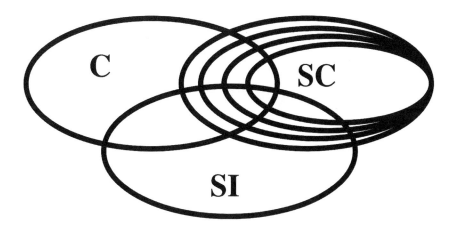

helps on both counts. However, aerobic fitness takes time to build, and while it provides a good base, additional measures may still be required in a stressful situation.

Breathing, while highly desirable most of the time, is problematic for shooters because (as Keith likes to say) "if you're breathing, you're moving." The main idea, then, is to hold your breath while firing the shot. Competition shooters will be familiar with the "respiratory pause." This is the natural pause at the bottom of the breathing cycle that the shooter extends briefly in order to fire the shot without movement. However, if the shooter is stressed (having just run a distance, for example), we have generally found it better to use the "gulp of air" technique. The shooter takes a gulp of air, which satisfies the need for oxygen just long enough to get the shot away before the body realizes that it's been tricked.

Both of these techniques work best when the shooter is aerobically fit, because the transfer of oxygen to the blood is more effective. If the body is short of oxygen in the blood, one of the first locations that gets less is the eyes, and this directly affects the shooter's vision. The shortage of oxygen will also soon affect the brain (decision making) and fine-motor control (trigger finger).

Whether or not the shooter is aerobically fit, extreme stress (fear or pain, for example) will affect breathing. The body is physiologically designed to hyperventilate during extreme stress; it's preparing you for fight or flight. When you do neither, the buildup of carbon dioxide can prevent the absorption of oxygen into the blood. The idea, then, is to get control of your exhaling (to expel the carbon dioxide) and the body will take care of the inhaling part.

Under some situations, "forced breathing" is required. The shooter forces the exhale and ensures that lots of oxygen is taken in. This technique works really well before the run in a fire-with-movement competition or situation, as well as during the brief recovery period after the run.

Under other situations, "controlled breathing" is required.[3] Lt. Col. Dave Grossman's "combat breathing" is a great name for something that competition shooters have known for years as "four-square breathing." Here, the shooter, in order to take control of his breathing and therefore his body's level of stress, follows this pattern:

- ➣ Inhale for a count of four.
- ➣ Hold for a count of four.
- ➣ Exhale for a count of four.
- ➣ Hold for a count of four.
- ➣ Repeat as required.

The fact that both Lieutenant Colonel Grossman and Linda's Olympic smallbore coach both advocate the same technique (under different names) highlights the similarity of operations and competition—which, at the risk of stating the obvious, is an underlying theme of this book.

Secrets of Mental Marksmanship

Military Story—Fitness in the Military

Every summer that Keith spent in the Canadian Army, he was put in charge of the regimental rifle team. For someone who was interested in shooting and developing the marksmanship skills of soldiers, it was the perfect job. Physical training was an important part of this program, and although he usually ran the PT sessions himself or had a senior NCO run it, this year he decided to make use of the military PT staff at the gymnasium on base.

He spoke with the officer in charge of the gym and outlined his request. The officer smiled and said he had the perfect instructor for the job. Keith was soon introduced to a young and extremely fit corporal who spoke with a heavy French-Canadian accent. The corporal was hard as nails and projected himself in a most regimental and professional bearing. This actually caused an element of worry, as PT staff were well known for their driven desire to run infantry soldiers into the ground. There may have been lots of reasons why they wanted to do this, but the main one was, simply, because they could.

And so it started—from the very first PT period, the young corporal took charge. He put the team through warmups, stretches, an upper body workout, and finally outside for a road run. There was some grumbling among the team, with such comments as, "Where did this guy come from?" and "Has anybody understood him yet?" and "Wonder where he might want to take us now?" and "Who's idea was this anyway?"

Already dripping in sweat, the team struggled to keep up with the pace. The entire time the corporal was running up and down the line of runners barking out comments and commands that, with his heavy French accent, no one understood, and all the while looking as if he had just joined the run. But he almost lost the entire rifle team when, as he sprinted by us to the front of the formation, he said, "Now, we pick up the pace. If you think you sweat now, I make you sweater." Choking laughter rippled up and down the line as individual team members caught on to what he meant.

Military Story—Military Fitness and PTSD

It is a well-known fact that combat requires fitness. What is less well known is the fact that physical fitness is directly connected to the soldier's ability to withstand the mental stresses of battle. Further, the level of physical fitness is directly connected to the ability of the soldier to avoid post-traumatic stress. In the two following citations the message is clear: fitness is important to mental capability.

The following is excerpted from the CoachNet *newsletter (March/April 2004). The source of the military data referenced here is not identified, but it clearly stated that the more fit and the healthier you are, the better your chances of withstanding the effects of post-traumatic stress disorder (PTSD). "Healthy" was not defined, but we believe that nutrition, hydration, and a strong immune system are key factors.*

One of the great benefits of being physically fit and healthy is that you can cope with higher stress levels. The military has found that among soldiers, the higher the level of fitness, the less likely the occurrence of post-traumatic stress disorder (PTSD). At a more day-to-day level, we have all felt our coping skills drop when we're tired or hungry or ill. We have also all felt how quickly we rebound when we're well rested, properly nourished and hydrated, healthy, and have been exercising outdoors in the sunshine. Soldiers are often physically over-stressed before they even start to need their marksmanship skills. They need to focus on physical fitness and health as one of their paths to excellence.

The following is excerpted from a recent thesis entitled "Physical Fitness Influences Stress Reactions to Extreme Military Training."[4] It substantiates earlier findings of a direct relationship between physical fitness and PTSD: in general, the higher the fitness level, the less the PTSD. This study did not include the health of their subjects but was otherwise rigorous in methodology.

Tools to Increase Your Subconscious Powers

There are two important strengths of the current study [which examined the relationship of physical fitness and incidence of PTSD]. First, our findings regarding the link between physical fitness and military stress reactions is novel and may open the door to a new line of inquiry that may improve our understanding of prevention and treatment for combat stress and PTSD. Second, this study was conducted within the survival training environment, offering an unprecedented level of ecological validity. Specifically, SERE training[5] is a standardized and systematic, yet realistic and intense, course of training modeled after the experiences of American prisoners of war from the Korean and Vietnam conflicts. Short of actual military combat, it's among the best forums in which to examine human reactions to acute military stress in a controlled fashion.

POLICE

Law-Enforcement Story—Fitness and the Police Sniper

The physical requirements to be on a tactical team are understandably very high. The team members must carry a considerable weight in body armor and equipment; they must be able to move quickly; they may get into physical confrontations with powerful individuals; and they must always win.

Police snipers, you might think, would have an easier go of it. They just sit in place and wait for the word. Well, when we're preaching the need for fitness on our sniper courses, we like to relate the scenario of the police sniper making his way up several flights of stairs when he gets the call that ". . . this guy is killing hostages. Green light, green light. Shoot him . . . shoot him now!" The sniper is wearing all his armor and carrying the required equipment, and now he must run up several flights of stairs. He arrives in his position with his legs burning and feeling like rubber and his lungs are coming out his nose. And now he must fire a shot that will take one life to save others. Good people are depending on him.

When it's over, no one will care how he felt physically. They will only care whether or not he made the shot.

And when it's all over, the police sniper can have a very lonely time of it. He needs to be robust in every way—mentally, physically, and psychologically—in order to deal with post-traumatic stress.

> "I learned to lose myself so effortlessly in the breathing that I sometimes had the feeling that I myself was not breathing but—strange as this may sound—being breathed."
> —Eugen Herrigel in *Zen in the Art of Archery*

> "Success depends on your backbone, not your wishbone."
> —Author unknown

HUNTING

Hunter Story—Hunting and Fitness

Sitting around the campfire with our professional hunter friend Neville, we have heard many stories of hunter clients who have arrived for a hunt in (to be polite) a less than ideal state of physical fitness. Some are so overweight they breathe heavy just getting out of the hunting car and cannot be expected to walk at all. Others, although of an appropriate weight, have no aerobic fitness and can go only a short distance before giving out. Their leg muscles are so unaccustomed to hiking that after the first day they suffer from horrific leg cramps and have to give up the hunt. And all of this is on relatively flat ground.

Can you imagine what it must be like to go bighorn sheep hunting? If there is a need to be fit on an African safari, can you imagine having to climb mountains (real mountains) and do this in thin air?

Even a comparatively simple deer hunt in Canada usually requires some fitness in order to get the most enjoyment out of the experience. You're active from daylight until dark, walking distances you don't usually walk, enduring the cold frosty days as well as the warm days. And then if you have to drag a big buck some distance to get it to a vehicle . . . well, an element of fitness will make this experience much more enjoyable.

COMPETITION

Competition Story—Commonwealth Games Trials

In 1993, Keith had made a goal to be a member of the Canadian Target Rifle team going to the Commonwealth Games. The team consisted of only two members, so it was important to perform well in the team trials and stay at the top of the scoreboard.

The trials were being conducted at Connaught Ranges near Ottawa in the month of August. August at Connaught is almost always hot—very hot. The trials were progressing; Keith was shooting well and was in the lead, but not by much. He was in good physical shape, among the best on the range. He was also following his jungle warfare training and experience in Vietnam by knowing the importance of staying hydrated in order to keep thinking clearly and be in control physically. The matches ground along throughout the day, and after each match, he drank a liter of his favorite sports drink, prepared his rifle for the next match, and monitored the wind. All he could do was keep firing perfect shots, and when it was over, he would go look at the scoreboard.

The last match was 15 shots at 900 meters. The winds were calm and steady. It was going to be a hold and squeeze type of shoot, the very kind that he was best at. Once the shooter figured out what was needed for wind, he would only need to stay there and fire perfect shots.

Keith fired his first sighter and it was indicated as a miss. "Oh no," he thought. "I hope that target marker has been staying hydrated and can do his job. I really need him to do that right now." He checked his sights to make sure they were tight and challenged for a hit. It came back as a miss.

While his shooting partner fired his first sighter, Keith went through everything he could think of to figure out what had to be done to fix this problem. The sights were tight; there was no need to check the sight setting, as he had done that and double-checked it before coming up to the firing point. What could it possibly be?

With nothing apparently wrong with the rifle and sights, he went ahead and fired his second sighter with everything the same as the first one. Surely the problem was a dehydrated butt marker. The second sighter came back as a miss. "So this is how it's all going to end," he thought.

Again he made sure the sight was tight on its mount and had a quick look at the sight setting. It was all okay. What could he do differently for the next shot, the first shot on score?

Now ready to fire his first shot for score and with everything as it was for the two missed sighters, he was in the aim with tension on the trigger when he heard a voice say, "I would check my sight setting if I were you." The voice was his shooting partner, an older, wiser, and very experienced shooter who had coached many rifle teams. Keith, still in the aim, thought, "You silly old fool. I've checked the setting twice now, and it's correct." He settled back into his sight picture to fire his shot.

And then suddenly a picture came to his mind. It was a picture of his sight scale—the one he had looked at to confirm his elevation setting for this range—except in this mental picture the scale was blurred. It now dawned on him that he had looked at the sight setting, but he hadn't seen it. Despite being in good physical condition and understanding dehydration, conditions were such that even his efforts to remain properly hydrated weren't enough to maintain proper focus at that key moment.

He came out of the aim and this time made his eyes see the little lines that were the Vernier scale on his sight. He counted them very carefully and realized he was one major line off—this was 10 minutes of elevation. He was 10 minutes off in his elevation setting. "Now who was the silly old fool," he thought as he quickly corrected the sight setting.

His first shot was just slightly out of the bull's-eye. He made the appropriate corrections for his second shot for score and hit the bull's-eye with his next 14 shots to score 74 out of a possible 75 points for the match. He won the trials and represented Canada at the Commonwealth Games.

Incidentally, one of the other competitors, considered Canada's top shot and arguably a better shot than Keith, was carried off the range on a stretcher suffering from dehydration.

Tools to Increase Your Subconscious Powers

CHAPTER SUMMARY

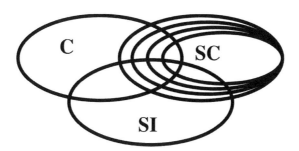

The purpose of the subconscious mind is to fire the perfect shot. The subconscious mind learns this through repetition. Every complex skill requires practice to ensure that the muscles learn their parts and that they can perform flawlessly with no conscious intervention. You usually need to train about four or five days a week for best results. The quality of this practice is critical. "When you're shooting good, shoot lots" because "correct repetition is the mother of skill." Get lots of good practice. Take every opportunity. As Lt. Col. Dave Grossman says, "Piss on golf. Real men go to the range." As Rob Leatham says, "Train hard and test yourself in the arena of competition," because those who master a shooting skill in match conditions are "more likely to do well in a pressure situation." Train with the best shooters. Your practice time will be well leveraged if you can spend time with good shooters. Learn to shoot quickly by focusing on the key elements and doing them as smoothly as you can.

It's critical that the intensity be matched to the training level of the shooter. Low intensity should be used whenever you're learning something new. The focus during low-intensity training is to be as smooth as possible, and then work on getting smoother. Doing it right is the most important thing; doing it on demand and fast will come later. Low-intensity training has no stress in it. The student takes the time to learn the skill and imprint it on the subconscious. This training provides the strong foundation that the student will draw on when the intensity increases.

High-intensity training gradually introduces stress, a little at first until the marksman is able to deal with it and still fire a perfect shot. The key is to add the stress in progressive increments and to teach the student how to deal with each type and amount of stress.

The type of training should also be matched to the shooter. Dry training should precede controlled training and rehearsals, and all of these should ideally be completed before the shooter has to go on an operation (or to a competition). The trick to working through the types of training is to build skill progressively and make sure each foundational piece is solid before moving on to the next building block. Anytime the shooter adds something new (equipment, position changes, types of fire, etc.), he needs to start back at the dry type of training.

The training phases (experimental, training, recovery) each have their own purpose, and the main idea is to understand which phase you're in and ensure you stay in the phase without dabbling in the others inappropriately.

Of all the complimentary physical skills that marksmen require, the one that contributes the most to the subconscious skills is aerobic fitness. Aerobic fitness is all about being able to deliver oxygen to the blood, and oxygen to the blood results in clear vision, clear thinking, and controlled performance. The marksman must learn to apply the breathing techniques that will support his shooting performance: respiratory pause, "gulp of air," forced breathing, and combat (or four-square) breathing.

These tools and techniques will enable your subconscious to fulfill its purpose: to fire a perfect shot . . . any gun, anywhere, anytime.

Secrets of Mental Marksmanship

NOTES

1. This demonstrates the controversy in the training field about getting the desired subconscious or semi-conditioned response: this trainer was working on repetitions, whereas the trainer quoted in the earlier story was working on hours and intensity of training.

2. These drills and exercises are the foundation of the marksmanship training that we teach to police tactical officers, military and security personnel, competition shooters, and hunters. "Holding and aiming" has the student acquire a position and focus on the holding pattern he is able to achieve, and then put that holding pattern on to a target. A "safety-on drill" has the student, with the safety on or with the firearm in a fired state, acquire a position and a sight picture and then squeeze the trigger with two to three times more pressure than usually required to fire live. "Dry-firing" means firing a shot without using ammunition. "Trigger tapping" means tapping the trigger (always dry, usually with the firearm in a fired state to get the desired "tap" sound) whenever the sight picture is perfect—useful in less stable positions like standing unsupported. "Hot and cold" exercises have the student firing without knowing whether the firearm is loaded with a live round (with the loading done by the coach).

3. Controlled breathing techniques will be revisited in Chapter 8 on advanced tools, where we talk about deep breathing and "centering" as stress-control devices.

4. The thesis by Marcus K. Taylor, Amanda E. Markham, Jared P. Reis, Genieleah A. Padilla, Eric G. Potterat, Sean P. A. Drummond and Lilianne R. Mujica-Parodi was published in *Military Medicine*, August 2008.

5. SERE is an acronym used in relation to two related training programs: the United Kingdom military's Survive, Evade, Resist, Extract training, and the U.S. military's Survival, Evasion, Resistance, and Escape training.

— Chapter 7 —

Tools to Increase
the Power of Your Self-Image

SECTION 7-1: THE KEY IS SELF-TALK

The purpose of the self-image is to provide the ultimate picture for the conscious and subconscious to follow. This is the true picture of how you see yourself. One of the best ways to improve your self-image is through self-talk. Self-talk is our internal voice, the monologue (or dialogue) that we carry on in our minds. Stop reading this for a few moments, close your eyes, and relax. What you just heard is your self-talk. It's the spokesperson for

The Power of Self-Image—The Key is Self-Talk

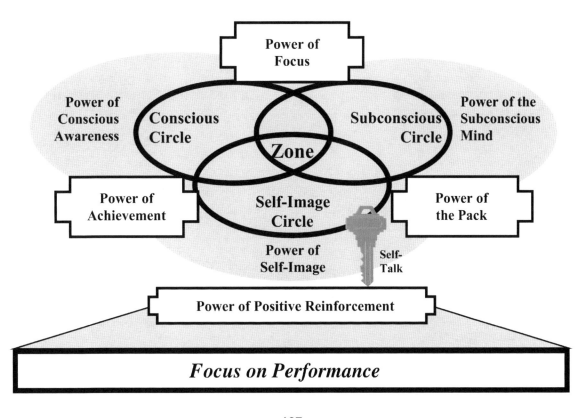

our mental attitude . . . you know, the mental attitude that determines our altitude.

Your self-esteem, attitudes, beliefs, and motivation are determined by the mental programs you carry around with you. Most people (experts estimate about 97 percent) spend more time fighting failure than they spend enjoying success.

The brain operates like a powerful personal computer. The keyboard is our five senses. Our senses develop the programs that run our lives. Since the moment you were born, every single message you have ever received from any source has been programmed into your personal computer—imprinted and stored in your brain. Your onboard PC stores all its programs in the subconscious mind. Just like the memory of a PC, the subconscious mind doesn't know the difference between something that is right or wrong, bad or good, positive or negative. It just stores the information and acts on the programs it receives.

Some of the negative programming we might have received as a child may have been as a result of input like this:

> "Jimmy, you're just no good at anything. You're going to end up just like your Uncle Bubba."
> "Timmy, you'd lose your head if it wasn't screwed on."
> "Johnny is a slow learner. I don't think he'll ever do well in school, and I don't think he will ever go to college."

The subconscious mind is

> "Got a better way of saying that?"
> —MilCun instructors

> "Altering your self-talk may be the most important undertaking you will ever begin."
> —Pamela E. Butler in *Talking to Yourself*

> "The programs you carry on board determine your course, your altitude, your speed, and your destination."
> —Author unknown

> "If you aren't thinking about what it is you have to do right to accomplish your goal, then what are you thinking about?"
> —Author unknown

designed to always act on the strongest programs it has. The subconscious mind is designed to get more of or duplicate the programs it already has that are the strongest. Whatever programs we already have, we consciously and unconsciously seek out or attract more programs just like them. Instead of constantly getting rid of the programs that work against us, we duplicate them.

About 77 percent (again, an expert's estimate) of our programs may be wrong, counterproductive, or work against us. Can you imagine flying on an aircraft that has only 23 percent of the right programs for its onboard flight computer? The programs you carry on board determine your course, your altitude, your speed, and your destination.

Every time you do the same thing, think the same thought, hear the same message, or say the same message, you're using the same neuron paths in your brain again and again. Each time you use the paths, you're actually feeding the neurons in those pathways. You're giving them chemical nutrients, so the pathways get stronger. Over time, the paths you use most become highways and superhighways.

Just to give you a picture of what we're talking about, here are some negative self-talk phrases that you may recognize, either from your own internal dialogue or from friends, co-workers, or family . . . or a most insidious source, TV programming or computer games:

> "I just know it won't work!"
> "Nothing ever goes right for me."

➤ "There's that Murphy's law again."

➤ "Today just isn't my day!"

➤ "If only I were smarter . . ."

➤ "If only I had more money . . ."

Instead, what if we rewrote these programs so that what we had in our mind's eye were more positive phrases like these:

➤ "I know I can make it work."

➤ "I can make things go right for me."

➤ "The heck with Murphy—I make my own luck."

➤ "Today will be my day before I'm done."

➤ "I'm smart enough to do this."

➤ "I can work on getting more money."

Wayne Sorenson, one of Canada's gold-winning small-bore shooters at the Commonwealth Games (Victoria 1994), used the song "Takin' Care of Business" (Bachman Turner Overdrive) as his self-talk solution. This would affect his attitude, which would cause him to do just that . . . take care of business. Our self-talk makes us focus on the important things that can make a difference in our performance. We can talk ourselves into taking on the conditions and getting every point possible, or we can talk ourselves into not bothering to try, being beat before we start. It's our choice.

The strongest program always wins. Every time

"You want me to improve my scores by 10 points? Great advice, coach, but how?"
—Linda K. Miller & Keith A. Cunningham in *How to Build a Training Plan . . . That Works!*

"If you aren't pulling with me, you are pulling against me (because I'm moving toward my goal)."
—Linda K. Miller, coach (1952~)

"The first order of business of anyone who wants to enjoy success in all areas of his or her life is to take charge of the internal dialogue they have and only think, say, and behave in a manner consistent with the results they truly desire."
—Sidney Madwed, businessman

we hear the words, say them, think them, or when they cross our mind unconsciously, one more program is being recorded and reinforced chemically and electrically in our subconscious mind. If you were to stop using a program path long enough, that neuron pathway would, in time, stop being fed and begin to break down. The process of breaking down our old programs doesn't even begin to take place until we have stopped using the old programs for at least three weeks.

To get rid of an old program, you have to replace it with something else. To truly change what we think, we first have to change the programs that created our thoughts in the first place. (While this borders on the subject of psychology, this is not psychology. This is all about how to improve your self-image so that you can become a better marksman. If something in these pages can help you become better in some other way, it's up to you.)

Learning to control your self-talk is the most natural way to get rid of the old programs in the brain and replace them with new programs. This time, the programs will be ones you consciously choose.

A new self-talk program must:

➤ Be clear and to the point. It must be specific. For example, "It's like me to train four times a week."

➤ Use repetition. This type of motivational self-talk is like a personal contract. You need to see it and say it often; for example, write it down and post it all over the house.

➤ Be strong. The self-talk phrase that is vivid and memorable works the best. For example, Muhammad Ali's self-talk (which he reinforced by making it public) was, "I am the greatest!"
➤ Be tied to a goal. The changed self-talk must have "pay value" for you. You must want the change badly enough that you will stick to it.
➤ Have duration. It takes a minimum of 21 days to work.

There are three steps to positive self-talk:

➤ Be aware.
➤ Evaluate.
➤ Replace.

Step one is to be aware of your own self-talk. Listen consciously to everything you say out loud for several days. Watch for the self-talk statements you say about yourself. Monitor the self-talk of others around you. Is the "power of the pack" working for you? Analyze what you hear as to whether it's moving you toward your goal.

Step two is to evaluate your own self-talk. Turn your self-talk around. If you're saying something that isn't moving you toward your goal, then you must replace it with a positive statement. For example, if you catch yourself thinking, "I always have trouble with my CCB shot," consider what your world would be like if you thought instead, "I

> "Whether you think you can or you think you can't, you're probably right."
> —Henry Ford, businessman (1863–1947)

> "Self-talk can either work for you or against you . . . your choice."
> —Keith A. Cunningham, soldier (1950~)

> "One person with a belief is equal to a force of ninety-nine who have only interests."
> —John Stuart Mill, philosopher (1806–1873)

> "Everything that's around you right now in your life, including the things you're complaining about, you've attracted . . . This is one of the hardest concepts to get, but once you've accepted it, it's life transforming."
> —Dr. Joe Vitale, Msc.D, metaphysician

always get my CCB shot because I always set up my position just right, I always follow the marksmanship principles, I always mentally rehearse the shot, and then I just do it with confidence."

Step three is to replace your dysfunctional self-talk with your new, chosen, productive self-talk.

When we hear a student say something negative, we stop and ask them, "Got a better way of saying that?" We each make many little 10-second choices every day. Victory doesn't come in a single moment. It comes in a hundred little moments throughout the day and along the way.

New self-talk would sound more like this:

➤ "I shoot only perfect shots."
➤ "I am taking control of me—right now!"
➤ "When I set a goal, I stick to it."
➤ "Right now I choose to be successful."
➤ "Right now I choose to make this shot."

Give yourself 10 seconds as many times a day as it takes to be successful. And when you practice your new self-talk, make it always "perfect practice" . . . because only perfect practice makes perfect.

One of the motivations for writing this book is to counteract the frequent negative comments written in shooting articles or voiced in shooting programs on television. The writers of these articles may feel a need not to brag, or it just may be the way they think. Either way, they often fall into the habit of using negative self-talk. This does nothing to improve their own performance, and, worse yet, it can harm the listener's ability to think positively and constructively.

Some of these comments sound like this:

> "Was having a good shoot until I shot an eight . . . missed a wind shift . . . what a dummy!"
> "Was having a good shoot until I turned the sight the wrong way . . . I can't believe what an idiot I was."
> "Everything was going well until I realized I had brought the wrong ammunition. . . sometimes I think I couldn't organize a drunk up in a brewery."

We have all been there and understand the frustration, but if that is how we leave it, then we're focusing on the problem and not the solution. And by calling ourselves degrading names, we're lowering our self-image. Even when a coach berates us in a joking manner, the conscious mind knows it's a joke, but the subconscious only records the offense.

It's a critical part of the coach's role to help the shooter identify the negative comment for what it is: an opportunity to find a solution. The coach can help the shooter turn his attitude around by rewording the negative analysis into positive performance statements to create the right picture to be used next time. As the shooter becomes familiar with the technique, he will learn to identify his own solution opportunities and will start to build a positive, constructive attitude into his own performance analysis. For example:

> "Having a good shoot . . . missed a wind shift . . . *I always check the flag or mirage just before firing and then I always quickly fire a perfect shot . . .*"
> "Having a good shoot . . . turned the sights the wrong way . . . *I have engraved arrows on the adjustment knobs and I always check them before I turn . . .*"
> "Brought the wrong ammunition. . . *I have a detailed list for going to matches and I always carefully check it before leaving home . . .*"

Which set of pictures do you think will have the best opportunity to solve the problem and thereby move you toward the success you desire?

> "All that we are is the result of what we have thought."
> —Buddha
> (c. 563 BC–483 BC)

> "Focus on what you want, not what you don't want."
> —Jack Canfield, writer (1944~)

> "You are born to add something, to add value to this world, to simply be the best that you can be."
> —Lisa Nichols, writer

Military Story—Military Unit Mottoes

Nearly every military unit has a motto. The purpose of the motto is to summarize the attitude of its members, to provide a short-form creed to perform by, and to get everyone in the unit thinking in the same direction.

Keith served with "G" Coy, 75th Rangers in Vietnam. The Rangers and their training have imprinted very powerfully on him. The motto of the Rangers is "Rangers Lead the Way." This motto is based on the job of the Rangers, which is to "go in first." It can also imply that Rangers set the example for others to follow. It's a very positive and appropriate motto.

Secrets of Mental Marksmanship

The motto of the U.S. Marine Corps is "*Semper Fidelis*," which is Latin for "always faithful." This means that Marines are forever faithful to their country, the Corps, and to the individual members. The Marines pride themselves in accomplishing every mission given to them by their country and never leaving a Marine behind.

When Keith joined the Canadian Forces, he became a member of the Royal Canadian Regiment (RCR). This is Canada's oldest infantry regiment and has a proud history. Its motto is "Never Pass a Fault." This means that everyone is always vigilant to ensure that everything is done correctly. In the context of this book, this motto isn't as positive as it should be. It begs the question, "Gotta better way to say that?" Although we understand the meaning of the RCR motto, it's actually not saying it. A better way to say it would be, "Always Make It Right."

MILITARY

Military Story—Just Stop . . . and Just Start
From "Can I Give You a Little Honest Feedback?"[1]

Linda once had a Canadian military team member seek her out at the National Service Condition matches. He was doing very well; in fact, he was outperforming his capability level. He said, "I keep thinking that this glorious success is going to stop soon, that I am going to have a miss in the next match, and that I'll never be a champion."

Linda listened patiently to his description of the problem and then gave the plainest coaching feedback she could. "Stop it," she said. "Just stop giving these thoughts attention they do not deserve. You are the only one who can control what you are thinking. If you need an image to help you set aside your concerns, take each one of your negative thoughts and picture them on their own little piece of paper, file the paper, in a cabinet, lock the cabinet, and promise all these concerns that you'll be back later, after the match. Just stop thinking about 'success and failure' and start thinking about what you want to replace those thoughts with. Start thinking about what you need to do to shoot good shots. Focus on each match, your positions, the way the rifle feels, the recoil. It's your choice what you think about. You are in control. It's your brain."

Sometimes that kind of coaching doesn't reach the negative person, and you just have to take the individual aside. We have occasionally told someone that "when you say A, the group hears X. When you say B, the group hears Y. We need you to support the needs of the group." For some people, it is easier to change a behavior by focusing on the benefit that others will derive.

POLICE

Law-Enforcement Story—"I'm Sorry"

We were invited to hear a lecture on post-traumatic stress disorder (PTSD) in policing. There were two speakers: one was a cop who suffered from PTSD and the other was a psychologist who treated PTSD. The cop spoke first, telling the story of his traumatic incident and the aftermath.

He flashed a quick slide of a pistol. He was telling his story about the incident. He flashed the same slide again. "Can you tell what the pistol is?" he asked the audience. He put the same slide up again and left it up. "I'm sorry if you can't see this very clearly, but it's a picture of the weapon that the perp had."

Later in the presentation, he walked in front of the overhead projector, interrupting the projected image for a moment. "I'm sorry," he said.

Later he noticed that one member of the audience was straining to see around him to read a slide. "I'm sorry," he said, moving and checking to make sure that he wasn't blocking anyone else's view.

At one point, someone got up and closed a window blind to stop the sun from shining in his eyes. "I'm sorry," the cop said, as though he were responsible for the behavior of the sun.

He put up several images of normal things, like the view from his cottage. The first few images were lovely, but then they got progressively more distorted and flicked more and more rapidly. It was an effective presentation of a panicked mind not being able to stay in control. At the end of the sequence, he said "I'm sorry I can't make it more realistic."

After the lecture, we spent a few moments talking with the cop. "Do you realize that you're still saying that you're sorry?" we asked, watching his face for a reaction. When we explained that he had used the phrase "I'm sorry" at least a dozen times in his hour-long lecture, he was totally surprised, completely unaware that he was using this phrase at all. We suggested that he start weaning himself from this self-talk by using the phrase "excuse me" instead of "I'm sorry," as this would at least move him one step away from constant repentance.

Law-Enforcement Story—Police Brotherly Ragging
From "Can I Give You a Little Honest Feedback?"[2]

The number one type of relationship behavior that we change during our police sniper courses is the brotherly "ragging." We want the snipers to adopt the same positive reinforcement style that we use to teach them so they are all hearing positive reinforcement more often and are making positive reinforcement statements. Our theory is that the more you listen, talk, read, and write about a thing happening, the more likely that thing is going to happen.

We have heard a sniper student razz another student who just fired a beautiful group that landed five inches above the point of aim, "Look here, Dave just put one in over the top. Good thing your life wasn't relying on that one, Dave!"

What we want to hear them say is, "Holy cow, Dave! Look at that pretty little group. One more sight adjustment and you are going to have it nailed."

Getting the snipers to change their habitual ragging is not easy. It's their comfort zone. It's how they relate. It's what they "usually" say to each other. After two days with us, we rarely hear another word of it because we give them feedback on it, we give them replacement phrases, and we give them lots of positive reinforcement.

Hunter Story—You Can't Sneak Up on a Deer
Keith tells this story of a recent hunt:

A while back we were hunting deer on our range property with a good friend of ours. I set him up in a good place on our 400-meter firing point, with good signs that deer were using the range as a grazing area. Sure enough, he wasn't in place for 30 minutes when a nice buck came out. I was nearby, heard the shot, and came over to help him. He is a fine shot, but signs were that he missed this deer. He and I spent the rest of the morning searching the area to make sure, but in the end we gave it up.

I was a bit miffed at him for missing such an outstanding opportunity as I carried on with my hunt. I was going to "sneak and peek" down an old logging road. Part way along I stopped and had my lunch. As I continued, I noticed I was still bothered about the morning I spent looking for a deer that should have been an easy shot. I also noticed that it was very difficult to sneak along this old road because it was covered with autumn leaves. It was like walking on cornflakes. My mind went to thinking about the chances of actually seeing a deer. Surely it would hear me long before I got close enough to see it.

I soon recognized that the way I was thinking was going to ruin the rest of the day's hunt. I needed to forget about what was bothering me and get on with the day. Besides, I too had missed easy shots on deer and spent the rest of the day looking for it. I decided to get back into the hunt. "Well," I thought, "just because you might not be able to walk up on a deer doesn't mean you shouldn't try." So I switched on "stalking mode" and actually tried to walk quietly.

Ten minutes later I spotted a nice eight-point buck just off the road. He was busy freshening up a scrape and didn't notice my approach. Just because you think it might not happen only means that you need to try harder.

COMPETITION

Competition Story—Cadet with Nine Bulls
Linda tells this story in "Snatch the Pebble."[3]

I enjoyed shooting with some of the cadets . . . there was one in particular who seemed to be very keen. She told me that she loved shooting and that her father did everything to encourage and support her in the sport. She was thirsty for knowledge, very interested in any tips and support I could give her. I was pleased that she loved the sport that I love and took every opportunity to encourage her.

I certainly wasn't the only one. Most of the competitors will help the younger shooters, and as a case in point, Keith went out of his way to help this youngster understand how some of her self-talk was working against her and how she could change her behavior to help herself.

She had had a disappointing match and had left the firing line moaning, "That was my worst shoot ever. I can't believe I could be so bad."

Keith walked over to talk to her about the match. It turned out she had shot nine full-value shots and one disappointing magpie (taking two points off her score). Keith pointed out that she had given the one shot way more attention than it deserved and was ignoring the nine shots that had been very successful. Keith acknowledged that a magpie is always disappointing but that everyone shoots them once in a while. The point is to keep focused on what went right for the other nine shots and keep making them happen.

COMPETITION

Competition Story—Got a Better Way of Saying That?
From "Can I Give you a Little Honest Feedback?"[4]

For competitive rifle shooters, the problem is more often that they are down on themselves . . . or at least that's the self-talk they use. We hear phrases like, "If I don't screw this one up, I'll have a good target," or, "If only I could stop snatching the trigger," or, "Last time I shot possibles back to 600 yards. I doubt I can do that again." They are excusing their performance before it is completed. They are making excuses before they need them. They are thinking about outcome instead of performance.

We give them lots of feedback on this habit. We tell them how to change their thinking, their self-talk, and especially what to let us and the other shooters hear. Whenever we want to tell them, "Don't say that!" we instead give them a positive phrase to say.

For "If I don't screw this one up," we tell them to replace that phrase (and that thought) with this phrase: "To get the same result on this one as I have on all the others, what do I need to do? Well, I need to get into a solid, comfortable position. And I need to get me and the gun naturally aligned to the target. Then I need to make sure I've got my eye and sight(s) properly aligned. Then I launch into my mental program, which gets me that sweet trigger release and relaxed follow-through. Yeah, that's how I did it and that's how I'm going to do it this time."

For "If only I could stop snatching the trigger," we tell them to focus not on stopping but on starting. We tell them to do lots of dry-firing and think about that "smooth, steady, subconscious squeeze" and when they have given their trigger finger lots of physical training, then they can move on to mixed dry and live fire. We tell them, "Start focusing on the sight picture and follow-through intensely enough to be able to report the exact location of the crosshairs at the moment of firing and after the recoil has finished."

For "Last time I shot . . ." we tell them not to focus on past outcomes but to focus on the present (wherever you are, be all there) and to focus on performance. "Tell me about all the things you do right to produce great performances. Build on those strengths. Be very specific. Start with your position, your body alignment, your sight picture, your trigger release and follow through, your mental program. Tell me everything, every single little detail."

What we need is a strong, compelling image of the behavior we want so it will replace the old habit. We want them NOT to focus on what they are doing wrong; we want them instead to focus on what they need to do to get it right.

SECTION 7-2: MORE TOOLS—ATTITUDES, SOLUTIONS, PRETENDING

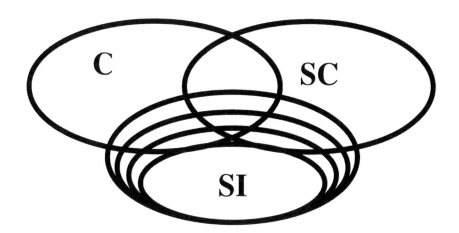

While self-talk is probably the single most important thing you can do to align your self-image with your goals, there are other tools you can use to mold your self-image. They include:

➤ Mastering the positive attitude
➤ Being solution oriented
➤ Confirming through congratulating and complimenting
➤ Setting an example
➤ Pretending to make it so

Mastering the Positive Attitude

The winning attitude for both the recreational and the operational marksman is this: "Regardless of the situation, I am always going to shoot well." If you have any other attitude, you're allowing yourself to open the door for failure. We have zero tolerance for an attitude that accepts failure as an option. Our attitude accepts—expects—winning.

It's not that we have an unrealistic attitude; it's that we think the only realistic attitude is positive.

It's not that nothing bad ever happens to us; it's that we feed on adversity. As we wrote in a story

"A high tide raises all boats."
—Author unknown

"It's not whether you get knocked down; it's whether you get up."
—Vince Lombardi, coach (1913–1970)

"It's not how far you fall, it's how high you bounce."
—Author unknown

called "The Challenge of Adversity,"[5] while victory is sweet, victory against poor odds is sweeter still . . . and victory with grace under the challenge of adversity is a personal victory and is the sweetest of all. And while we don't seek adversity, we do seek challenge. And those of us who strive for victory recognize that any greater challenge is an opportunity for greater victory.

When you're firing in training or in competition, never let on what the last shot was. We have watched shooters who swear or stamp a foot when they have a shot land outside where they wanted it to be. These shooters seem to think that if they show displeasure, they're proving how much they want to shoot well, and that this will help them shoot better. In fact, the opposite is true. Every shot you fire is merely information to use on the next shot. Never give a bad shot the attention it doesn't deserve. Having an emotional reaction to a shot doesn't further your objectives, and it can impair them. As Anthony Robbins says in his book *Unlimited Power*, successful people believe there are no failures, only results. This is particularly important for competition shooters. A shot that lands in the eight ring isn't a failure, it's an outcome; it's data; it will inform the shooter's decision making for the next shot.

At the range and in life, be around the type of people you want to turn out to be. It suddenly becomes easy to have a great attitude when all the people around you have one. If you feel like you're struggling to stay positive, find a positive person. Collect positive people in your life. They will appreciate it, and you will too.

Another application of the "power of the pack" is to attract people into your life who have truly "been there" and who can share their wisdom and experience with you. We learn best from those who have been there.

In addition, read the right books. There are many books on positive thinking. Not many deal with operational marksmanship, but some focus on competitive marksmanship. Many deal with other sports or businesses or social themes, but they can offer a wealth of ideas about the power of a positive attitude.

You don't have to have years of experience to apply positive thinking to maximum benefit. One of our then junior shooters, Neil Bowers, was faced with shoulder surgery, a serious operation for anyone, and especially critical for a shooter. Linda called Neil the day before his surgery hoping to give him a boost of confidence. Instead, she found he had his mental program well in

> "The average pencil is seven inches long, with just a half-inch eraser—in case you thought optimism was dead."
> —Robert Brault, writer

> "Positive thinking is the key to success in business, education, pro football, anything that you can mention. I go out there thinking I am going to complete every pass."
> —Ron Jaworski, football player (1951~)

> "The person who says that something can't be done should never interrupt the person who is doing it."
> —Author unknown

> "When the conscious mind has a positive thought, it cannot, at the same time, be thinking negatively."
> —Author unknown

hand. "The force," he said, "is with me." He knew he was going to sail through the surgery because he had a positive force with him—the force of positive thinking and powerful self-talk.

Being Solution Oriented

When things aren't going in the desired positive direction, how do you react? Ignoring things isn't the answer. Getting bent out of shape about things isn't the answer. When things aren't going in the desired positive direction, you must correct the course.

The key to positive correction is to be solution oriented. Point out what should be done rather than what was done wrong. Think this way when correcting yourself. And think this way when coaching.

What you say is never as important as what you cause someone (or yourself) to picture. Make sure you picture positive thoughts.

Never talk about problems; find solutions. If you don't have a solution, then say to yourself, "I need a solution for . . ." This creates a positive approach and attitude toward solving a problem.

Confirming through Congratulating and Complimenting

Reward through praise. Take every opportunity you can to give someone praise—there is no maximum amount, so long as the praise is genuine and deserved. Hearing praise gives everyone a good positive feeling, and it always gets the best results. And be quick to give yourself some praise. If you don't feel comfortable saying it out loud, then at least say it to yourself. Notice when you have done something well and enjoy the moment.

Encourage others by complimenting them on good performance. This is a pleasant thing to do, and it increases the chances of improving your own performance through positive reinforcement.

Congratulate the best performer during any of your training and the winner of any competition. This should be a religiously followed habit. Talk to the winner. Strive to be around winners. By giving lots of positive reinforcement, you will start to feel like the winner you want to be.

Setting an Example

Develop a positive approach for yourself and stick with it. Maintain a positive approach with others. Be consistent with yourself and others.

Set a positive example for others to follow. Be the most positive and cheerful person on the range and in your life.

A high tide raises all boats.

Pretending to Make It So

This is probably one of the most controversial things we advocate. Pretend that things are the way you want them until your self-image changes and things actually become the way you want them. As they say in *The Secret*,[6] you attract what you expect. And pretending that something is already done is the clearest statement of expectation that you can make.

Military Story—Vimy Ridge

History shows us that battles have been won and lost based on attitude and the initiatives of subordinate leaders and individual soldiers. The victory for Vimy Ridge in World War I was credited to Gen. Arthur Currie, whose attitude was simply this: planning and coordination save lives. He encouraged and trained subordinate leaders to solve tactical problems to keep the momentum of the attack moving forward, and he spent considerable time building models of the ground and rehearsing. He developed and used the "rolling barrage" that kept enemy under cover until the attackers were on them.

Currie had the attitude that he wanted to accomplish his mission, but with the absolute minimum number of casualties, and he worked and planned to accomplish this. This idea, particularly the part about the minimum casualties, wasn't always foremost in the minds of the generals of the day. He used his staff and listened to soldiers at the front to come up with solutions to influence and gel his plan. And then he created models of the ground over which the attack would take place, and he rehearsed and practiced the plan until everyone understood their part in the attack.

Law-Enforcement Story—Police Sniper Selection Grid

Police agencies have many different ways of selecting their tactical teams, and tactical teams have many different ways of selecting their snipers. We have always found it somewhat ironic that the members of the tactical team are usually gung-ho react-mode kinds of people, and they are the group from which the sniper (who is usually a more laid-back, deliberate kind of person) is selected.

In our entry-level police sniper course, we introduce the students to our Police Sniper Selection Grid so they can prepare themselves for the requirements of their new role. The following are several excerpts from that material.[7]

The attitude and personality traits of a sniper have to be carefully considered. Not everyone is suited for this important tactical position. The tactical entry teams, which are pumped and motivated by being part of a team about to engage in a sudden life and death situation, will kill in a reactionary manner. The sniper is often out of immediate harm's way and when required must kill deliberately and most intentionally. He is often the last resource called upon and is expected not only to incapacitate but also to most certainly destroy his target.

He is called on because the target area is small, often partially hidden behind innocent hostages, or he has to shoot among or near his team members. He has little or no room for error. Any error could result in the injury or death of someone who is counting on him to produce and who, most certainly, doesn't deserve to die. He will often have to do this job after waiting for hours or days for the right opportunity or the command to fire. He may have only a fleeting moment to engage his target, and his one well-placed shot could end this whole intense, stressful, and dangerous situation.

If he makes the shot, he will likely be the hero to everyone—his peers, his superiors, and most certainly the hostage.[8] If he misses or hits someone other than the intended target, he will be shunned by his peers for fear they might get caught in the crossfire of what will surely be coming down from above. His superiors will be looking for a scapegoat to shift the blame despite the fact that they're ultimately responsible for everything, including his training or lack of it.

The sniper selection grid covers the following categories of sniper characteristics:

- ➤ Marksmanship skill
- ➤ Physical condition
- ➤ Mental/emotional condition
- ➤ Field skills
- ➤ Preferred personal characteristics

This selection grid can help the police officer think about his choice to become a police sniper, to make sure that what he is planning to become is something he will do well, without hesitation, without conscience, and without error. He will be prepared to act resolutely, with readiness and resolve. The grid can help the selection officer determine an officer's suitability. The grid can also be used to help the police sniper select areas for further development. However, the grid won't replace the personal interaction between the candidate and the selection officer, or the sniper and the team.

On the subject of emotional balance and mental conditioning:

The entry team will kill emotionally and instinctively as a matter of survival. The sniper must kill calmly and deliberately, shooting carefully selected targets. He will see the eyes and the expression of his target. He will know that he is killing one of his own kind. He must not be susceptible to feelings of anxiety or remorse. He must be able to acknowledge the humanity of his target and at the same time be at ease with the requirement to end the target's life.

If an officer is motivated toward being a sniper mainly for the prestige of performing a unique function, he may not be capable of the cold rationality that the sniper job requires. The sniper needs to be able to "draw the curtain," to compartmentalize.

A proper mental condition cannot be taught or instilled by training. Psychiatric screening may be necessary to determine if certain essential mental qualities are possessed. Can this candidate live with making the hit? Can he live with missing the hit or hitting someone other than the target? The sniper must have this clear in his mind before he is called upon to fire the shot. He cannot afford to balk and must act correctly at a critical moment when others are depending on him.

Years ago the British army would conduct a simple test with their sniper candidates to see if they were of the right mindset to kill a selected target on command. They would get all their snipers onto the firing line and ready to fire. They would then turn loose in the area in front of the snipers a number of long-eared, pink-eyed, white rabbits. The rabbits would hop about nibbling on bits of clover, minding their own business and harming no one. A sniper instructor would crawl up beside one of the students and direct him to shoot the rabbit that was, for example, second from the right. If the student hesitated or refused, he was removed from the course.

On the subject of intelligence as a job requirement:
A police sniper's duties require a wide variety of skills.

He must know everything about his rifle and its use, ballistics and ammunition, optical devices, communication equipment, and how to use a map and compass or a GPS. He must have the ability to observe and see details and pass this information on to the appropriate authorities. He must be able to read the situation as it develops and be prepared to advise his superiors. The sniper must display decisiveness, self-reliance, good judgment, and common sense.

On the preferred personal characteristics of the police sniper:
Although these characteristics aren't absolutely necessary to be a good and effective sniper, they describe some life skills that the sniper may be able to call upon to better carry out his mission.

- Organization—The successful sniper possesses organization skills. He is a list maker. He keeps a logbook. His equipment is properly maintained and easy to find quickly. He has taken action to ensure that he will always have the right equipment in his bag when he goes on operation. He has a plan.
- Experience as a hunter or woodsman—This provides fieldcraft experience and will develop confidence to operate effectively in this environment.
- Experience as a competitive marksman—This gives the sniper the opportunity for extensive practice with his equipment. Many shots are fired under the stress of wanting to do well and win a match. Stress management techniques are developed and practiced under a very controlled environment. It's an excellent opportunity for the sniper to get good before he needs to be good in operations. As well, the sniper gets to meet many competent marksmen, and through social activities he learns new ideas and techniques that will help him become more efficient and effective.
- Ability to make rapid, accurate assessments and mental calculations—The sniper must have the ability to quickly and accurately assess the situation and decide on the correct course of action. He must understand the calculations and adjustments of his equipment and know how to make them to get the desired results. His observation skills go beyond the accurate observation of the current situation to include the skill of patterning and the accurate anticipation of conditions.
- Ability to maintain an emotionally stable personal life—The sniper must be able to carry out his functions in an emotionally stable manner. He must then be able to leave his professional activities at work and be able to function properly in society.
- Ability to function properly under stress—The stresses placed on the police sniper are, in many ways, greater than those experienced by other members of the tactical team. His one shot will be the difference between a dangerous situation ending or causing more complications. He holds the lives of others within his own skill level.
- Possess the traits of patience, attentiveness, and perseverance—The sniper must have the patience to wait and wait until he is suddenly and sometimes rapidly called into action. He must have the attentiveness to detail that allows him to plan ahead and be prepared for any eventuality. Changes in the wind must be noticed and allowed for in advance. The police sniper must have the perseverance to stay alert, to train at every opportunity, and to do the things that must be done to improve the chances of a successful shot.
- The ability to work alone—Although it's always best to deploy snipers in pairs, there will be times when the sniper will have to work alone. He must have the ability to make the correct decisions without the benefit of a second opinion.
- The ability to work closely with another individual in confined spaces—Sometimes the sniper will

have to remain with his sniper partner in a confined location that will limit their movements. They must have the ability to accomplish this without affecting their efficiency. This requires the sniper to be more or less unself-conscious, as well as be highly tolerant and considerate of others.

➤ Team player—In the police situation, the sniper must work effectively as a member of the tactical team. He must be willing to sacrifice his own interests for the good of the team. Although he is fundamentally an individualist, he behaves well in a team setting.

➤ General personal character—In our experience, snipers are a different breed than the rest of the tactical team. They're generally quiet in nature, letting their work speak for them. They're often more introspective than extroverted. They're generally optimistic by nature and find it easy to be positive. (They're rarely a pessimistic personality type.) They're generally levelheaded and display a calm intelligence. They're capable of creative thinking and enjoy solving problems (which they usually see as challenges). They possess a high degree of mental stamina and can stay focused on the task for extended periods of time. They are resistant to tunnel vision and can select a broad or narrow focus as required. They possess a depth of character not always required for other types of police work. They're often the most likely to be promoted from the tactical team.

In the conclusion of the Police Sniper Selection Grid, we characterize the police sniper as follows:
There are three personal traits that clearly separate the ultimate sniper from the other members of the tactical team or from lesser snipers:

➤ He can outwit the enemy.
➤ He can hit anything.
➤ He marches to his own drum.

While in an agency setting, the sniper must temper these personal traits with the requirements of agency policy. However, these traits are the most definitive of the successful sniper: successful at getting into the right situation to have a shot, successful at making the shot, and successful at dealing with the aftermath.

There are many reasons why a person might want to be a police sniper. Each individual has to decide if his reasons are the right ones. When it's time to make the shot, he must be prepared. He must not just think he is ready, he must know he is ready. There will always be others depending on him. He must be confident that he is the right person for the job and that the job is right for him.

Law-Enforcement Story—Simunitions
One of the greatest training aids to come along lately, especially for police, is "simunitions."[9] This is nonlethal ammunition that can be fired through police duty weapons and allows for very realistic armed encounters in a training environment. Trainers are limited only by their imaginations as to the scenarios that can be developed.

When simunitions were first used, a problem was quickly identified: as soon as the officer was shot with this ammo, he stopped. This would seem to be a logical reaction to being shot, but it created the wrong attitude when you're in a life and death gunfight.

Our police students brought this situation to our attention, and later we read about it in Lt. Col. Dave Grossman's book *On Combat*.

The solution was simple: train the officers to ignore being shot and continue the fight until the threat is neutralized. This doesn't mean that the officer is to think of himself as being bulletproof. Feeling like you're bulletproof will cause you to ignore important lifesaving tactics. But, just because you're shot doesn't mean you're dead or that you should stop or quit the fight.

Remember the story about Stacy Lim. Despite being shot through the chest, she continued the fight until the threat was neutralized. This has to be the only attitude to have in such a situation. It has to be the only solution to win a gunfight. This has to be the only way to train and have imprinted on the subconscious mind.

HUNTING

Hunter Story—Falling Through the Ice

Keith does like to hunt. And the one animal he likes to hunt more than any other is the wolf. We're not sure why this is so; perhaps it's some of the old sniper spirit still alive and well within his soul, or it could be from a Native American belief that you take some of the spirit of what you kill. But on this particular hunt, he would need to call on many of the points we teach our students just to survive—not to survive the wolf but to survive the land and its elements.

Shortly after we had purchased our range property and while Linda was away somewhere in the world with her consulting job, Keith decided he wanted to spend the day hunting. It was a clear but cold day in February. The purpose of this hunt was twofold: he wanted to range out as far as he could to become familiar with the terrain of the 1,000-acre wilderness property, while at the same time hunt the several wolf packs that roamed the land. He planned to be out for the whole day and packed his daypack accordingly. The snow was about a meter deep so snowshoes were a must, as, of course, was his favorite hunting rifle.

The property had no road access at that time of year. Just as it was getting light, he parked his pickup truck near a snowmobile trail and, after making a last-minute check of the topo map and his planned route, he was off.

The going was difficult in the bush where the snow was soft, for even with snowshoes he still sunk nearly to his knees with every step. So he kept to the ridgelines where the snow was easier to walk because it had less chance to accumulate and was wind packed. Here he picked up the tracks of a wolf pack and the hunt was on. The wolves, however, soon realized they were being pursued and began their own counter tactics. The game went on throughout the day.

Eventually Keith realized that the day had very little light left, and it was important to use it to get back to his vehicle. The wolves would win this one. He got out his map and GPS and planned a route. He had about five kilometers to go and, the truth be known, he had broken off the hunt a bit later than he should have.

The shortest route was down the length of a long and narrow lake, then along a waterway out its south end, eventually coming to the snowmobile trail and finally to where the truck was parked. The lake was solidly frozen, so it was safe to use. The snow on it was wind packed, so it would make the going a bit easier. He figured he would make the truck in about two hours and just after dark.

All was going according to plan. Traveling down the center of the lake was relatively easy going, and he covered the two kilometers to its south end on schedule. Here he stopped briefly to rest and appreciate the terrain, covered in its wintry blanket. This little lake is a bit peculiar because it has a small inlet waterway coming into it and, about 50 meters to one side, a small outlet waterway. Normally inlets and outlets were never this close to each other. He would be following the outlet.

He adjusted his pack, checked the safety on his rifle, and started off. He was thinking he would be at his vehicle soon and the heater would feel good. The day was cooling off as the sun sunk further toward the horizon. Tufts of swamp grass could still be seen sticking out of the snow, marking the edge of the waterway.

"Self-esteem—high or low—tends to be a generator of self-fulfilling prophecies."
—Nathaniel Branden in *The Six Pillars of Self-Esteem*

"To be there without ever having been there—that is the goal of simulation."
—Terry Orlick in *In Pursuit of Excellence*

"We are what we pretend to be."
—Kurt Vonnegut Jr., writer (1922–2007)

Secrets of Mental Marksmanship

After taking three steps the snow gave way beneath him. He knew instantly what was happening but couldn't understand why. The snow and ice had all been so solid; why would it give way here? The cold, icy water eagerly accepted him, and he threw himself toward a large tuft of swamp grass. He figured there should be solid ground below it and he could use the grass to help pull himself out.

Struggling in the cold water he realized he had to get out quickly, and after such a long walk he would have a very limited amount of energy to use. Holding onto the tuft of grass, he paused to think of the best way to get out, the way that would get him out on his first attempt and use the least amount of energy. He thought of jettisoning all of his equipment, especially his snowshoes, as it would be difficult to climb out with them on. But he had three kilometers yet to go to reach his vehicle and he would need them. His plan to get out would have to include his snowshoes. And leaving his rifle behind . . . no, that wasn't going to happen either.

Hanging onto a tuft of frozen grass with one hand, he removed his pack and rifle with his free hand and placed them on the snow behind the grass. He then slowly drew his feet and snowshoes up under him and, when ready, tried to stand up. The snowshoes gave just enough resistance against the water and, while reaching for the next tuft of grass, he was able to get further out of the water and onto the snow. After several more attempts, he lay on the snow catching his breath beside the watery hole.

After several minutes, he recovered enough to stand up. He wasn't sure if his body was shaking from the cold or the effort he had just expended to get out. Either way, he still understood the situation he was in and what he had to do to save himself. He was okay, thinking properly, but wasn't "out of the woods" yet. As he put on his pack and rifle, he smiled at the double meaning of that thought. Yeah, he'd be okay, but he needed to get going. His clothes would freeze up soon and he would be cold, but he had only three kilometers to go and he was certain he would make it.

He looked about, thinking that he couldn't trust walking on the waterway. He decided he would go the rest of the way along the tree line on the edge. The snow would be deeper there, but he would have to accept that; it was the safest way to go. And he needed to get going.

He took five steps toward the tree line and suddenly found himself, yet again, up to his armpits in icy water.

If there can be any humor in the life-threatening situation he was again in, it was the thought he was now having: "Well, I have just rehearsed this, so getting out this time should be easier."

It wasn't easier. He had expended a lot of energy getting out of the first hole and now didn't have that reserve to get out of this one. He looked at the water trying to pull him down. There was only one option: he would, little by little, pull himself out of this hole. It would take longer, but it would come to pass.

He followed the first plan; it had worked well and was the obvious solution. It took much longer but he eventually got out. If he thought he needed to get going before, he certainly needed to now. Once at the tree line, he looked back at the two holes, somehow to reassure himself that it had actually happened. He felt smug about having gone through this and still have all is equipment. Some old sergeant, somewhere, would be pleased.

The going in the deep snow was difficult. He stopped often to rest. He checked his map to look for the terrain features that indicated he was progressing. He checked his GPS to see how many actual meters were left to the snowmobile trail. He had only gone 300 meters. Yeah, this was going to be hard, but he would make it just like he got out of that last hole—bit by bit until he was there.

He tried to make himself go at least a hundred meters before he stopped to rest. The GPS didn't always tell him what he wanted to know. He was stopping more often than he wanted. There were still two kilometers to go—but he was feeling so tired. His clothes were frozen and felt like cardboard. He shivered continually. He knew about hypothermia, how the core temperature would cool down, how he would eventually not be able to move any more, how his muscles would just stop working.

So, then, the idea was to keep moving while they were still working. This was hard and getting harder, but getting out alive was the only option, and it would happen. It would just take some time, and right now there was nothing better to do with his time but to keep going.

Although his entire body was aching and near exhaustion, it was his left hip that gave in to the strain first.

Every step became painful. He had to stop more often. He gave up checking the GPS to see how far he had gone—he could just look back at his trail and see where he had stopped last. He would stop doing that as well. From now on he would only look ahead. He wondered if this was what it was like—would the mind keep on wanting to go but the body would eventually just give up? He still had a kilometer to go.

He started to think about the truck and how nice the heater would feel. He could see the truck now and started to get his keys out of a pocket. He unlocked the door and put his kit in the back. He crawled into the driver's seat and just sat for a moment feeling how good the seat felt. He started the engine and soon had heat in the cold air around him. It all felt so good and was worth the extra effort to get here. Yes, it was worth the effort . . . just keep on, keeping on.

He decided he would give the GPS just one more chance. It said he had 800 meters to go. Wow! He had covered 200 meters in that last thought. He hadn't even felt the hurt in his hip—and that was a good thing.

He unlocked the front door to the house. He walked in, dropping his pack and rifle on the floor and went straight to the washing machine. His clothes reeked of the smell of swamp water. He stripped down and put each item into the washing machine and then, naked, went straight to the shower. He turned the water on full blast and as hot as he could stand it. He had no idea how long he was there, letting the hot water bring him back to life. Yes, this too was worth the effort.

This time the GPS said he had 500 meters to go. Wow! "That's nothing," he thought. He pictured the distance as it appears on the range. He had shot a lot of shots from that distance. He would be there in no time. That hip was sure hurting now. But he could endure that if it meant getting home tonight.

And finally, there it was. The snowmobile trail became visible right on cue. The trail was hard packed and he took his snowshoes off for the last 200 meters to the truck. The rest went absolutely according to plan and as he had imagined it.

Throughout he had maintained a positive attitude, even humorous at times. Getting through this successfully was the only option. He kept his mind busy thinking about solutions, focusing on what had to be done to get the desired end results. He also kept the mind occupied with what a successful result would be like, pretending he had already accomplished it. *"Keep the mind focused and the body will follow."*

Competition Story—The Last Three Shots
This is Keith's story from "The Power of Self-Talk."[10]

I once had difficulty with my last three shots on score. If I had a good shoot going, I would say to myself, "I've got a good shoot going here if I don't blow these last three shots." This would cause me to think about failure and subconsciously list off all the ways I could blow these shots.

If I had a bad shoot going, I would say to myself, "I could still salvage a mediocre score if I don't blow these last three shots." I would then spend the last three shots thinking (and telling myself) what a rotten score I would have if I blew these shots.

I talked with a friend of mine from New Brunswick about this situation. George Chase is an outstanding shooter and has coached me several times in team events. I have fired some of my best performances under his guidance, and I have a great deal of respect for his opinion. He asked me if I was thinking the same thoughts at the start, when I had a good shoot going, as I was for the last three shots. I replied that if I thought that way at the start, then I wouldn't have a good shoot going when I got to the last three shots. He smiled. Sometimes we just have to be slapped in the face with the obvious before we see it. Stop thinking of the last three shots as being different. Tell yourself that each one of them is just the same as the others—no more or less valuable, just the same.

As part of a mental program, I tell myself for each shot that I am "going to shoot this shot just like the last shot." I shoot these shots quickly before I have a chance to tell myself anything different. The subconscious mind propels us in the direction that we're picturing. So tell yourself to picture positive thoughts.

Secrets of Mental Marksmanship

COMPETITION

Competition Story—Leo the Lion-Hearted
From "Snapshots from Canada."[11]

The first ever F-Class World Championships were held in Canada in August 2002. Participants from around the world were delighted to be a part of this landmark event.

Leo D'Amour was our anchor shooter on Jim Bullock's firing point. Leo is a veteran shooter, having been on more Canadian shooting teams than he would probably care to remember.

We were at the 700-meter mound, and Leo was calmly firing a string of uninterrupted V-bulls. At one point in the string, the target did not respond. The target markers in the butts were very good, and only the best were retained for the final day of the Worlds. Jim called for a hit (i.e., to have the target pulled down for scoring). The target came back up empty, signaling a miss. Jim asked Leo if there was any possibility that he had cross-fired. Leo was certain that he had fired on the correct target. Jim exhausted all the challenge procedures, and there was still no bullet hole to be found.

There was really nothing to do but to carry on. Losing six points (what the miss would cost the team) was a hardship for the team score, especially in the light wind conditions on that day, but all we could do was hope for the best and carry on.

Leo's next shot was a V-bull.

After the next shot was fired, the target did not respond. By this time, Keith's firing point was finished and Keith was watching the proceedings. He said, "I don't think they'll find that shot. I don't think it made it to the target. I think I saw a little puff of smoke about 200 meters downrange." When bullets blow up in flight, you will often see a little puff of smoke or a wavy air disturbance. Sure enough, after exhausting all of the challenge procedures yet again, Team Canada had another miss.

Jim reached into Leo's ammo box and said, "What bullets are you using?" Jim's company (Gold Cross) makes some of the finest police and competition ammunition available. As Jim examined the bullet, the ballistic tip came off in his hand. He said that they were old bullets with a faulty tip and that the manufacturer no longer made them like that. This is a vivid example of the considerable dependence shooting (and particularly F-Class shooting) has on the technology that supports the sport.

Leo said that he had more ammo with different bullets in the car.

Jim said, "Go get them."

Leo's next shot was a V-bull, as were the rest of his shots at the 700-meter mound.

The real story here is not the ammunition and not the team score. The real story here is Leo. Throughout this very unhappy situation, he maintained an attitude of professionalism, an air of calmness in adversity. Without this attitude, the bullets that made it to the target would not have been V-bulls. Without Leo and Jim's significant experience in shooting and teams and international matches, this situation could very quickly have degenerated into a real embarrassment for the team. With his professional attitude, Leo helped all of us retain our professionalism.

We didn't fully appreciate how very important this was until after the match was over and one of the first-timers on the team said, "I was really nervous, and the first point I lost I was really upset. But Leo really set the example. If he could have that kind of problem and just keep on doing his job, then what else could I do? Leo didn't get angry or upset; he just looked for a solution and kept on shooting his shots."

In fact, Leo was both angry and upset, but he never let it show. His attitude was that it was bad enough to lose team points with something he could not control; it would be horrible to lose team points with something he could control. And while he had no control over the bullets blowing up, he certainly could control his reaction to the situation. While he and we all knew that any possibility of victory had been blown to bits along with those bullets, we still had the opportunity to act with grace in the face of adversity and thereby achieve a personal victory.

The first ever F-Class World Championships were held in Canada in August 2002. Participants from around the world were delighted to be a part of this landmark event.

— 144 —

Tools to Increase the Power of Your Self-Image

Before we left the 700-meter mound to move back for the next phase of the match, Keith (our team captain) called the whole team into a circle. "We've had a tough go here at the 700," he said. "I think now's the time to bring out Sandy Peden's 'don't quit on me now' speech. Even though we've had a tough time here, we still have a job to do at the 800- and the 900-meter mounds." At these words, the team relaxed.

Keith continued: "We still want each and every member of the team to continue to do a professional job. We still need to make every shot count. We have the best wind readers on the range, and this is more and more important as we move back. We still need to focus on performance and do the best job we can." The team was now ready to move on, to set aside our adversity and to move on to the next challenge.

Just to set the record straight, the points those faulty bullets cost us would have moved Team Canada to third place overall. But as all experienced team shooters know, no single team member's score determines the team results. It always takes top performances from every team member to win team events.

Competition Story—Not Just Shooters
We actively collect stories about people who set good examples in marksmanship and in mental marksmanship. We also collect stories about good examples of positive attitudes and effective self-talk from other sports and endeavors. Occasionally, we throw in an example of the other end of the spectrum (negative attitudes and dysfunctional self-talk) just to ensure that new people who come on our courses can relate to our teaching. What follows is a small sampling of some of these stories.[12] All of these athletes set examples that we can use in our own lives (either by following or by countering their example).

One day we happened to be watching a sports announcer interviewing a baseball pitcher on the upcoming game and season. We have all heard this type of interview many times and look on it as being pretty innocent. Except this time, this professional athlete, who has the finest coaches in the world and is paid an enormous salary to perform better than anyone else, replied to one question with, "Yeah, I've had a real good training camp and my arm is feeling good, so we should have a good game unless I blow it."

Unfortunately, baseball pitchers get more credit than they deserve for losing a game when they have such limited control over so many other factors that influence the outcome. As in shooting, we can take responsibility only for the delivery of the shot. There are many other influences that decide the outcome. When we focus our self-talk on the outcome instead of on our own performance, we lose sight of just where we do have control. Self-talk must be positive and about the immediate things that we control.

Bruce Wilkins, formerly one of our national shooting coaches, liked to tell the story about a baseball pitcher who is about to pitch against the other side's top hitter. The coach comes on to the field to bolster his pitcher's confidence. "You're doing good, Bob. This guy can be beat. Why, just last week Wilson with the Red Sox struck him out. Now, this guy really likes a pitch that is down and right. He can really hit those ones out of the park." The coach affectionately pats his pitcher on the shoulder and as he turns to leave the mound, his last words are, "So whatever you do, don't pitch one down and right."

Our pitcher takes his position on the mound with his self-talk influenced by the one person he trusts the most in the world, his coach. As he winds up to deliver his first pitch, the voice in his mind is screaming, "Whatever you do, don't pitch one down and to the right!" The more we think about or talk about something happening, the more we improve the chances of that thing happening.

It would have been better if the coach had said, "You're doing just fine, Bob. You can beat this guy by just doing what you have been doing all this game. Now, have fun with him." This won't guarantee that Bob will keep this guy from blasting one out of the park, but it will help our pitcher perform at his best. The pitcher has no control over how well the hitter will perform on this day, but the pitcher can control how well *he* performs on this day.

In our seminars, we have also used an outstanding example of a professional athlete with the most positive self-talk. Unfortunately, most of the shooters were under the age of 20 and didn't know who Muhammad Ali was[13] or how he would, during prefight interviews, tell the world of his positive self-talk and what his mental program was going to be for the upcoming fight. "Float like a butterfly, sting like a bee" became a familiar saying to any of us who lived through the Ali era. He would also announce his goal to the world, as if making a contract with those of us listening, and then was motivated and compelled to live up to it: "I am the greatest." Ali really thought he was the greatest and was therefore willing to work hard and work smart to live up to that self-image. He had announced it to the world and wasn't going to let himself down . . . and, of course, he didn't.

I'm not much of a golf fan, but I watch it sometimes to see how the professional players handle the pressure. Most, of course, handle it very well and with a professional touch. By the time they get to this level, they have a good grasp on the importance of thinking the right thoughts because you can't get there from here without it.

Arnold Palmer was being interviewed one time about how lucky he had been lately with his putting. He replied, "Funny thing about that. The more I practice, the luckier I get." Arnold was focusing on the things he could control, working hard and smart, and he just kept getting luckier. Although I have never heard Tiger Woods talk specifically about his mental approach to his game, I have heard his father make comments about his son's strong positive mental attitude. I'd bet the deed to the farm that Tiger has a mental program to control his self-talk leading up to a perfect swing . . . because you just can't get there from here without it.

SECTION 7-3: MORE TOOLS—FAME AND FORTUNE (MAKING A SCRAPBOOK)

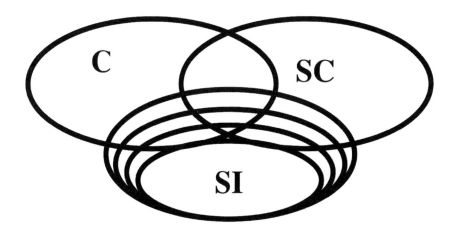

The final tool we use to support a healthy positive self-image is making a scrapbook. If you haven't started one yet, start one today! It's a surprisingly positive thing to make, first because it helps you pay attention to all the little successes in your life and then because it gives you irrefutable evidence that you have had many successes in the past.

What do you put in the scrapbook? (We have a bias for a print scrapbook rather than an electronic one. This may have to do with our age and era, but we think that the substantial nature of paper makes it more pleasurable to leaf through.)

Photographs are the easiest thing to collect. Make sure you take pictures of any significant events in your marksmanship career, whether training, competition, or operations. Keith's first scrapbook is mainly comprised of pictures from his time in the U.S. Army and his tour in Vietnam. He knew at the time, of course, that he was participating in history, but he had no way of knowing that his first significant life event would turn out to have a powerful link to the rest of his career and life. But there it is, laid out in pictures, along with the occasional newspaper clipping (for example, about Typhoon Hester that hit Vietnam while he was there) or a promotion letter or a certificate of accomplishment.

If you're a competition shooter, there are lots of possibilities for pictures of winning. If you're not winning your own trophies yet, make sure to get into the pictures of the winners and put them in your scrapbook. As soon as you do win something, make sure you get pictures of every little medal and badge. If you travel somewhere to compete, make sure you get a picture of the venue. Try to find a flyer announcing the match and put that in the scrapbook. Get a copy of the results and highlight your own name and score. If the local newspaper reports the event, make sure you get a copy of the article, whether or not they mention your name. If the organizers have a blog or website, print something from it and put it in the scrapbook. (If you're keeping an electronic scrapbook, put more than just the link in your scrapbook—links become obsolete too quickly. You're building a lifelong artifact, and you want to be sure it isn't dependent on someone else's technology.)

If you're an operational shooter, get pictures of training locations and situations (within the security specifications of your agency). Get someone to take a picture of you in your operational kit, with your weapons. If you have a particular role, like first in the stack, get a picture of it and put it in the scrapbook. Many of

"Pictures like these [with awards and background of ISSF targets] are important for your scrapbook. This scrapbook is the perfect place to 'feast on success,' which in turn creates motivating positive self-talk and a positive attitude. In your mind's eye, you look like a champion and so you believe you can think and do what it takes to be a champion."
—Linda K. Miller & Keith A. Cunningham in *The Power of Self-Talk*

"God gave us our memories so that we might have roses in December."
—J. M. Barrie, writer (1860–1937)

"So live that your memories will be part of your happiness."
—Author unknown

the military members currently overseas are being encouraged to take pictures and make videos of their experiences. This is part of the same scrapbooking process we're advocating.

If you're a hunter, always take a picture of your game. If you travel to hunt, make sure you include a picture of the location, perhaps a map or a flyer from the outfitter you're using, or even an airplane ticket stub, a visa, or a copy of the page from your passport that has your in-country arrival stamp. Even if you don't bag your own trophy, get a picture of the game you were after. If someone else at the camp brings in a big trophy, get a picture of them (and you). Take a picture of the rifle you use and include the datasheet for the ammunition you load, and maybe include the test group you shot.

Gathering these materials provides a great deal of the value of the scrapbook, but the best use of it follows later . . . sometimes years later. Anytime you're feeling just a little blue, take a look at the scrapbook. Maybe you're a police officer or a soldier and you've had some accident that's put you on desk duty for a while. There's nothing like looking at pictures of your success to put renewed hope in your heart. If you're a hunter or a competition shooter and you've had a tough streak lately, take out the scrapbook and remind yourself how good you can be and will be again.

Military Story—Visiting the Doc

There is another wonderful use of the scrapbook. It ties a cord of continuity through your life, one that others can relate to. We saw this happen in a particularly touching manner a few years ago.

When we were watching the television series *Band of Brothers*, we were especially taken by the episode about the medic. It started Keith thinking about the "Doc" on his team during his last fateful mission near Firebase Linda west of Da Nang. He hadn't seen or heard from Doc for over 30 years. We decided to look him up.

It turned out that he was living near Gettysburg, a place we were planning to visit in a few months on our return to Canada from a job in Florida. Doc's family made us wonderfully welcome at their farm home, and as we sat around after dinner, Keith brought out his Vietnam scrapbook. Two of Doc's four teenage daughters were home, and they sat on the couch with the big book on their laps, turning page upon page. There weren't very many pictures of their dad in the scrapbook, but the pictures were all about their dad's experience. They were spellbound. They finally had a link to their father's past that they hadn't had access to before. You could see their understanding of him deepen with every moment. It was a magical use for a scrapbook, one that underlined and magnified its value.

Law-Enforcement Story—A Room-Size Scrapbook

Occasionally our students will send us photographs and newspaper clippings of calls they were involved in. Usually it is a picture of them in some kind of activity related to what they learned on a course with us. We enjoy these clippings and pictures and hang them on the walls of our classroom. We also take pictures, on all of our courses, of students carrying out activities related to operations. These pictures are, of course, of them doing that activity correctly. We also hang the best of these pictures on the wall. This is us creating a scrapbook of them.

When our police students are creating their own scrapbook, they should include newspaper clippings of every call they were ever on, whether or not they're mentioned or photographed. If they were there, then it's part of their life's experience and should be included.

Hunter Story—"Deer Diary"

One version of the hunter scrapbook that we keep is a "Deer Diary." Keith's record starts back when he was a teenager and describes the circumstances of every deer he has ever taken while hunting. Linda's diary starts much more recently and recounts every deer and moose story. First and foremost, these records pay respect to the animals who gave their lives for our table. Secondly, they record the circumstances of each hunting situation so we have a history of lessons learned and lessons employed. Finally, these stories have helped us introduce our sons to hunting, giving them a wealth of deer hunting "experiences" before they climbed into their first tree stand.

Keith also keeps a photo album of his hunting experiences. He always keeps a camera with him and takes lots of pictures at the kill sight. As all hunters will attest, it seems that while at the kill sight the deer is still a deer, but once you remove it from that location, it becomes just meat. Out of respect for the creature, Keith takes lot of pictures while it's still the animal.

Tools to Increase the Power of Your Self-Image

COMPETITION

Competition Story—Our Competition Scrapbooks

We have always been lucky to have lots of material for our competition scrapbooks. We're involved in a lot of different types of shooting competitions: pistol, service/tactical rifle, precision/sniper rifle, smallbore rifle, target rifle, air rifle. We have organized, coached, and competed at clubs, regionals, provincials, nationals, and a variety of international matches. We have traveled within our province, within our country, and around the world to participate in shooting matches.

Some of our exploits have been covered by local press, some by national press. Sometimes we wrote articles about the event, just to ensure that a shooting match got the right kind of coverage in the press.

We don't have to win to include a match in our scrapbook. We sponsored the MilCun Shield for the F-Class (long-range rifle) world champion. Neither of us has won it, but we're pleased to have our picture taken with the winner every time we can.

We don't even have to shoot in a match to include it in our scrapbook. We have run the CFSAC (Canadian Forces Small Arms Competition) matches where we aren't eligible to compete, but we have pictures of them in our scrapbooks. Similarly, we have coached the CFCST (Canadian Forces Combat Shooting Team) to Bisley, England, and we have pictures of the team and their winnings in our scrapbooks.

Our scrapbooks are a rich source of recollections and confirmations. Anytime we feel like we aren't getting enough done, we take a look at the scrapbook. Anytime we feel we aren't getting enough success, we take a look at the scrapbook. Anytime we need a boost, a little perspective, a context for our current work . . . we turn a few pages in the scrapbook.

Competition Story—The First World Champion
From "Snapshots from Canada":[14]

COMPETITION

The first ever F-Class World Championships were held in Canada in August 2002. Participants from around the world were proud to be a part of this landmark event.

The winner of the individual grand aggregate, presented with the MilCun Shield, was Wolfgang Scholze of Germany.

Wolfe was a great example of someone who didn't win much in the way of individual matches but just kept on keeping on. His best finish in an individual match was a bronze medal (third place) in Match 4. The Monday Aggregate (Matches 1 to 4) was dominated by U.S. shooters (Bob Crone, Larry Bartholome, and Carlos Hathcock) and the Tuesday Aggregate (Matches 5 to 8) was dominated by shooters from the southern hemisphere (Bill Hallam, Philip Blakely, and Tracey Short) . . . and Wolfgang quietly "moved up the middle" to overtake them all in the Grand Aggregate.

Wolfe has been around F-Class for a while and has shot in Canada several times. He won the Farquarson Trophy (top F-Class shooter in the DCRA[15] National matches) in 2000. He is among those who were accustomed to Bisley-style Target Rifle shooting with the shooters paired "two to the firing point"; i.e., two shooters share one target, shooting one shot each, alternately. The target is pulled down and scored for each shot fired. This means you are unlikely to be able to "go off your last shot" unless conditions are very, very tranquil (most unlikely at Connaught). Since there is a time limit for each shot, the tactic of waiting for "your condition" is not going to work either. You must shoot your shot when it is your turn, regardless of the conditions. As one shooter who was new to this style of shooting was heard to mumble as he left the firing line, "Every shot a sighter."

After the prize ceremony was over, Wolfe came over and asked if it would be okay if he picked up the trophy. For those who know Wolfe (he is a big man), he is probably the only guy in the room who could comfortably pick the trophy up and hold it in his arms for pictures!

And so we now add a line to our "trophy timeline" . . .

1999
- ➤ We (and many others around the world, we later discovered) started thinking about a world-level F-Class shooting match.

2000
- ➤ An e-mail dialogue started the ball rolling, and Canada volunteered to be the host of the first F-Class World Championship (FCWC).

2001
- ➤ We decided to provide the trophy for the world champion.
- ➤ Winter—We started talking to our shooter/artist friend Craig McLeod about its design.
- ➤ Spring—Craig introduced us to local cabinetmaker Henry Vant Erve.
- ➤ Summer—Henry selected the wood for the trophy, laminated it, and fashioned the overall shield.
- ➤ October—Craig sanded and polished the walnut and carved out the letters "MilCun Shield" in a banner across the top.
- ➤ November/December—Craig worked on the relief carving that was to become the centerpiece of the shield.

2002
- ➤ January—Henry glued the relief carving into the shield.
- ➤ February—Engraver Michael O'Donnell[16] completed the brass work.
- ➤ August 28—The shield was awarded to Wolfgang Scholze, the first ever world champion, a most deserving recipient for the award "given to recognize uncommon excellence in the skill of Long Range Marksmanship."

CHAPTER SUMMARY

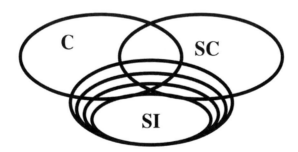

The purpose of the self-image is to provide the ultimate picture for the conscious and subconscious to follow. One of the best ways to improve your self-image is through self-talk. Self-talk is the spokesperson for our mental attitude—the mental attitude that determines our altitude. Learning to control your self-talk is the most natural way to get rid of the old dysfunctional programs in the brain and replace them with new achievement-oriented programs.

While self-talk is probably the single most important thing you can do to align your self-image with your goals, there are other tools you can use to mold your self-image. They include:

- ➤ Mastering the positive attitude
- ➤ Being solution oriented
- ➤ Confirming through congratulating and complimenting
- ➤ Setting an example
- ➤ Pretending to make it so

Tools to Increase the Power of Your Self-Image

The final tool we use to support a healthy positive self-image is making a scrapbook. It's a surprisingly positive thing to do, first because it helps you pay attention to all the little successes in your life, and then because it gives you irrefutable evidence that you have had many successes in the past.

Gathering these materials provides a great deal of the value of the scrapbook, but the best use of it follows later . . . sometimes years later. Anytime you're feeling just a little blue, take a look at the scrapbook. Maybe you're a police officer or a soldier and you've had some accident that's put you on desk duty for a while. There's nothing like looking at pictures of your success to put renewed hope in your heart. If you're a hunter or a competition shooter and you've had a tough streak lately, take out the scrapbook and remind yourself how good you can be and will be again.

NOTES

1. "Can I Give You a Little Honest Feedback" by Linda K. Miller was originally published in the *CoachNet* newsletter (September/October 2001) and has been republished in *Favorite Stories for the Competition Coach*.
2. "Can I Give You a Little Honest Feedback" by Linda K. Miller was originally published in the *CoachNet* newsletter (September/October 2001) and has been republished in *Favorite Stories for the Competition Coach*.
3. "Snatch the Pebble" by Linda K. Miller was originally published in *Precision Shooting* (July 2000) and has been republished in *Favorite Stories on Winning*.
4. "Can I Give You a Little Honest Feedback" by Linda K. Miller was originally published in the *CoachNet* newsletter (September/October 2001) and has been republished in *Favorite Stories for the Competition Coach*.
5. "The Challenge of Adversity" by Linda K. Miller and Keith A. Cunningham was originally published in *Precision Shooting* (October 1996) and has been republished in *Favorite Stories on Attitude*.
6. *The Secret* is a controversial book (and film) based on the centuries-old idea that your perceptions determine your world and that you can attract the things you desire into your world. Some people would call this a "self-fulfilling prophecy." We use a similar technique in performance analysis, where we focus on the things that must be done correctly in order to fill the mind with only the correct way of firing the shot, thus "attracting" the correct shot execution into our range practices.
7. In addition to using this sniper selection grid material in our Police Sniper 1 course, we published it as an issue of our *SniperNet* newsletter (Number 2, Summer 2005).
8. We are distressed that some agencies do not provide the internal support that is due to and needed by the successful police sniper. We are outraged that the hostage, whose life has undoubtedly been saved by the police actions, sometimes sues for "mental hardship" caused by the officers who provided the rescue. The idea of suing because you were mentally traumatized by being sprayed with your captor's red mist doesn't hold a candle to the physical trauma of becoming red mist by his hand. This type of opportunistic litigation is beyond belief.
9. We acknowledge the contribution of the word "simunitions" to the vernacular by the company of the same name that produces a popular brand of paintball ammunition. By "simunitions" we mean any type of nonlethal substitute used to simulate live fire during training.
10. "The Power of Self-Talk" by Linda K. Miller and Keith A. Cunningham was originally published in *Precision Shooting* (April 1998)
11. "Snapshots from Canada" by Linda K. Miller and Keith A. Cunningham was originally published in *Precision Shooting* (February 2003) and has been republished in *The Dream Team*.
12. "The Power of Self-Talk" by Linda K. Miller and Keith A. Cunningham was originally published in *Precision Shooting* (April 1998) and republished in *Favorite Stories on Attitude*.
13. Fortunately, the movie about Muhammad Ali and his fabulous career eventually solved this problem, as most young army guys saw the film.
14. "Snapshots from Canada" by Linda K. Miller and Keith A. Cunningham was originally published in *Precision Shooting* (February 2003) and has been republished in *The Dream Team*.
15. Dominion of Canada Rifle Association is the Canadian national organization for military-oriented shooting disciplines and Target Rifle.
16. Michael O'Donnell is a local engraver who has the distinction of being in high demand for prestigious engraving projects, including being the official engraver for the world-famous Stanley Cup hockey trophy.

— Chapter 8 —

Advanced Tools—Your Powers Applied

SECTION 8-1: APPLYING ADVANCED TOOLS

Success in the world rarely "just happens." Although all of us have a childlike belief that good things happen to good people, the reality of life is that good things happen to people who know how to make them happen.

When the intensity of your situation is relatively low—you're a recreational plinker or a small game hunter, or perhaps you're Andy Griffith in Mayberry in the 1950s—you can probably get by without the power of mental

Mental Marksmanship Map—Applying Advanced Tools

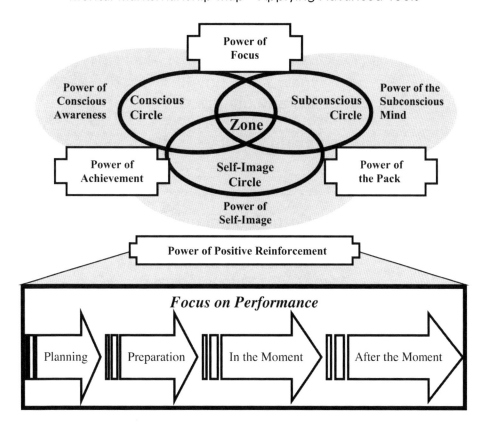

marksmanship, and you're even less likely to need any "advanced tools." However, if you think you might ever be in a tense situation in your professional or recreational shooting, you will need all the power you can muster . . . and the higher the intensity you must deal with, the better you need to apply all the skills.

In this chapter, we describe the advanced power tools you need for high-intensity situations:

- ➤ Planning
  - Goal setting
  - Contingency planning
- ➤ Preparation
  - Using available resources
  - Visualization
  - Mental rehearsal
  - Stress control
- ➤ In the moment
  - Attention control
  - Using situational stress relievers
  - Making situational pressure work for you
- ➤ After the moment
  - Post-traumatic stress

This toolbox provides you with the big dark secret used by Olympic and world-class competitors. It includes techniques used by GSgt. Carlos Hathcock (U.S. Marine sniper in Vietnam) and soldiers past and present. It includes techniques advocated by law-enforcement officers who have "been there, done that." All these tools, working together, will increase the likelihood that you will be able to get into "the zone," to produce an "ideal performance state," under pressure and on demand.

SECTION 8-2: THE POWER OF PLANNING

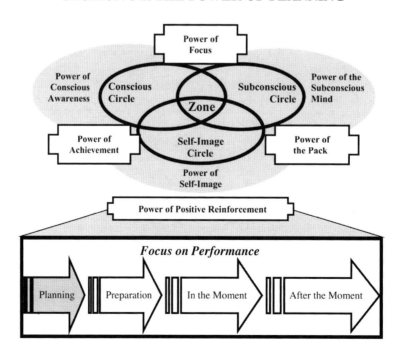

As Keith is fond of saying, "a plan is a common point from which to make changes." The power of the plan is that it tells you what the delta is between what you originally had in mind and the reality you now face. It gives you a measure of the correction you need to apply to your course in order to meet your destination.

There are two key types of planning: goal setting (and the resource/logistics planning to support the goal) and contingency planning (what to do when the first plan isn't working).

Goal Setting

To begin with, you must set goals. You must become goal-oriented. If you're floating through your marksmanship career without a goal, you may have an enjoyable time of it, but you're very unlikely to become a consistently good shot and certainly not likely to become a great shot in a high-intensity situation. You need to set big goals and you need to set little goals. Big goals may cover a career or a year. Little goals cover a short time, like a training phase or a single practice session.

Setting goals will help you to focus your efforts and energies in the direction that has the most pay value for you. None of us has unlimited resources (time and energy, particularly), so we can't just do everything. We have to be selective about what we will work on achieving. And we must channel our efforts toward accomplishing the things that are most important to us.

Decide just what it is you want to do in your shooting world

> "Set goals out of reach, not out of sight."
> —Author unknown

> "When setting goals, aim high—push hard."
> —Author unknown

> "We're all born under the same sky, but we don't all have the same horizon."
> —Konrad Adenauer, 1st Chancellor of West Germany (1876–1967)

> "If you don't want to win, no one will stop you."
> —Author unknown

> "Flaming enthusiasm, backed up by horse sense and persistence, is the quality that most frequently makes for success."
> —Dale Carnegie, writer and lecturer (1888–1955)

and focus your efforts in that direction. Goals require you to make plans, to work hard, and, even more importantly, to work smart. Goals will help you to organize for success.

So what exactly is a goal? A goal is a statement of desired end-state. A goal describes only a thing that you can control. The key thing that a goal must be is performance-oriented. The end-state that it describes must be an element of performance that you can control; that is, the goal must be in fact "doable." The test for whether a goal is doable is to ask the following question: "Great advice, coach, but how?"

For example, Linda's coach once said to her, "Your prone and kneeling scores are great. If you could just bring your standing scores up to world-class levels too, you'd be in the top eight all the time." So, the goal is to bring the standing scores up, right? WRONG! Ask the question: Great advice, coach, but how? How do you bring your standing scores up? Well, improvements to the structure of the shooter's position, equipment adjusted specifically for the shooter, a mental program specific to the standing position, workouts in the gym that focus on stabilizer muscles, visualization, mental rehearsal, shooting a faster pace, more training time in that position, etc. Now we're getting somewhere; now we have lots of constructive, productive goal ideas. We're now talking about elements of performance. Now we need to just get those elements described (quantified and qualified) as an end-state.

A helpful mnemonic popularized among competition shooters in Canada by Bob Todd (Canada's grandfather of coaching programs for Olympic shooting) is useful to remember when describing a goal: a goal needs to B-SMART:

➤ B—Believable. You need to believe you can accomplish this goal. An unbelievable goal might be to have zero movement in the standing unsupported position. Instead, a more believable goal description would be to have the movement "slow, smooth, and small."

➤ S—Specific. The goal must state exactly your intentions. "To become a better shot" isn't specific enough. You must answer the question, "How?"

➤ M—Meaningful. The goal must have pay value for you. If it doesn't, you will move on to something else that does.

➤ A—Achievable. If you make your goal results-oriented (e.g., scores), you don't have control and the goal can be unachievable. Your goals must be performance-oriented. You have total control over your own performance, and therefore performance-oriented goals are totally achievable.

➤ R—Relevant. If you're

"Victory always starts in the head. It's a state of mind. It then spreads with such radiance and such affirmations that destiny can do nothing but obey."
—Douchan Gersi, filmmaker and writer

"In preparing for battle I have always found that plans are useless, but planning is indispensable."
—Gen. Dwight D. Eisenhower, 34th U.S. president (1890–1969)

"It is a bad plan that admits of no modification."
—Publilius Syrus, writer (1st century BC)

"A plan is a common point from which to make changes."
—Author unknown

doing very well in your deliberate matches and not very well in the sitting rapid, your goals must be oriented toward your performance in the sitting rapid.

➤ T—Timely. Timely goals are ones that fall into the right place in the sequence of learning. For example, you need to learn to group all your shots onto the target surface before you try it under match conditions.

You must write your goal down, because the more we talk about, hear about, write about, and read about something happening, the greater the probability of that thing happening. That's the power of positive reinforcement in action. Also, by writing your goal down, you're making a contract with yourself to accomplish that goal, and if you announce your goal to your training partner, your family, your coach, or anyone else you respect, it can be an incentive to stick with it.

A goal should have a time frame in order to ensure you're reminded to keep your perspective and stick with it. But the real test of reaching a goal isn't that a specific amount of time has elapsed, but that you have achieved the desired end-state. The goal time frame is "do until . . ." For practical purposes, of course, a training goal might be "to run my mental program for every shot" and you have successfully completed the goal when the training session is over. The larger goal might be "to fire each shot subconsciously" and the training goal is repeated until the larger goal is met.

When setting a goal, aim high. If some people fell just short of their goals, they would still finish higher than the goals set by others. As the old saying goes, "Shoot for the stars; you may reach the moon."

If you don't want to win, no one will stop you. If you're going through the effort, time, and money to train, then push yourself for excellence. Competition shooters can set some national or international objectives. Hunters can work on accuracy, distance, positions, and moving targets. Police and military shooters can set objectives relevant to their annual qualifications. What's the worst that could happen—you become the best shot on the team?

Contingency Planning

The dictionary defines a contingency as an unforeseen event or an emergency. The purpose of contingency planning is to think about what kind of events or emergencies could occur and think up solutions for them. You plan for and rehearse the solution for any problem that might come up on the range or on operations so you're as prepared as possible.

What are you going to do if . . . ?

What is the worst thing that could happen to me now?

Some of the contingency planning we must deal with in competition includes:

➤ Your event timings don't allow you time for normal meals.
➤ The weather is inclement (rain, snow, extreme heat).
➤ Another competitor tries to play mind games with you.
➤ Your firing point equipment fails (the target carrier breaks, for example).
➤ Your own equipment fails (rifle or pistol breaks, sight breaks).
➤ There is a last-minute change (e.g., range officer moves you to a different firing point).
➤ The range staff is incompetent.
➤ The spectators are noisy and inconsiderate.
➤ When you need him most, the team coach or team armorer isn't there.

For operations, you will have other contingency plans to make. Only you know these best, but examples we discuss with our sniper students include:

➤ Your callout doesn't give you sufficient warning for normal meals.
➤ The weather is inclement (rain, snow, extreme heat).
➤ Just as you leave the house, your spouse reminds you that tonight is your daughter's first ballet performance.
➤ You get to the location and your equipment fails.
➤ There is a last-minute change and you need to move to another location.
➤ There are civilians moving in your area of operations.
➤ Your sniper partner isn't on the callout with you.

If you have a plan for such contingencies and have rehearsed it, it will be as if you have been here before. "Nothing new," you think to yourself. "This is no problem. Here is my solution."

"If you don't know where you are, even a map won't help."
—Watts Humphrey, software engineer (1927~)

"If you don't know where you are going, any road will do."
—Chinese proverb . . . and *Alice in Wonderland*

Secrets of Mental Marksmanship

MILITARY

Military Story—Cy Clayton

Here the term "situational awareness" is as valuable as a loaded weapon. Operations in a hostile environment are always exhausting. It's times like this when leaders at all levels earn their keep. As an instructor at the Canadian Forces Infantry School, Keith spent some of his time training officer cadets and junior NCOs.

When in the field, he would continually push one of his combat-learned points. While moving forward, just about everyone would spend most of their time looking at the ground just in front of their feet. Now, looking where you're putting your feet is important, but so is looking around you as well. He would often let them walk into their first training ambush and then take that opportunity to make his point—the unaware die unaware. He would continually coach them to "look up, look around." If he spotted wildlife, he would announce to the group, "You're under observation! Who will find it first?" In combat, survival is doing the little things that swing the odds in your favor. Having situational awareness improves those odds.

One way to help your situational awareness is to keep thinking like your enemy. When Keith was a private soldier in the Canadian Army, his platoon warrant officer, Cy Clayton, who later became the regimental sergeant major, was one of the best NCOs he knew. He particularly remembers that at any time on a field exercise when the platoon needed a boost, he would ask them, "What's the worst thing that could happen to you now?"

Everyone would quickly look around and someone would answer, "If we took fire from that tree line."

"Yes," Cy would say, "and what could we do about that?" This would cause everyone to think tactics, and there would be a fun discussion on the possible solution.

By this time the platoon would have moved further along, and the warrant would start it all over again. The miles got shorter and the packs got lighter, and we were thinking like the enemy would think, and this minimized surprises and kept us alert and aware.

POLICE

Law-Enforcement Story—"Give 'er"

In our experience, lots of cops just "give 'er" and get the job done. We enjoy watching the students on the second level of our police sniper courses where we up the ante by introducing stress: physical stress, mental stress, and tactical stress. Success in the high-intensity situations requires planning.

One of our favorite students is a young constable from a northern jurisdiction. When he joined our entry-level course, he realized that (compared to the other students on the course) he was a little flabby. In fact, he weighed more than he had ever weighed in his life, and not enough of it was muscle.

The following year he joined us for the second level of the courses, the one that focuses on performing well in stressful situations. He had taken his fitness level seriously, and he had transformed himself into the more usual hard-body tactical guy that we're accustomed to seeing on our courses.

He performed well on the first day, with stress exercises that are somewhat challenging. On the second day, he was still going strong. The stress exercises were a little more intense, but nothing he couldn't deal with by using his natural enthusiasm, good humor, and ability to apply himself.

On the third day, the main stress exercise required tactics to ensure that the student could successfully complete the task. Ben threw himself into the exercise, gave it all he had, and failed at the task. When it was over and he had recovered his breath, he said, "That's the first time I haven't been able to do something by just givin' 'er. That's the first time I needed to actually think my way through it before I started it."

The exercises on this course got progressively more challenging through the rest of the week. Ben had learned his lesson. He planned each one and performed well at all of them.

We were delighted with his progress. He had truly learned a skill that would serve him well in his police work . . . and in any other endeavor he chose.

HUNTING

Hunter Story—Hunting is Like a Military Operation

There is a reason why the best operational snipers often have a hunting background. That is because hunting can be, or perhaps should be, conducted like a military operation. By the time the hunter becomes a sniper in the military, he already has considerable experience. And as you may have guessed, there is an underlying theme in this book that relates the training value of hunting and competition to operations.

A number of years ago, while Keith was still in the military, he decided he finally wanted to shoot a deer with his muzzle-loading rifle. The rifle was a replica of the .50-caliber Hawkins as made by Joseph and Samuel Hawkins in the early 19th century. He would hunt on the home farm where he grew up and where he knew the terrain and the habits of the deer. He chose a place where his hunting mentor had years ago told him was a good place to kill a deer, and he decided to treat it just like a military operation.

The first thing to do was to send out reconnaissance patrols to locate and pattern the enemy. This was accomplished over a couple of days during the week before the muzzle-loading season was to start. He quietly and carefully moved about the area looking for signs of activities. He found the bedding areas in the thick cedars, then located and followed the game trails from there to the feeding areas.

Next he located likely ambush sites along these trails, selecting several in the event he was compromised or the wind was wrong at one. He chose them for their camouflage potential and for their proximity to the trail. He spent some time quietly adding to the existing camouflage and ensuring the trail into the site was free of branches and leaves that might give away his approach.

And finally he selected routes to the area so that, no matter which way the wind might be blowing, one of the routes would allow him to come and go without being detected. He then left the area for several days to wait for the opening day of the season.

Next to go in was the ambush patrol. On opening day and just as it was breaking dawn, he quietly made his way along the chosen route to the ambush site. Here he waited. He had prepared a daypack with all he would need to stay the day without moving from this location. His food was of the type that didn't need preparation and was wrapped in quiet material. He had even planned for the "call of nature" and brought an appropriate jug so he wouldn't have to leave the site for this reason and was still able to control the scent that just "going" on the ground would leave. A more serious call of nature, if needed, would have to be dealt with by means of moving away from the area far enough to carry out "cat sanitation." (With this plan, he had smiled to himself remembering how his old sniper instructors had told him that in this situation on operations, you would just "mess your pants." Well, maybe, but only in a life and death situation, and then . . . well . . . maybe . . .)

During the first day his target didn't show. Several does and lesser bucks came by, and he used these opportunities to make sure his attention to detail was working. Since he wasn't detected, he thought likely it was.

On the second day the wind changed direction at midday. Since his scent was now blowing directly onto the game trail, it was necessary to move to an alternate position. He accomplished this with the least amount of fuss and was quickly set up again. On this day a nice buck came by, but it wasn't his target.

On the third day, about mid-morning, his target showed up. A beautifully racked big-bodied buck cautiously moved along the trail. Forever wary and continually on the alert, this was how he had lived long enough to grow so big. It reminded Keith of the way Viet Cong point elements had moved as they approached the kill zone of the ambush patrols he had been on in Vietnam.

He carefully thumbed back the big hammer on the Hawkins .50 in such a manner, as he had practiced, to cock the rifle without making a sound. The buck was still unaware. He moved the rifle to the aim, moving only when the buck was looking away, and finally drew a bead on its chest. The .50 rocked against his shoulder, and he peered through the cloud of smoke to see if he could see the deer running off. He saw nothing—this was a good thing. He sat quietly in his ambush site, reloading and waiting for some sign of activity in the kill zone. Still nothing.

He waited 15 minutes before he stood up, rifle at the ready, and approached the place where he had last seen the deer. Moving out into the relative open made him feel uncomfortable, and he continually scanned the area around him. But within a few steps he could see his deer. It had fallen into a low spot that kept it out of sight.

The big buck was there. He had met his goal. It had all gone according to his plan, and even his contingency planning was put to good use.

Competition Story—A Coach to Remember

Joe Liota, a beloved Canadian pistol coach, told the following story about Olympic gold medalist Linda Thom.

COMPETITION

There were a lot of head games going on in the international shooting sports at that time. I wanted Linda to develop her own game plan and then be able to deal with the distractions presented by the other competitors, their coaches, the media, and the spectators. We talked about it for a while, and then we decided that she didn't need to have an answer for every question or situation; she just needed to have a response.

We chose two responses she could use no matter what comments or questions came her way. The first was, "You can talk to my coach about that," and the second was, "We'll see about that later." These two simple statements covered all the contingencies. They made Linda relax because she had an effective plan for dealing with all the uncomfortable situations that can arise at an international match (or in any other competitive or stressful circumstance). With these tools, she knew she could deflect unwanted attention and carry on with her own plan to focus on her shooting. And focus she did, winning the gold medal in the Ladies Match Pistol at the 1984 Los Angeles Olympics.

SECTION 8-3: THE POWER OF PREPARATION

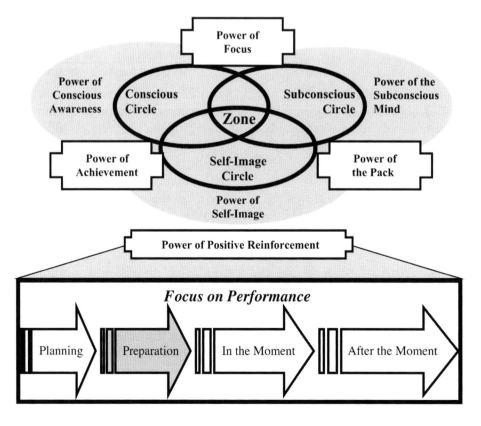

Preparation is all about acquiring, organizing, and improving your resources prior to the event that will require you to use them. Some of the elements you can bring to bear from a mental marksmanship point of view include:

➢ Using resources available in your environment.
➢ Employing methods that help you control stress.
➢ Specifically preparing for the event with visualization and mental rehearsal.

Using All Available Resources

If you know you have done everything possible to accomplish your training goals, you will go into an operation or competition with confidence and therefore less stress. Consequently, it's important to ensure you have used all the available resources that you can call upon to accomplish your training goals.

There are four basic resources for you to use to help you improve your shooting: time, money, effort, and people.

Command of time is a critical life skill. Being able to manage the time available to you is the hallmark of success. Are you using the time you do have? Competing priorities in our lives must be given their place (and time), but not at the expense of training time. Are there periods of time that could be better spent? Since it's typically very limited, our training time requires careful management. When you do train, are you working as steadily as you could? Each moment of the training opportunity needs to be used effectively to get the most out of this precious resource.

Money seems to be a limited resource in all our lives and so it requires careful management. Again, competing priorities will need to be managed. Do you think you could perform better if you had better equipment? Police and soldiers may not be able to use duty equipment on personal time, which means they need to buy their own equipment with which to train. If you need more training time, you may need to join several shooting clubs. Get your financial priorities in line with your personal goals. (At the height of her

smallbore training, Linda belonged to five different clubs in order to get sufficient range time with the right coaching.)

Effort is a way of multiplying your resources. What you get out of training is in direct proportion to what you put into it. If you don't expend effort, you can't expect the results. Are you working as hard as you could? Are you working as smart as you can? Are you getting the most out of every moment and every piece of equipment? If you want better performance, work harder to get it.

Arguably the best resource you can have around you is people. Talk to people who have been successful. Talk to winners. Talk to people who have been there, done that. Find out what techniques and tactics they used. Talk to them about the training they had leading up to the event. Find out what they thought in order to complete the mission successfully or to win a major competition.

All these resources are governed by "The Secret":[1] you attract what you expect. Expect the time, money, effort, and people that you need to fulfill your mission and your dreams. And when you attract them into your life, recognize them for what they are and use them well.

Methods That Help You Control Stress

Stress is an important factor that can work for you or against you. Some stress will keep you alert and focused, give you energy and stamina, and provide you with the edge you need to succeed. Other stress will cause you to panic, lose control, or act irrationally. It will cause you to worry and fret, and your performance abilities will drop below your standards. The idea then is to control the stress so you can benefit from it and make it work for you.

Some of the methods of controlling lifestyle stress[2] are being organized (and therefore prepared), controlling the way you think, being physically fit, and having a strong social support group. (Methods to help you control stress in the situation will be addressed in the next section of this chapter.)

Being Organized

Being organized and knowing you are is an

important factor in controlling stress. The key to being organized is ensuring that you and your equipment are in a state of readiness at the appropriate time. You need to be fit and well rested, and your equipment needs to be in good working order. If you don't train often, then you will have doubts about your equipment and your abilities. Specifically, keep your rifle and sight maintained, zeroed, and ready for competition or operations. Keep your equipment bag maintained with the equipment you need.

Develop and use checklists and equipment lists. This helps keep you mentally organized. Update them as necessary. Remember that they're of no value to you unless you have them handy (in your shooting logbook) and you take the time to read them. Always "run your list" and be certain that each named piece of equipment is there. If you haven't gone over your list at least once per training day, you will eventually get caught without a piece of equipment when you need it.

Using lists, especially checklists, leads to routines. Develop and religiously follow a routine that will guarantee your preparedness. If you're interrupted in your checklist routine, deal with the interruption and then finish your routine.

The Way You Think

The way you think is something you can control, and therefore it's your responsibility. Some people resist this idea, believing that the outside world is what

"I took the visualization process from the Apollo program and instituted it during the 1980s and 1990s into the Olympic program. It was called Visual Motor Rehearsal. When you visualize, then you materialize. And the interesting thing about the mind is, we took Olympic athletes and then hooked them up to sophisticated biofeedback equipment and had them run their event only in their mind. Incredibly, the same muscles fired in the same sequence when they were running the race in their mind as when they were running it on the track. How could this be? Because the mind can't distinguish whether you're really doing it or whether it's just a practice. I think if you've been there in the mind, you'll go there in the body."
—Denis E. Waitley, motivational speaker and writer (1933~)

"makes" them think and feel certain thoughts and emotions. The fact is that there is only one person who is in charge of what is in your brain . . . and it's you! What you think will determine how you feel.

Positive thinking and a positive attitude come with confidence. Confidence comes with the right kind of training. Only perfect practice makes perfect. Make sure your training has credibility, that it's the right training to develop the skills you need the most.

Positive self-talk will help keep things in proper perspective. It will provide the right kind of picture in the conscious mind and allow the subconscious mind to propel you in a successful direction. Success breeds success.

Develop and use a mental program. Col. Lones Wigger, one of the best shots from the United States Army Marksmanship Unit (USAMU), has probably shot more shots under stress than all of us put together. In 1978, he was preparing to shoot the World Championships in Korea and the weather was cold and snowy. Being from USAMU, located in Fort Benning, Georgia, he and the team were accustomed to warm, sunny weather. He was approached by another shooter who was near panic and saying, "My God, look at this weather! The snow is coming down so thick that sometimes you can hardly see the targets and the wind is howling! What are we going to do?"

The competition they were about to shoot was the men's three-positon match, 40 shots in each of prone, standing, and kneeling, for a total of 120 record shots. Colonel Wigger's reply was, "I am going to run my mental program 120 times, and then I am going to look at the scoreboard." He won this World Championship using the stress of the situation in his favor. When you're expected to make an impossible shot, just run your mental program and let God (or other deity or physics or the Fates) sort it out.

Physical Fitness

Maintaining a good level of physical fitness will help you control stress. Follow good nutrition habits, eating the proper food at the proper time. Limit your indulgences. Stay properly hydrated. Develop and follow an exercise program. It's well established that proper exercise will relieve and control stress. Include exercise that strengthens muscles, ensures flexibility, and develops aerobic condition. Make at least some of your program outdoors, in the sunshine. Keep your immune system strong. Get proper rest. On operations and during competition conditions, it's sometimes hard to get the amount of rest you need. In the army there's a saying that a good soldier sleeps whenever he can because he will never know when the next opportunity will come along. Get rest when you can.

Social Support

Maintaining a good, sound relationship with family and friends will help to control stress. Knowing that you have someone you can talk with about anything

> "I would rather have a B-grade plan with an A-grade execution than an A-grade plan with a B-grade execution."
> —Author unknown

> "The greatest achievement of the human spirit is to live up to one's opportunities and make the most of one's resources."
> —Luc de Clapiers, Marquis de Vauvenargues, writer (1715–1747)

> "Don't be afraid of the space between your dreams and reality. If you can dream it, you can make it so."
> —Belva Davis, journalist

> "Small minds are much distressed by little things. Great minds see them but are not upset by them."
> —Francois de la Rochefoucauld, writer (1613–1680)

will allow you to vent stress and prevent it from building up. Being involved with recreational activities and having a hobby will pull you out of stressful situations and let your positive thinking have its effect.

Visualization and Mental Rehearsal

A special type of mental preparation involves picturing yourself already there, already doing the real thing. For this specific preparation, there are two techniques: visualization and mental rehearsal. Visualization is a detailed picture of a specific thing (for example, a perfect sight picture), and mental rehearsal is you going through the event or a key portion of the event (for example, setting up your shooting position and firing a perfect shot).

The purpose of this type of training is to provide:

➢ Relaxation—Provides a plan, therefore calming anxieties.
➢ Focus—The focus is always on performance.
➢ Positive image of a perfect shot—Since we do the mental rehearsal of the actual skill being conducted in a perfect way, we have a perfect image.

Visualization is the forming of a detailed picture in your conscious mind. Since we directly control the conscious mind, we can make it picture anything we want it to picture and whenever we want it. Since our powerful subconscious mind always moves us toward what the conscious mind is picturing, we can now control the subconscious mind by simply picturing the right picture. We can make this work for us when we're about to fire a shot. For example, just before we look in the sight, we visualize what the sight picture should look like. For our standard sniper target, the crosshairs should overlay exactly in the center of the white aiming patch and our students often visualize this as "four squares in the crosshairs."

Mental rehearsal is simply an extension of this. It's the visualization of ourselves carrying out a particular skill activity. A common mental rehearsal for shooters is the firing of a perfect shot, but

"Are you counting the days to Friday, or are you making the days to Friday count?"
—Author unknown

"You can make more friends in two months by becoming more interested in other people than you can in two years by trying to get people interested in you."
—Dale Carnegie, writer and lecturer (1888–1955)

a mental rehearsal can include the entire event or operation.

There are two types of mental rehearsal that we can use:

➢ Within the body—We visualize an activity as if we were viewing it through our own eyes (also known as first-person mental rehearsal).
➢ Outside the body—We visualize ourselves carrying out an activity as if we were standing back watching (also known as third-person mental rehearsal).

Both types work well, and sometimes a combination of the two is best. Generally, first-person rehearsal is used for those portions of the event that are mostly

"Four squares in the crosshairs"

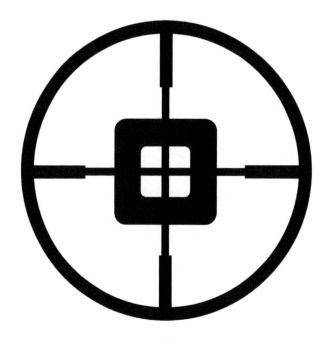

mental (like acquiring a sight picture and firing a subconscious shot) and the third-person rehearsal is used for more physical skills (like arriving at the range and setting up equipment). A complete mental rehearsal of you preparing for and taking the shot will switch between the two types of visualization.

We must always visualize ourselves conducting the activity perfectly. The subconscious mind doesn't distinguish between mental rehearsal and reality; it's imprinting your pictures either way. Make the pictures perfect and, when the time comes, your subconscious will do everything it can to make your reality perfect.

This is the key advantage of visualization and mental rehearsal: the subconscious mind doesn't know the difference between visualization and live-firing. You can therefore train to fire a subconscious shot anywhere and anytime you want. You simply stop what you're doing, relax, close your eyes, and imagine firing a perfect shot as many times as you want.

This technique is used by Olympic-level shots who, like the police officer or the soldier, must make every shot count, every time.

Military Story—Zero Confirmation

With all the preparation that a military unit must do to get ready for operations, the one that most often gets overlooked is confirming the zero on all weapons. Most people in supervisory roles seem to think that if a weapon has been zeroed once in its life, it will be zeroed for everybody for the rest of its life.

A professional hunter or guide won't take a hunter out until that hunter has confirmed the zero on his rifle. On most hunts there is a whole lot less at stake than there is on a military operation, namely some very nice back straps from an elk or moose and maybe somebody's reputation. But if the professional hunters have found it necessary to confirm zeros, anyone who can think must certainly see the need to confirm zeroes before a military operation.

Keith has witnessed, back in the day of iron sights, a senior NCO going through all the rifles in a platoon and adjusting the rear sights to make them appear more centered on the weapons. This, even though the rifles had just come back from the zeroing range where the shooters had zeroed them. Of course, the platoon officer thought he was lucky to have such a conscientious and knowledgeable NCO because the "Sir" didn't know any better himself.

Keith was once on a military exercise in northern Norway. This was "just an exercise" where both sides would shoot lots of blank ammunition at each other. He was in charge of the reconnaissance platoon in the combat support company within an infantry battalion. After landing in Norway, the company commander got all his officers together and asked each one what he wanted to do with his platoon to prepare for the upcoming exercise. When Keith's turn came, he asked for a "live-fire range and real ammo." Everyone laughed, and the company commander was a bit miffed because he thought Keith was just fooling around.

"We're here just shooting blanks," he said. "Why do you want to waste time shooting live ammo?"

The reply was something like, "Well, if we were here on a real military operation, it's exactly what I would want to do because it's the exact thing that we should be doing. Train like you want to fight, as you have often said." He got his range and ammo.

When our older son, Wes, was in Bosnia, then a captain in the Canadian air force, we stayed in constant contact with him by e-mail. In every e-mail, Keith asked if he had gotten out to zero his personal weapon, a Browning 9mm pistol. In fact, it almost became nagging until we finally got an answer that we sort of liked. He told us that he had been putting in requests to his superiors for such an opportunity and finally got a response. They would fly by helicopter to a range, be put through a zeroing exercise by an air force warrant officer, and fly back as soon as possible. Well, better than nothing.

However, once at the range they were issued 10 rounds and everyone was put on the firing line. Downrange was a single Figure 11 (charging man) target. Everyone was to shoot their 10 rounds at the center of visible mass on the same target . . . at the same time. Wes had the presence of mind to shoot his group at the face of the target, figuring everyone else would follow orders. He was right. There was only one group that formed on the face of the target, and the odds were good that the group was his. They were soon on their way back to their home base, and Wes was the only one who actually knew where his personal weapon was shooting.

During the Falkland Islands war, units of the British army were launched very quickly and had minimum time to prepare. They also knew that once they arrived, there would be a very good chance that they would move directly into battle. In order to confirm their zeroes before arriving, they set up targets overlooking the stern of the ship. They then processed everyone through a zeroing practice. You might wonder how they could do this effectively on a rolling ship. Well, with the target and the shooter both rolling together on the same deck, the sight pictures appeared to be remarkably still.

Proper preparation and planning prevents piss poor performance, as was once said, likely by a sergeant major.

"Fatigue makes cowards of us all."
—Gen. George S. Patton, soldier (1885–1945)

Law-Enforcement Story—Preparing for Stress

In our Police Sniper 2 course, the aim is to fire a perfect shot under stress. In PS1 the students learn to fire a perfect shot, so in PS2 the emphasis is on retaining the marksmanship skill in stressful situations. We have several ways of adding stress to the situation:

"All things are ready, if our minds be so."
—William Shakespeare in *Henry V*

➤ By teaching progressively more demanding types of fire:
  • Deliberate fire (one shot at a time, on the shooter's own time)
  • Snap fire (one shot at a time, on demand and timed)
  • Rapid follow-up or double-tap snap (two shots, on demand and timed)
  • Rapid (multiple shots, on demand and timed)
  • Multiple targets
  • Fire with movement
  • Scenarios with tactics
➤ By adding stress in progressive increments:
  • Changing targetry
  • Pushing timings
  • Adding physical activity
  • Using distractions like noise
  • Requiring problem-solving and tactics
  • Shooting from longer ranges (known distances and field firing)
  • Shooting with wind as a factor
  • Shooting with limited light (night, dawn, dusk)
  • Shooting from supported positions other than prone
  • Shooting from unsupported positions
  • Shooting through materials (glass, cinder block, car doors)
  • Using realistic scenarios
  • Adding surprises and novelty situations, especially with lack of planning time
  • Adding unknowns, unexpected and frequent changes

➤ By keeping score. Throughout the PS2 course, scores are kept and posted in the debriefing room. Each stress exercise is scored and at the end of the course, the students are measured by type of stress exercise as well as ranked by overall grand aggregate.

Each of the skills required to complete the stress exercises is taught prior to being put into a stress scenario. The intensity of the scenario tends to cement the skill deep into the subconscious of the student, storing it in a place from which it will emerge when the officer is called on to perform during operational stress.

A key feature of the way the officers are trained is this: for the major (daily) stress exercises, the students have an opportunity to assess the results of their first attempt and then do the exercise again. Between attempts, the class is debriefed about what worked and what would work better. This gives everyone a chance to think through their plans and tactics and make sure they are using the best approach for each exercise. This is where the real learning takes place, a type of learning that you rarely get on operations. While you may get an immediate debrief with your peers on operations, you don't usually get a retry to see if you can perform better.

Hunter Story—Hunting Heritage

In Canada, most recreational marksmen live in fear of having the government decide that they ought to give up their guns and go play golf instead. The only recreational form of shooting that seems to be sacrosanct is hunting. Hunting is considered part of the Canadian heritage, and when anti-gunners get together to decide what guns are "bad guns" and what guns are unassailable, they usually know that they need to leave the hunting guns alone.

This phenomenon has resulted in some very unlikely folks taking up hunting. Now, the easy way for people to do this is to simply take a hunter safety course and get their small game license. They don't need to prove they go hunting small game; as long as they have the paperwork, they are considered hunters.

However, this wasn't enough for our friends Deb and Doug. They decided they would actually take up big-game hunting. Deb is really the driving force on this adventure because she just loves venison. Deb, however, has never hunted anything. So she came to us and said, "Can you teach me how to hunt deer?"

She was already an outstanding marksman, so that part would be easy. "What would you like to learn?" we asked.

"Everything," she said, "from what equipment we need, what clothing we should wear, what you do to find the deer, what to do when you find them, how to field dress them, how to butcher them. Everything, from beginning to end."

Deb paused and looked at me. "I may have a little trouble with the 'end' part. But, well, I eat venison, so I should be okay with the rest of it."

"You know," Linda said, remembering her first hunt, "it's quite quick. The deer is beautiful. The deer is a target. The deer is a carcass. The deer is meat." Linda watched Deb's face and caught the startled look of acceptance. "You'll be okay," she added.

We have a lot of respect for people who put this much emphasis on preparing for an operation. Deb and Doug not only wanted a weeklong course, they also wanted to have a "pro" with them for their first hunt. It's really the right way to do it. If you don't have the heritage of being taught by your grandparents and parents, hire a pro! It's the best way to learn to drive, and it just may be the best way to prepare for your first hunt.

COMPETITION

Competition Story—Set Up for Failure

From "One Thin Wire."[3]

A couple years ago, a shooter at an Ontario Rifle Association's Service Conditions match complained that he had shot 20 points below his "average" because he was cold. It had rained (he didn't have rainwear), and then the wind was cold as he dried out (he didn't have warm outerwear either).

We don't mean to sound smug, but we truly believe this shooter set himself up for failure. He was not prepared for the weather and, in Canada as in most places, you can always expect to have weather! It wasn't so much that he couldn't shoot well when he was feeling cold; it was that feeling cold gave him the excuse he needed to justify not shooting well. His ability to perform was held back, not by the weather, but by his attitude toward the weather.

Compare this to Ken Ferguson, one of Canada's top Service Rifle competitors, in the 2009 RNBRA (Royal New Brunswick Rifle Association) Championship. The weather was brutal. It didn't just rain all day; it rained continuously, it rained hard, it rained until we could barely see the targets, it rained until the ground had soaked up all it could, it rained until the shooters were not only soaked, but they were firing from puddles. Ken quietly shot his shots and wiped his sights and kept on keeping on. He never commented on the weather or complained about the conditions. He knew that he needed to focus on seeing the sights and the target in poor visibility, but otherwise, he just fired his shots as best he could throughout the 12 matches fired that day. At the end of the day, he not only won the championship, he shot a personal best.

COMPETITION

Competition Story—Rory's Solution

From "Competition Rifle Course."[4]

We're always pleased with the competition shooters who realize that in order to properly prepare for competition, they need some training . . . and that they will benefit from a properly structured course. Rory was an excellent example of exactly the right kind of student. Here's his story.

On the first morning of the competition rifle course, we spend several hours covering the marksmanship principles, both in theory and applied. First we talk about the principles and tell the students what each one means and how it applies to shooting well. Then we demonstrate, and then we coach the students in setting up their positions with their own equipment.

Then they do safety-on drills, then they do dry-firing. We noticed that when the first trigger went "click" at the other end of the room, Rory flinched. Hoo, boy! We knew that Rory usually shot a big boomer, a .300 Win Mag with a 210-grain bullet screaming out at over 3,000 fps. We knew he had earned his massive flinch, and earned it well. We were very pleased that Rory had asked to use a MilCun-built .308 for the first three days of the course because we thought we might have a chance at curing his flinch. When he dry-fired in the classroom, his flinch was so habitual he was completely unaware of it.

On the mound that first afternoon, we let Rory shoot a five-shot group along with the other students. This first group the students shoot is five live shots, fired this way:

- ➤ 10 safety-on squeezes
- ➤ 10 dry fires
- ➤ 1 live fire
- ➤ 10 safety-on squeezes
- ➤ 10 dry fires
- ➤ 1 live fire

. . . and so on, until five live shots have been fired. Rory's group was average, probably about 1 1/2 MOA—amazingly good, considering the flinch.

Advanced Tools—Your Powers Applied

Then it was time for the first step of flinch-curing, using the same drill we use for helping shooters "discover" the perfectly relaxed shot, which helps lead them to a perfectly subconscious shot.

Keith used Rory as the demonstration shooter. Rory gave us a whole-body flinch on the first dry fire, even knowing it was a dry fire.

Linda took on the job of coaching Rory. The drill was this:

> ➣ The coach loads the rifle for the shooter, rattling the case in the breech area, and sometimes loading a live round and sometimes closing the bolt on an empty chamber.
> ➣ The shooter looks away while the rifle is being loaded so he doesn't know whether the rifle is loaded or not.
> ➣ The shooter focuses on firing a perfect shot, regardless whether it's dry or live.
> ➣ While the shooter is preparing to shoot, the coach watches the shooter's body and face, looking for any significant changes that indicate the shooter will flinch.
> ➣ The coach tries to "catch the shooter doing something right" by giving him a live round only when he is expecting a dry one.

Linda pretended to load a round for Rory and told him to go ahead and shoot. She looked for the signal characteristic that a flinch is about to develop and explode. In Rory's case, a crinkle in his forehead, just between his eyebrows, was the hallmark that he would flinch on the shot. Just prior to that crinkle, though, was the "signal," a little muscle in the left eyebrow that tightened. Aggravating the situation was the fact that Rory was closing (or half closing) his non-aiming left eye while setting up his sight picture and firing. She asked him to keep both eyes open while firing.

Linda gave Rory about 10 dry fires before his first live one. For every shot, she asked Rory to open his eyes wide and focus on the sight picture, keep his forehead smooth and clear, relax his face, and think about the perfect shot. She repeated "smooth" over and over and put her finger on his forehead over the crinkle to help him relax the muscles. Anytime it looked like a flinch was setting up, Linda would stop his shot and ask him to reset (start over). Whenever it looked like he might be able to shoot a perfect dry fire, Linda would let Rory click the trigger. Finally, after about 10 dry fires, she thought Rory had had enough success to risk giving him a live round. She quietly slipped the round into the chamber and noisily rattled a spare round in the tray as she had for all the dry shots. Then she closed the bolt.

Rory squeezed the trigger with Linda repeating "smooth, smooth, smoo-oo-ooth" all the while. The rifle cracked and the recoil rippled through the length of Rory's body. He looked up from the rifle with an expression of total amazement on his face. He had fired a dry shot with a live round; that is, he was totally relaxed, totally focused on good shot execution, and totally surprised when the shot went off. Linda and Rory talked about what that felt like for a little while and then continued with the exercise. By the time Rory had fired three live rounds (and probably about 25 dry fires), Linda decided he needed a little break.

On returning from the break, Linda decided that the last thing Rory would expect would be to fire a live round first. So that's what he did. It was a good shot, smooth and subconscious. Linda then figured that the last thing Rory would now expect was a second live one in a row. She loaded the rifle with a live round. Rory set up to shoot and Linda could see the crinkle starting in his forehead. She put her finger on his forehead and said "smooth." Rory relaxed and started over. Again, Linda could see the crinkle starting. The last thing she wanted was to spoil all Rory's hard work by letting him flinch on a live round. She put her finger on his forehead again. The third time, she said to Rory, "I'm just going to keep my finger here on your forehead, sort of a reminder." And Rory fired his fifth live round completely flinch-free.

The group was perfectly centered in the 1-inch patch. It was a single raggedy hole, about a 1/2-minute in diameter. It was evidence that a very fine shooting performance had taken place.

Rory continued to shoot the MilCun .308 on Tuesday and Wednesday and continued to shoot beautiful little groups.

Several times during these days, both Keith and Linda spoke to Rory about his shooting ability being revealed by shooting the .308, about how we thought he would be a top-notch shooter if he chose an efficient caliber that didn't beat him up as badly as the .300 Win Mag. He said he had thought about the 6.5x284, and we agreed that this would be a very competitive long-range caliber that would be far easier to shoot than the Win Mag.

On Thursday, Rory had planned to shoot his Win Mag but forgot to bring his ammunition. So he carried on with the MilCun rifle and continued to shoot tiny little groups.

On Friday, Rory shot his Win Mag. He continued to shoot the same smooth, subconscious shots he had learned to shoot on Monday, and he produced outstanding results. He fired a 15-shot match with a score of 75-14v, winning that portion of the MilCun Invitational. In the second phase, a 10-shot match, he scored a 50-8v, coming second to a 50-9v. His aggregate was 125-22v and he won the first ever MilCun Invitational Competition Rifle Course Match by one "v."

SECTION 8-4: POWER IN THE MOMENT

In the moment, those few seconds or minutes where you need maximum power, requires a few special skills. You have a good plan, you're well prepared, and now you must bring all your force to the situation. You need the following tools:

➤ Situational stress relievers
➤ Making situational pressure work for you
➤ Attention control

Situational Stress Relievers

It's always a good idea to have a collection of stress relievers in your toolbox, something you can pull out and use when a situation is threatening to get the best of you. No matter how well prepared you are, no matter how well you control your thoughts, sometimes the situation just crashes through all of that and your adrenaline spikes and you need to deal with the stress NOW.

We have already discussed several things that will help you deal with stress. Your lifestyle strategies for nutrition, rest, fitness, and exercise are vital to enabling you to deal with situational stress. Your relationships with friends and family and your social support network provide a healthy, resource-filled context for you. Your ability to relax and take a break from training and/or operations is essential to refueling your mental gas tank. We have discussed coping tactics like planning and preparation in this chapter. And while we haven't specifically talked about them in this chapter, we have throughout this book emphasized other key coping tactics like maintaining perspective, having a positive attitude, and focusing on performance.

Sometimes, however, what you need is an immediate fix to relax in a stressful situation. Following are some stress-relieving techniques that can help. Some are "instant"—you can learn them and use them immediately. Some take a little more time to develop skill, but you can start to use them within a few days and they tend to endure through a longer stressful situation. Most of these techniques can become lifelong skills, ones you can use in work, sport, and social situations . . . ones that you will probably want to pass on to your family.

➤ Stretching—This is simply the physical or yoga stretching that causes the tense muscle to relax.
➤ Fake yawn—Even if you don't feel sleepy, make yourself go through the motions of a big yawn. Yawning actually releases a chemical in the brain that causes you to relax. (It also distresses the competition.)
➤ Deep breathing—Whether you call it combat breathing, four-count breathing, or four-square breathing, this technique is easy to learn, easy to use, and very effective. First, breathe in to a count of four and hold for a count of four, then breathe out to a count of four and hold for a count of four. (And repeat.) When we become anxious, our breathing tends to become shallow, and this simple breathing pattern forces the body to breathe deeper. When the mind notices that breathing is deep and regular, it thinks, "Well, we must be relaxing now," and it calms down.
➤ Centering—This is a technique of focusing your thoughts to a single physical point in order to give

"Anyone can hold the helm when the sea is calm."
—Publilius Syrus, writer (1st century BC)

"I believe that hunting is the only peacetime experience which will allow us to consistently tap into a 'primal toolbox' of skills and experiences that is completely unknown to anyone else."
—Lt. Col. Dave Grossman in *On Combat*

"Fear is that little darkroom where negatives are developed."
—Michael Pritchard, motivational speaker

"Courage is . . . mastery of fear, not absence of fear."
—Mark Twain, writer (1835–1910)

yourself a break from the stressful situation. Close your eyes and, while performing the deep breathing exercise above, focus on a point at approximately the center of your body, just in behind your navel. Continue for several deep breaths. This helps you exclude all the thoughts that are competing for your attention, giving you a momentary break and allowing you to refocus.

➤ Disassociative thinking—This technique is simply thinking about something completely different. We prefer to make that "something" an element of performance that we can control, but for some people, a relaxing image (for example, a beach at sunset, their dog at play, or the flame of a candle) has the desired effect.

➤ Association—This technique requires a little training and can be very helpful. The idea is to associate something very pleasant with something difficult. Linda has used this technique to good effect for competition. When she was training for smallbore competition, she pinned up drawings of a perfect sight picture all over her house, each with the word "RELAX" written under it. Each time she

"Ability to focus attention on important things is a defining characteristic of intelligence."
—Robert J. Shiller, economist (1946~)

"Relaxed body, focused mind."
—MilCun instructors

"I think I can, I think I can . . ."
—*The Little Engine That Could*

"No one knows what he can do until he tries."
—Publilius Syrus, writer (1st century BC)

"If you wait for the perfect moment when all is safe and assured, it may never arrive. Mountains will not be climbed, races won, or lasting happiness achieved."
—Maurice Chevalier, entertainer (1888–1972)

saw one of the drawings (on the bathroom mirror, on the fridge door, in the clothes closet, by the phone, etc.), she would pause for a second and relax. The association stuck. Once trained, whenever she saw a sight picture, she automatically relaxed.

➤ Music—Many athletes use a personal device to play music prior to a training session or competition. This can work in several ways. The music provides a cocoon and keeps you from hearing distractions around you. In most shooting circles, if someone has earphones on, no one goes near him. The music can be used to help you either associate or disassociate some helpful images. And, most interesting of all, music can be selected to reinforce a slowed heart rate. The Baroque style of music (for example, the Brandenburg concertos) is so-called "60-cycle" music; that is, it has 60 beats per minute, which is a desirable resting heart rate. The theory is that when the body hears this music, the heart empathizes and slows to the same rhythm.

➤ Compartmentalization—This is a handy tool. All you do is acknowledge

Advanced Tools—Your Powers Applied

the stressor or distraction, give it a label, and put it away in a mental storage area, promising you will get back to it when the time is right. This relieves you from having to deal with thoughts that are stressing you and lets you focus on the truly relevant things. For example, some people imagine a filing cabinet: they imagine themselves writing the distracting thought on a piece of paper, putting it into a file, and closing the drawer.

And finally, if you're part of a team, pep talks can be a big stress reliever. The best pep talks focus on what you can do; that is, they speak to your strengths and they focus on performance. (If you're not part of a team or the team leader doesn't give effective pep talks, develop your own mental pep talks as an extension of your self-talk.)

There are a wealth of stress-relieving techniques that take a little more time and attention. For marksmen, the fundamental thing is the mental program, which gets the conscious mind focused on a productive task while giving the subconscious a clear picture of what is required. It's a simple technique to learn, but it takes weeks of training to ensure you will automatically use it in a stressful situation.

Other stress management techniques that are very effective in the right circumstances include:

> Hatha yoga—A combination of stretching and focus.
> Progressive Muscle Relaxation (PMR)—A technique to focus on individual muscle groups in turn and consciously tense and relax them.
> Autogenic training—Similar to PMR in results, but autogenics uses the mind to get the muscles to relax by imagining, for example, that the muscles are fluid.
> PMR with guided imagery—A coached technique where you're led through a series of pleasant images and finally, in a completely relaxed state, you're brought through a mental rehearsal of an incident, with you performing at your very best.
> Hypnosis—A fairly controversial technique, but most people report a feeling of being reenergized after being hypnotized. It's perhaps only one step further than PMR with guided imagery, where you're in such a relaxed state that you're very suggestible. If the suggestion that is made is something like, "Whenever you see a sight picture, you will be intensely focused and completely relaxed," you may be able to make use of this technique.
> Meditation—Often performed in combination with the physical relaxation techniques above, this is usually clearing the mind to a single thought (like a meditation candle, or a single word like "Om") and eventually to clearing the mind of all thoughts.
> Biofeedback—This technique employs a device that measures an indicator of your state of relaxation (heart rate, for example) and lets you know when you're successful in achieving a state of greater relaxation (lower heart rate, for example). How you do this usually involves one of the other relaxation techniques described above.
> Video games and simulators—This is a simple technique of

"Adversity causes some to break; others to break records."
—William A. Ward, writer (1921–1994)

"It is a rough road that leads to the heights of greatness."
—Lucius Annaeus Seneca, writer (54 BC–39 AD)

"Don't be afraid to take a big step. You can't cross a chasm in two small jumps."
—David Lloyd George, statesman (1863–1945)

"Energy flows where attention goes."
—Rev. Dr. Michael Beckwith, DD, visionary

— 173 —

using games and simulation to prepare for operations. Obviously, this training must be operationally relevant. There is some evidence that adults (like children) learn best when they think they are playing. The best thing about video games is that many people enjoy the endless repetition and can therefore tolerate a much longer "training session" than they otherwise would. And the best thing about simulation training is that it is possibly the closest thing to operational reality that isn't going to be truly dangerous or fatal.

Above all else, focus on performance. This is the one big thing you can control, and it's in the end the only thing that counts. It's hard to put into words just how empowering it is. When you focus on the thing you can do, the thing you're doing now, and there is complete focus on it, you're free from all anxiety and you can take pleasure in being totally engrossed in your task. This is one of the most marvelous feelings you can have—that feeling of total absorption, total engagement—what we call "relaxed body, focused mind."

Making Situational Pressure Work for You

Making situational pressure work for you is partly how prepared you are and partly attitude control. The more prepared you are, the more experience you have, the easier it is to thrive on the stress of the moment. And as the sports psychologists put it, the attitude you need is one of "positive self-expectancy." It's what we learned in kindergarten—you can because you think you can.

Situational pressure or stress is a tool that you must make work for you. Situational pressure causes a level of physiological arousal that creates:

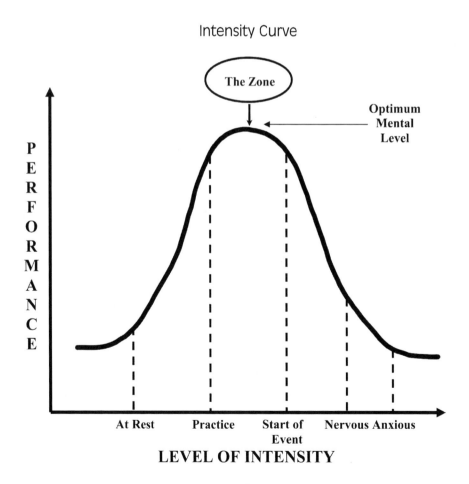

Intensity Curve

Advanced Tools—Your Powers Applied

➤ Visual acuity
➤ Faster reaction time
➤ Increased endurance
➤ Greater strength

In order to achieve great things, you want to be just on the edge of control. If you're out of control, you can't achieve much of anything: you have panic, and the situation will rapidly overtake you. But if you have significant pressure working for you, and you can stay in control, it can give you an advantage.

Situational pressure is usually stress caused by fear of the unknown and fear of failure. (Occasionally, it can also be caused by fear of success.) The key is to allow these fears to produce the (optimum) intensity while keeping everything under control. You maintain control by having confidence in your ability and your equipment, by having a plan and knowing what you're going to do, and by proper preparation and training.

The "intensity curve" diagram[5] shows that your performance level improves as the level of intensity increases . . . to a point, and then your performance level deteriorates as the level of intensity increases further, beyond your ideal performance state, or "the zone." When you're at rest, you aren't performing. During practice you have some intensity, but most of us don't get to our optimum mental level during training. At the start of the event (whether it's a police incident, an enemy contact, a competition, or the appearance of the game animal), most of us slip into a state of excitement that is just a little beyond our most effective mental state and need to pull ourselves back into the zone. Beyond that slightly excited state, we're nervous and anxious, and then we can slide into the totally unproductive panic state.

To keep your excitement under control when firing a shot, mentally rehearse it a few times until you have everything under control. The subconscious mind sees the picture of the calm, patient, in-control professional about to fire another perfect shot, just like all the other shots. Once the subconscious mind has a clear picture of what you want, it will do everything in its power to reproduce it, so long as you can keep the conscious mind from interfering.

To bring intensity levels up in practice, use some of the high-intensity techniques described in earlier chapters. And always, imagine firing a very important shot. Vividly imagine the scenario of this shot and just how you're going to perform it in the most perfect way. Perhaps you're training for the Olympics and this is the last shot of the finals . . . you're in a tight race for the gold . . . you hear the crowd cheer as your rival shoots his shot . . . you need the shot of a lifetime, and this is it. Or perhaps you're a police sniper and you need this one shot to end a lethal situation and save the lives of the hostages and your entry team. Picture the details of the view in your scope as the bad guy shouts orders . . . feel the familiar contact with your rifle . . . there is nothing in this world except for you and this all-important shot . . . you have the green light and it's going to be perfect.

During training, simulate situational pressure with contests: make bets for a dollar, a soda pop, etc. One police tactical team tells us that they all put in a couple of dollars and then the whole pot goes to the winner of the little competition. The competition doesn't have to be complicated; it just has to put some pressure on the participants. We often use our "Last One Standing"[6] match as a simple and effective exercise to develop superior marksmanship and nerves of steel.

The best relaxed state you can be in during a stressful situation is the "zone," also known as the "ideal performance state." Learning to produce the ideal performance state on demand and under stress is the hallmark of the great performers, whether they're athletes, artists, or marksmen. The stress you feel while in your shooting location will certainly be the kind you want to have working for you. You must be able to keep things in proper perspective. There are those things you can control and those things you cannot. Quickly identify the difference. Those things you cannot control, don't fret about: you have no control over them. Those things you can control, control them in your favor. You may not be able to control the situation, but you can control what goes on in your mind.

Secrets of Mental Marksmanship

Attention Control

There is one important tool that can help you control stress and effectively maintain vigilance in stressful situations. It is attention control. Attention control is the ability to focus at the correct level at the correct time.

You can't fire a perfect shot if someone is talking to you and you're actually attending to (hearing) what they're saying. If you're listening to what they're saying, you can't be running your mental program. We can only think one thought at a time. If you aren't running your mental program, then you aren't firing a perfect shot.

Within attention control there are three different areas of focus.[7] They are "position," "in the bubble," and "broad scan."

"Position" is the state of focus you employ when you're setting up your position. You focus on each body part, making sure it's just right, that it feels just right. If it isn't right, then you adjust it. If you don't make it right and you're somehow not comfortable or there is a haunting feeling that something is just not right, it could interfere with your "in the bubble" focus, which in turn could interfere with your shot.

"In the bubble" is the state of focus you use when you're about to fire a shot. Your focus takes in nothing around you. You hear nothing but your conscious mind flicking through the pictures of your mental program. You see nothing but your sight picture and your target. GSgt. Carlos Hathcock talks about this state of focus as "getting inside his bubble." When he was in his bubble, he didn't feel the rain that was getting him wet and cold, and he didn't feel the insects biting—he was totally focused on the firing of a perfect shot. For sniper pairs, when the sniper is getting inside his bubble, it would be a good idea to remove his earpiece and let the spotter relay any important communications.

"Broad scan" is the state of focus you use to scan your entire environment. For the police sniper, it means looking to see where all the containment officers are, whether there exists the threat of civilians moving into your target area, what the wind is doing, where your shot might go if you miss or when it goes through your target, what the wind is doing, your own security in your present location, what the wind is doing, what the range is to the target area, observing the situation as it unfolds, what the wind is doing.

You may have to flick from one of these areas of focus to another. But when you're in one, be all there. You must be aware of each area of attention and move from one to the other as required. Remember the power of focus: "wherever you are, be all there."

Attention control is used every day in your life; driving a car, for example. The "position" focus happens when you first get into the car and you adjust the mirrors or the seat belt because it isn't just right or you're sitting on something that will draw your attention away from driving. You use broad scan when you're doing routine driving: watching for other cars and pedestrians or navigating. You will go into your bubble focus if the car ahead of you suddenly does a panic stop or a kid darts out in front of you. You would go into a semiconditioned response, something you may have practiced a few times and certainly have visualized and rehearsed in your mind . . . your automatic action in an emergency. This is just like firing a shot. Your foot on the brake is like your finger on the trigger—when the eye sees the right picture, your body produces the appropriate action.

Military Story—The Boxer's Flurry

The best story to show what your skill level should be like when you find yourself in an operational-type confrontation, particularly at close range, is from an old army buddy of Keith's. They served together while on the rifle team of the 2nd Battalion, the Royal Canadian Regiment.

This was just after the Canadian Army had decided that boxing was too aggressive for its peacekeeping soldiers and removed it from its programs. There were still lots of soldiers who had trained and boxed, and Roy was one of them. He was mild mannered, easy going, and fun loving. Whenever time allowed, he would talk about his experiences in the ring.

Roy told a story of a time he was fighting for the army championships. He had trained hard and steady for this fight and was hungry for it. His opponent wasn't only someone who wanted to win as much as Roy but was from a different regiment, and this alone was motivation enough to win or come home carried on his shield.

The fight was hard, both giving as good as they got and both determined to end it as quickly as they could. Shortly into the third round, Roy says he remembers going into a flurry of punches and counterpunches and the next thing he remembers is the referee holding his arm up and declaring him the winner, his opponent on the mat.

Roy had trained his punching routines and combinations so well that he didn't have to think about them. He reacted in a certain way because his opponent presented a particular opportunity. He didn't have time to think about the right thing to do; he just let what was imprinted on his subconscious mind do its thing.

This is what you must be able to do when firing a shot in combat. The conscious mind says it's time to fire a shot and the subconscious skill takes over and delivers exactly what you have been trained to do. In a combat situation you don't rise to the occasion, you sink to the level of your training. The training has to be adequate, and it has to be correct.

Law-Enforcement Story—Mike's Story

One of the things we like to hear the most is a success story coming back to us from our students, and Mike's story is a perfect example.

Mike is a training officer with one of Canada's major metropolitan police services. One day he was monitoring a group of recruits as they went through a day on the range. At the end of the day the instructors had the group go through a competition to gel the lessons being taught. The competition was a simple one involving the engagement of paper targets with a specific scenario and finishing with some steel plates. The recruits were expected to go through this course of fire as quickly as possible and get all their hits.

One recruit had a very good run and challenged the instructors to "beat that." The lead instructor smiled, looked about, and then yelled the name, "Mike!"

Mike was only a short distance away and was watching the situation develop. He knew what was going to happen when he saw the lead instructor looking around. Mike acknowledged with a wave as he went to get his duty rig. He was hoping that what he was feeling on the inside was not showing on the outside. His mind was flooded with the importance of doing well in front of the recruits. He may have felt a wave of panic as to what might happen to his reputation if he allowed this recruit to beat him.

So what was Mike to do? He needed to perform right now, because there was a lot riding on him. First thing, he needed a plan. Just how was the best way to deal with this course of fire? Mike carefully thought it through. He knew the first phase of the course, at the paper targets, was easy for him. This would not require any special attention. He would shoot this without thinking about it—just let it happen.

But the steel plates, they had caused him problems in the past. What was the best way to deal with them? Mike decided that here was where he needed a plan. The best way to hit a steel target, any target, was to see the front sight and then give a steady press on the trigger. His plan was to make sure this happened for every shot. Front sight . . . squeeze, front sight . . . squeeze, front sight . . . squeeze. He closed his eyes and visualized doing this over and over. Yep, this was going to be his game plan, and then he would see how it turned out. Now was the time to focus on performance.

Mike went to his challenge with confidence, focused on what he had to do to get the job done. And get it done he did. He breezed through the paper targets without even thinking about them, and when he got to the steel targets, he saw only the front sight and felt the squeeze as he moved smoothly from target to target.

He knew he had met the challenge when, as he cleared and holstered his weapon, he heard a gasp from the recruit and cheers and laughter from the other instructors. He had blazed through the course of fire, setting an outstanding example for the recruits. As pleased as he was for having done that, he was also pleased that he had proven to himself that he knew exactly what to do to meet this kind of challenge.

Secrets of Mental Marksmanship

POLICE

Law-Enforcement Story—Scottie's Subconscious Shot

One of our police sniper students was on a tactical team call when the team leader called, "Sniper up." Scottie was delighted to get an opportunity to put his sniper skills to use.

There was a barricaded gunman on the front porch of his house. The situation was fully contained. The negotiator was trying to talk the gunman into surrendering. The gunman was considered unstable and so Scottie was to get the crosshairs on him and keep them on him pending a green light.

Scottie found a great location in a house across the street from the gunman. He pulled the table into the center of the kitchen and set up a few feet back from the window. His rifle was fully supported and he was sitting on a comfortable kitchen chair. He checked his view of the gunman. The porch rail obscured most of his body, but he had a clear view of his head. He checked his ability to put the crosshairs on various locations in the porch area, just in case the bad guy decided to move and shoot. Everything looked good. He settled the crosshairs on the gunman's face.

The gunman's head exploded, sending red mist and bone chips everywhere that Scottie could see.

"Holy cow," Scottie thought, "was that a subconscious shot or what?"

His earpiece came to life. The situation was over. The gunman had shot himself.

Scottie laughed out loud. He still laughs when he tells this story.

HUNTING

Hunter Story—What Is Buck Fever?

Our hunter marksmanship courses, although just a weekend long, are always interesting. This is primarily due to the range of experience that the students have, each attending the course for their own reasons. There have been experienced African safari hunters and those who don't yet own a rifle or fluorescent vest. They all contribute to the character of the course.

One particular question we received was from a hunter with some experience. And although some students did smile when they heard the question, others thought it to be a proper question, with an answer that needed to be heeded.

"What is buck fever and how do you keep from catching it?"

Well, it's not the kind of fever that causes your body temperature to rise and where you need to drink plenty of fluids and get lots of rest and in a few days you will be right as rain again. It isn't likely life threatening, unless you could "just die" from the embarrassment and the kidding you're likely to get from the other members of your hunt camp.

"Buck fever" is caused by the excitement of the situation. As the name implies, this excitement can be caused by a buck, although depending on your experience level, it can be caused by any size or shape of the game you're after.

A local deer hunting guide once told us a story of a client he was taking to one of his favorite deer stands for a morning's hunt. They came to a small clearing and to one edge there was a small doe. The deer raised its head from feeding and looked at the hunters. The guide carefully pointed out the deer to his hunter, and although the doe wasn't their quarry on this day, it's always good for the client to see deer.

Once the hunter saw the deer, he began to shake uncontrollably. He pointed at the deer with his finger and stammered words that the guide couldn't understand. He drooled, and the guide was concerned he was having an epileptic seizure. The hunter's knees gave way and he sank to the ground sitting upright and leaning against a tree, still shaking violently. Now the guide thought he was having a heart attack. The deer by now had disappeared into the tree line.

"That was the biggest buck I have ever seen," the hunter finally gasped, the first words that the guide could understand. The guide now understood what was happening—the worst case of buck fever he had ever seen.

"If it was such a big buck, why didn't you shoot it?" the guide asked in a calming voice, hoping to get his client to come back from wherever he was.

"Well . . . I . . . I . . . didn't have my gun" was the reply. The guide carefully reached forward and removed the rifle from his hunter's hands, checked to make sure it was unloaded, and suggested that he would help him back to camp.

So, this story shows the extreme that some can be affected by buck fever. Any of us who have hunted can likely think back to a situation where we have experienced some kind of lesser exposure. Some of the nice bucks that we have missed were likely as a result of some level of buck fever. Some have said that they were shaking so badly when they saw the buck through their optic sight that they couldn't hold the crosshairs on the deer. Others talk about the surge of adrenaline that they feel when they first see the buck, but eventually they get themselves under control and calm enough to fire an effective shot.

All of this is because the hunter is focusing on results rather than the procedure needed to successfully take the animal. Their primary thought is likely, "Wow, what a buck—I hope I don't miss it," or, "I hope I don't screw this up." The less they have practiced for just this moment, the more likely they will suffer from buck fever.

It's hard to understand that someone would go hunting in the first place and then experience such a state of surprise when they do see the game they're after. What, did they expect to spend all this time and money on a guide and a hunt and not see anything?

The best way to overcome buck fever is through lots of prior preparation and planning. Learn to shoot your rifle and learn to shoot it very well. Get lifelike targets of the game you will be after and shoot at them from various distances and positions and as quickly as you can be effective. Go out and do some "rock hunting." (Have we mentioned this before?) Go on some varmint or small game hunts and get yourself desensitized to suddenly seeing game. Read hunting magazines about various hunting scenarios and watch DVDs about the hunting experiences of other hunters after this game. In short, do your homework and you will come off like a pro who has done this many times before. "Ho, hum, just another one," as Keith's good buddy and sniper partner used to say.

Competition Story—Linda's Movers
Keith is quick to tell this story of when he and Linda were shooting as a sniper pair in the Canadian National Sniper/Precision Rifle Championship. The Dominion of Canada Rifle Association, as part of its National Service Conditions Championship, sponsors the match. The matches are shot with each member of the pair firing each match, their combined scores going toward the championship. It's a very challenging competition.

Linda and I had just finished the 200- and 300-meter matches and had done very well.

If we just kept up this kind of performance, we would be in the running for another championship. But the key match was this one: the 400-meter moving target match, which could have a very heavy influence on the final outcome. We each had to shoot 10 rounds for a total of 20 rounds at a moving Figure 11 (charging man) target. In this match, if you get only 11 or 12 hits out of 20, there aren't enough matches left to make it up. But if you get 18 or 19 hits and just fired decent scores at the rest, you have a good chance to win the championship.

We set up our rifles on the firing line, one beside the other. I was always on the right because I shot left-handed. I shot first while Linda was in the role of the spotter, and with no sighters for this match we were soon into it. Linda was seeing the swirl very well and kept me informed as to whether my leads were right. I ended up with 10 hits with lots of them in the bull. We switched roles and Linda got ready to fire while I spotted.

Things were going very well and Linda was hitting the target with every shot. On about the sixth shot, nothing happened. I didn't hear the shot, nor did I see any swirl. I immediately asked what happened, and Linda said that the rifle had misfired. She tried to recock it and it wouldn't. I sprang forward to see if I could make it work any better, but the rifle would have none of it.

I stood up, frustrated and ready to quit. How can you win these kinds of matches if the equipment won't keep up with you? The conversation went something like this, with Linda asking the first question, and it all happened before the next target exposure (in about 10 or 15 seconds):

"What can we do?"

"We can't do much if the rifle doesn't work."

"I could shoot your rifle."

"It's left handed!"

"I've shot it before." Linda is now behind my rifle.

"We certainly don't have anything to lose at this point." I am getting my ammo box open and placing a round onto the feed tray.

"We know it's zeroed. You just shot really well with it."

By now the next target was up and moving, and I didn't have time to get the spotting scope set up. I decided I would stay where I was and help her load and unload what was a strange rifle to her. I would see what I could do to help her by watching the splash.

The match was over quickly, and I wasn't sure what had just happened. "They all looked good to me," she reported.

"Well, the splash looked good too, what I could see of it." I was wondering if our run at the championship was over so quickly, and having nothing to do with marksmanship.

Finally the target came up with the indication and score, and she had nine hits. The only one she missed was the one left in the chamber as a result of the rifle failure. But the real victory here was what she had done to keep us in the matches. Her mind was full of "what can we do to fix this in a hurry." Shooting right-handed on a left-handed rifle had at least a chance of keeping us in the competition. And if you give her just a chance, she will more often than not just make it happen.

By the way, we won the championship.

SECTION 8-5: POWER AFTER THE MOMENT (THE POWER OF PERSPECTIVE)

After the moment, those few seconds or minutes where the impact and implications of your actions register in your mind, you also need some special skills. There is currently a great deal of research and discussion about post-traumatic stress. The competitor feels it. The hunter feels it. The police officer feels it. The soldier feels it.

"It" is the aftermath of the incident, and it usually includes a physical reaction (for example, big-game hunters often tremble uncontrollably after the animal is down), a mental reaction (for

"There's no use crying over spilled milk."
—Moms everywhere

"It's not over until I say it's over."
—Author unknown

"Rule #1: Don't sweat the small stuff. Rule #2: It's all small stuff."
—Author unknown

example, many cops tell us that during the incident, everything is in slow motion, but immediately afterward everything feels like it's on fast forward), and an emotional or psychological reaction (for example, a soldier who "goes to ground" when a car backfires is responding to a psychological imprint that was effective in war and is almost comical in civilian life). Whether they win or lose, the most common reaction of the competitor is a feeling of being let down or disappointed ("Is that all there is?") or disassociated from the achievement if they win ("What if it's a fluke?").

As we have said several times in this book, we aren't psychologists, but we are avid marksmen who have applied our skills in

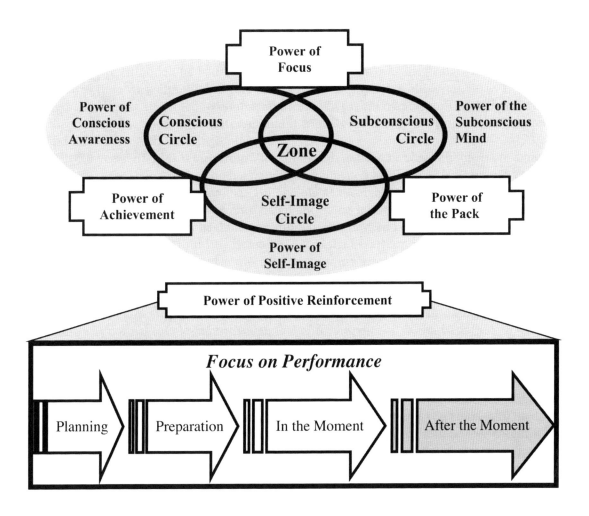

high-stress situations. We believe that the skills we have discussed in these pages will serve you well in the preparation, application, and aftermath of a critical incident. In addition, you may need some other information and skills to help you identify and accept some of your post-stress reactions. For this reason, we recommend that you include PTSD (post-traumatic stress disorder) reading and training in your curriculum.

From what we have read on the subject, the most important things for prevention (and for easy-to-diagnose and treat reactions) appear to be:

➤ Immediate validation of your actions in the incident
➤ Acceptance of the symptoms (by you and your superiors/peers/family)
➤ Implementation of SOPs (standard operating procedures) for debriefing, rest, refocusing, and reengaging

Military Story—Returning to the World

Keith was in the Vietnam War from 1971–1972. He served with "G" Coy 75th Rangers doing long-range reconnaissance and sniping in four-man teams. Later he was with "E" Coy Recon 2/1 196 Infantry Brigade doing the same jobs with a platoon-sized element. It's only within the last few years that he even heard of PTSD and started to look back over the years to see if he could recognize if he had any of these symptoms.

While doing this research, we spoke to and heard of others who suffered greatly from their combat and armed confrontation experiences. Lieutenant Colonel Grossman goes into great detail in his book *On Combat* about PTSD. (This book has to be considered a must-read for all warriors, both green and blue.) But the key point that came out was the spectrum of suffering that occurred. At one end of the scale there was virtually no reaction and at the other end there was suicide. Keith was at the "virtually no reaction" end and wondered why.

As he looked back over the years, he could remember only a few incidents that could be related to PTSD:

> "After 60 days and nights of constant combat, 98 percent of all soldiers became psychiatric casualties."
> —Lt. Col. Dave Grossman in *On Combat*

➤ Shortly after his return from Vietnam, his stepbrother took him on a getaway weekend back to his stepbrother's hometown. Keith knew it was a 4th of July weekend but made no further connection. They had parked on the main street of the little town, and Keith was leaning on the fender of the car while his stepbrother chatted with some old high school friends. His next thoughts were, "Why is this place so confined? Why can't I move?" He slowly began to realize he was under the car and having a difficult time moving. His claustrophobia began to set in and by the time he got out, he hadn't had a joyful experience. Embarrassed, he looked around to see if anyone had noticed. They had, and they were all laughing. Although embarrassed, he almost felt proud to have such a reaction to a burst of firecrackers. He had heard of returning soldiers having such a reaction and thought he must be normal.

➤ While in Vietnam he had recognized how his senses had improved. He could smell better, hear better, and see in better detail. But shortly after his return, he also noticed how these improved senses began to fade. Always an avid hunter, he spent more time hunting trying to keep these senses alive, but to no avail. They eventually faded back to normal because he was no longer in a life and death situation.

➤ About 10 years after his return from Vietnam and now in the Canadian Forces, he happened to be walking across a large parade square. In several locations around the base there were 25-meter outdoor ranges. These were built so they could safely be used in the populated area of the base, and there just happened to be one beside the parade square. A machine gun crew was setting up a C9 light machine gun to test fire. Keith was walking across the otherwise uninhabited parade square and was in the center of it when they fired their first burst. His next thought was, "Why is this ground so hard and how can I get further into it?" He then realized that he had reacted to the burst of fire, got up quickly, and looked around to see if anyone had noticed. He was again embarrassed as he dusted off his once clean and tidy uniform, but he was a bit proud to "still have the old reactions." He took 20 steps and repeated the whole thing again on the machine gun's next burst. Now he thought, "It's going to take me a long time to get off this parade square and to my office if this keeps happening." Again dusting off and tidying up his uniform, he now prepared his mind for the fact that there was going to be more firing and none of it involved him. He did remember his experience on that 4th of July weekend and wondered if his reaction to machine gun fire could be traced back to a specific incident in Vietnam.

➤ Throughout his military career in the Canadian Forces, Keith frequently was a member of the shooting team that went to Bisley to compete. These teams have been competing at Bisley for over a hundred years, and in 1896 the Canadian Army built a residence in which to house the teams. In front of the house, affectionately referred to as Canada House, is a cannon. It's an original cannon with a carriage and is very much a part of the Canada House motif. The tradition is that anyone who wins a match gets to fire the cannon. The cannon is loaded by someone who knows how with a small charge of black powder (no projectile), and everyone gathers around to watch it being fired. Keith was there chatting with other team members when the cannon was fired without warning the crowd. Although he had been present many times over the years when it was fired, the sound this time was slightly different and he went to ground. Getting up, he was feeling embarrassed and he was subjected to comments from other team members. But on that particular firing of the cannon, the sound was different and it triggered a deeply imprinted reaction. Perhaps this sound was very much like "incoming."

➤ Exactly 20 years after his return from Vietnam, Keith noticed he was thinking more and more about his experiences. They weighed on his mind and dominated his time. At least once every hour, he thought about one incident or another. But the one that came up the most was the day the team he was leading suffered one killed and five wounded, including himself. He hadn't experienced such frequent recollections before and was beginning to think he might need help with it. He decided to talk with a good friend who was a World War II veteran. Derek had seen considerable action, having jumped into Remagen and the Eagle's Nest. He was a sniper and just before being captured, he tossed his sniper rifle into the Rhine. He later escaped and eventually made his way back to Allied lines. They chatted for several hours, and Derek said he had had similar feelings and that what Keith was experiencing was normal. Derek's advice was that if it became too heavy, then by all means see someone, but know that this was normal for all combat veterans. From that point on, Keith went back to having things under control and keeping everything in proper perspective.

But there are other reasons why he didn't suffer PTSD like many others have. In talking with a member of the Toronto (Canada) tactical team who did suffer greatly from PTSD, we were amazed with the number of calls they have to handle. Two or three calls each and every day. And on each call you could get killed.

This kind of stress is far greater and of a different intensity than what Keith experienced. Keith was with reconnaissance teams whose main job was to avoid the enemy and report on his activity. He didn't experience any of the intense battles that would last for several days, with continuous firing and lots of casualties. Certainly if they were compromised, then they were in great trouble, and teams had been overrun and wiped out, but even then these teams were high on the priority list to be extracted if they needed. Even though he experienced the many dangers of combat (being shot at, being mortared, being in the beaten zone of a machine gun burst, dealing with booby traps, being at arm's length of an exploding grenade, being wounded, having a friend die in his arms, and so on), he doesn't feel it was the same as is experienced by tactical officers. All of Keith's experiences were short and quick, and once over he was back into a safe area and not likely to go out again for several days. Many of the missions he was on had no activity at all and it was very much like a camping trip. Certainly there was always the stress that something could happen at any moment, but it didn't. On every call that a tactical officer goes on, however, something will happen. Certainly some calls are more intense than others, but something will happen.

Without even knowing that PTSD was something, Keith received all the right cures. Every team that returned back to the rear from a firefight received immediate validation. They were debriefed by their superiors, who were always pleased with the action and eager to receive any intelligence the team could offer. That evening, everyone bought them drinks at the club and were eager to hear the story. The returning soldiers were made to feel like successful warriors and were the envy of everyone else.

When Keith returned from Vietnam and experienced some symptoms, he accepted them. He really did think that it was what veterans did and felt and thought it was okay. In fact, once in the Canadian Forces he was proud of these feelings and reactions; he thought that was what a real veteran of combat did. He was known within his regiment as that "Vietnam veteran" who was, for the most part, listened to and whose advice was sought out.

And although it took 20 years to happen, he was eventually debriefed. Even though Derek likely didn't know he was doing that, it was the right thing for Keith, and it worked.

Secrets of Mental Marksmanship

POLICE

Law-Enforcement Story—All's Well That Ends Well
We first met Jim B. when he attended one of our mental marksmanship seminars. We next met him when he invited us to an RCMP (Royal Canadian Mounted Police) seminar on post-traumatic stress disorder (PTSD). When we attended their seminar, we were impressed with their thorough, studied, and sensitive treatment of this "inconvenient truth" of police and military service. As part of the seminar, Jim told his own story, which is an outstanding example of what can go wrong "after the moment" . . . and how he is now working to make it go right.

Jim was a member of a major metropolitan tactical team. He had been having a rough week. One call resulted in him shooting the perpetrator. The next call, he was beaten up very badly and he might have wished he had shot the perpetrator. Then he went on a call at a hospital. An overwrought father with a sick infant son was in the emergency room demanding attention with a pistol. As the situation progressed, he eventually put the pistol to the surgeon's neck. Having already established that the father wasn't interested in "negotiations," as soon as he directly threatened the surgeon, Jim knew he had to act. Of his team members on scene, he had the best fire position: a clear shot at the perpetrator, a clear path with no risk to the surgeon, a clear background in the over-shoot area.

Suddenly it was over. The face-on head shot (from less than 10 feet) was indeed gruesome, but it was over . . . thankfully, blessedly over. The surgeon was saved, the baby was safe, and the hospital staff were all okay, as were Jim's team members.

After surrendering his gun and his badge, Jim went home. It was New Year's Eve, and Jim's wife (since Jim was working the nightshift) had gone to spend the night with family. So, Jim went home to an empty house. The image that troubled him wasn't the torn up face of the perp. The image that troubled him was that of the pistol. It was, as it turned out, an air pellet pistol.

Let's be clear now. The pistol was used as a firearm, and under the law it's considered a firearm during this activity. Also, even an air pellet pistol put to the neck of the surgeon could certainly maim, paralyze, or even kill the doctor. Yet, it bothered Jim. Alone in the house, he had lots of time to let this thought fester. He sat down in his favorite chair in the living room. The room was dark. He had a drink.

A year later, Jim finally started to get the PTSD treatment that he needed. But he didn't get it until he had a nervous breakdown and required full psychiatric care.

Now, with several years of treatment, Jim has become an advocate for getting police officers the right education and the right treatment for PTSD. It's his way of finding a good outcome from his very hard journey.

HUNTING

Hunter Story—The Wild World

Our favorite TV network to watch is WildTV. It's nonstop hunting, fishing, and sport shooting shows. We usually only watch another network if there is a rerun on WildTV. One thing we have noticed and find interesting is that after the kill, the hunter often shows some kind of emotion. Sometimes this is put on for the benefit of the camera and to improve the chances of selling this footage later to a sponsor, but mostly it's genuine and you can usually recognize the difference. We think this is a PTSD response to the sudden release of emotion, possibly connected to the primordial completion of the hunt, and certainly a relief to see the successful end of an endeavor that may have taken months to plan, weeks to prepare, and days to accomplish.

Advanced Tools—Your Powers Applied

COMPETITION

Competition Story—A Month of Ice Cream

When Linda came home from the Commonwealth Games in 1994, she felt very much "out of sorts." She hadn't performed quite as well as she would have liked, but she had won a medal for the Canadian shooting team, and overall it had been a very satisfying experience. But once home, she couldn't slow down to her normal routine and she couldn't sit still, even more so than normal. She jumped in her truck and drove the four hours to visit her shooting mentor.

Sharon was a very experienced competitor, having been to the Olympics several times, as well as most other Commonwealth and Pan Am Games and World Cups. She had been Linda's guide to international shooting competition and her supporter and friend. Sharon invited Linda to stay at her apartment for a few days to acclimatize to the post-Games environment.

Linda was shocked to find that Sharon was doing nothing! She slept late, she took the time to read the entire newspaper, she had clearly not been doing any serious housekeeping, she was eating—well, she was eating mostly ice cream.

Linda knew from her own coaching and previous competition experience that athletes need a recovery period following a major event. During that time, the shooter should leave his guns in the closet and go do something else. If the event was the final event of the training year, the shooter should have a recovery period of as much as two months.

Sharon smiled one of her Cheshire cat smiles. "Do y ou realize," she said as she set the empty bo wl down on the coffee table and stretched, "that following the Olympics, I didn't get out of bed at all for two days?"

"Reall y?" Linda replied, trying to hide her aversion to the idea with a small smile.

"Yup. And I didn't leave the apartment for about a week. The first time I went outside, I felt like the world was too bright, too noisy, and too busy. I wanted to wear sunglasses and earmuffs and I didn't want to be out there. I forced myself to walk down to the corner store and buy some groceries."

"And when did it all get back to normal?"

"Well, after about a month of mostly ice cream, I got in my car and went to the club. I didn't touch a gun for another month after that, but at least I was seeing people. Once I had enough of a break, I was ready to get back into training. The first time I picked up the rifle, it felt like an old friend."

Linda relaxed. She stretched out on the couch and picked up the newspaper with the intent of reading it from front to back, no matter how long it took.

CHAPTER SUMMARY

Success in the world rarely "just happens." Although all of us have a childlike belief that good things happen to good people, the reality of life is that good things happen to people who know how to make them happen.

When the intensity of your situation is relatively low, you can probably get by without the power of mental marksmanship, and you're even less likely to need any "advanced tools." However, if you think you might ever be in a tense situation in your professional or recreational shooting, you will need all the power you can muster . . . and the higher the intensity you must deal with, the better you need to apply all the skills.

In this chapter, we described the advanced power tools you need for high-intensity situations:

➢ Planning—The power of the plan is that it tells you what the delta is between what you originally had in mind and the reality you now face. It gives you a measure of the correction you need to apply to your course in order to meet your destination.
  • Goal setting—To become a consistently good shot or a great shot in a high-intensity situation, you must become goal-oriented.
  • Contingency planning—The purpose of contingency planning is to plan for and rehearse the solu-

Secrets of Mental Marksmanship

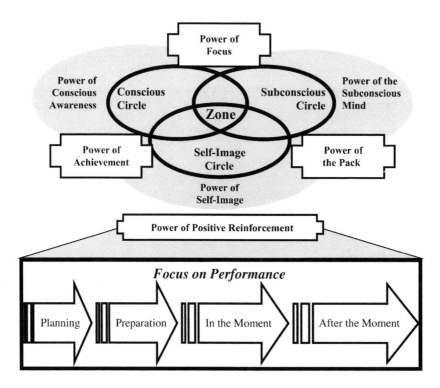

tion for any problem that might come up on the range or on operations so that you're as prepared as possible.

➤ Preparation—Preparation is all about acquiring, organizing, and improving your resources prior to the event that will require you to use them.
  • Using available resources—You have time, money, effort, and people at your disposal. If you know you have done everything you can to prepare, you will go into an operation or a competition with confidence and therefore less stress.
  • Stress control—Stress is an important factor that can work for you or against you. Some stress will keep you alert and focused, give you energy and stamina, and provide you with the edge you need to succeed. Being organized, and knowing you are, is an important factor in controlling stress. The way you think is something you can control and use to develop confidence and control stress. Maintaining a good level of health and fitness (including nutrition, hydration, exercise, and rest) will help you control stress. Maintaining a good, sound relationship with family and friends will help to control stress. Being involved with recreational activities and having a hobby will pull you out of stressful situations and let your positive thinking have its effect.
  • Visualization and mental rehearsal—A special type of mental preparation involves picturing yourself already there, already doing the real thing. Visualization is a detailed picture of a specific thing, and mental rehearsal is you going through the event or a key portion of the event. The purpose of this type of training is to provide relaxation, focus, and a positive image of you delivering the perfect shot.

➤ In the moment—In those few seconds or minutes where you need maximum power, you need a few special skills. You have a good plan, you're well prepared, and now you must bring all your force to the situation.
  • Attention control—Attention control is an important tool that can help you not only control stress, but also effectively maintain vigilance in stressful situations. Attention control is the ability to

focus at the correct level at the correct time. There are three different areas of focus. They are "position," "in the bubble," and "broad scan."

- Using situational stress relievers—No matter how well prepared you are, no matter how well you control your thoughts, sometimes you need a stress reliever—something to use when a situation is threatening to get the best of you. For marksmen, the fundamental thing is the mental program, which gets the conscious mind focused on a productive task while giving the subconscious a clear picture of what is required. You also need to train yourself in the use of the many stress relievers that can pull you back and help you maintain or regain control.
- Making situational pressure work for you—Situational pressure or stress is a tool that you must make work *for* you. It can give you visual acuity, faster reaction time, increased endurance, and greater strength. In order to achieve great things, you want to be just on the edge of control. If you're out of control, you have panic and the situation will rapidly overtake you. But if you have significant pressure working for you, and you stay just inside being controlled, it will put you at the advantage.

➤ After the moment—After the moment, those few seconds or minutes where the impact and implications of your actions register in your mind, you also need some special skills.

- Post-traumatic stress—There is currently a great deal of research and discussion about post-traumatic stress. The competitor feels it. The hunter feels it. The police officer feels it. The soldier feels it. "It" is the aftermath of the incident, and it usually includes a physical reaction, a mental reaction, and an emotional or psychological reaction. We believe that the skills we have discussed in these pages will serve you well in the preparation, application, and aftermath of a critical incident. In addition, we recommend that you include PTSD (post-traumatic stress disorder) reading and training in your curriculum.

This toolbox provides you with the big, dark secrets used by warriors of all types, as well as dangerous-game hunters and champion competitors. These tools will enable you to produce an outstanding performance in situations requiring all your resources to be marshaled effectively, just when it's both most difficult and most important to do so.

NOTES

1. *The Secret* is a book and a film that popularizes the idea that you attract what you expect. If you expect to have sufficient time and money to do what is important to you, you will eventually "attract" or figure out how to balance your competing priorities so you have sufficient time and money for the things that are truly important to you. If you expect to give enough effort to your cause, you will find a way to make it happen. And as we say in "The Power of the Pack," if you seek out the right people, the right people will seek you out.

2. Most professionals separate systemic and situational stress. Systemic stress can be mental or physical and generally has to do with your overall lifestyle or significant life events like births, marriages, and deaths. Situational stress can also be mental or physical and generally has to do with a specific situation; usually, situational stress ends when the situation is over.

3. "One Thin Wire" by Linda K. Miller and Keith A. Cunningham was originally published in *Precision Shooting* (February 2000) and has been republished in *Favorite Stories on Attitude*.

4. "Competition Rifle Course" by Linda K. Miller and Keith A. Cunningham was originally published in *The Accurate Rifle* (October 2001) and has been republished in *Favorite Stories for the Competition Coach*.

5. The intensity curve diagram has been around in sports for a long time. In *On Combat*, Dave Grossman presents the "Unified Model of Stress and Performance," and he maps heart rate to the intensity curve. While we generally agree that the heart rate increases as stress increases, the numbers that Lieutenant Colonel Grossman uses do not apply to the competition shooter. For example, Olympic-style prone shooters are usually performing best at about 40 beats per minute, with their subconscious timing the shot to be fired between the beats when there is the least amount of movement in the sight picture.

6. The "Last One Standing" match can be fired with any weapon; we just change the target, the fire position, and/or the distances to make it a challenge. This match is conducted in elimination stages. For pistol, use a target with an aiming mark of about 60 millimeters (about 2.5 inches). All shooters fire at the same time on their own target. (If there are more shooters than the range can hold in one relay, additional relays are formed.)

   - In stage one at 5 meters, each shooter has two minutes to fire 10 rounds. Only those shooters with all hits will continue to stage two.
   - In stage two at 5 meters, each shooter will have one minute to fire 10 rounds. Only those shooters with all hits will continue to stage three.
   - In stage three at 5 meters, each shooter will have 30 seconds to fire 10 rounds. Only those shooters with all hits will continue to stage four.
   - In stage four at 10 meters, the shooting will be "sudden death." Each of the remaining shooters fires one shot. Those who do not hit the aiming mark will retire. Those who do will again fire one shot (on command and under control of the RO) and continue in this manner until there is a winner decided. (If at any time all shooters do not hit the aiming mark, then everyone will remain for another shot.)

7. You will find that other texts identify four areas of attention: internal narrow, internal broad, external narrow, and external broad. While these are probably accurate from an analytical point of view, we find them unnecessarily complicated. We have therefore grouped them and renamed them with their application in mind.

— Chapter 9 —

Conclusion:
The Final Power—The Power
of Perseverance

The final power is completely yours to control. It's the most extraordinary of all the powers you have. It is the power to persevere.

The only unforgivable sin is to quit. We aren't talking about a tactical withdrawal. We're talking about bald-faced giving up. Whatever is happening to you on the firing point, in life, or on operations, always stay in the fight. The match, the hunt, or the mission is over only when the last shot is fired.

We aren't talking about a tactical withdrawal. We're talking about bald-faced giving up.

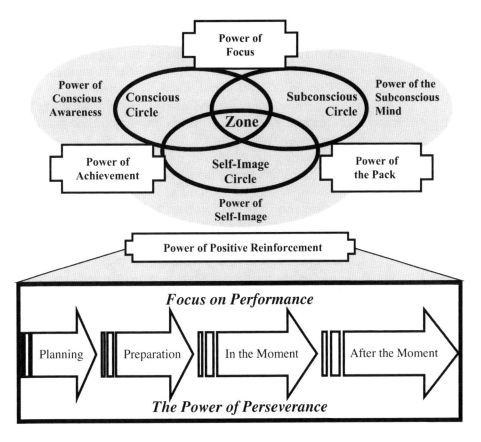

Always keep in mind who else you're affecting if you quit. For example, when you're a member of a tug-of-war team, if you get lazy on the rope while others continue to pull their guts out, you're affecting the whole team and can affect the outcome of the tug-of-war.

Remember the Stacy Lim story, where, having been shot through the chest, she took the fight to the bad guy. Her team was her family, her police agency, and every civilian that this bad guy would ever threaten. If he wasn't put down now, then when? If it wasn't her, then who? She focused on what she needed to do and didn't worry about whether it was a reasonable expectation. She just did it.

Always stay focused on your performance. Don't worry about your sore muscles or aching heart. Keep your mind on what you need to do now and keep doing it. Remember the story of the state trooper who, having received a shotgun blast, drew his sidearm and stitched the bad guy, pausing only when he needed to change magazines. His training was so ingrained that all he had to do was let his subconscious take over and perform the way his muscle memory dictated.

Modern training for police and military personnel emphasizes that if you think you're going to die, you will. The converse is also true. If you think you're going to live, if you count on it, you can very likely make it come true. This is one of the key values of paintball simulations: you are shot at, it hurts . . . and you live!

Always keep your attitude positive. Keep thinking you will be able to keep putting one foot ahead of the other until you have reached your destination. Keep thinking you will come out of this situation. Keep thinking you will come out of this situation victorious.

"Yeah, you're hit, but you're sure as hell not done."
—Ken Murray (author of *Training at the Speed of Life*) as quoted by Lt. Col. Dave Grossman in *On Combat*

"On the plains of hesitation bleach the bones of countless millions who, at the dawn of victory, sat down to rest, and resting, died."
—Author unknown

Military Story—Chamberlain at Gettysburg

The battle had been going hard and furious for two days at Gettysburg. The American Civil War could be decided then and there, and both sides knew it.

Lt. Col. Joshua L. Chamberlain and the 20th Maine were tasked to hold the left of the Union line on Little Round Top. He recognized the importance of his position, for if the Confederates could outflank him and "turn the line," they could easily defeat the Union army. As he laid out his position, he ensured that everyone knew the importance of holding it. He didn't realize just how soon they would be tested.

The Confederates had, the day before, attacked the right flank and been repelled. Gen. Robert E. Lee then made the decision to attack the Union's left flank, thinking that all the Union strength had been concentrated on the right and they would be weak on the left. In fact, his decision was correct, but the steep ground over which the Confederates had to attack and the determination showed by Lieutenant Colonel Chamberlain would make up the shortfall in the Union numbers.

The Confederates attacked with gallantry and dash but soon found the ground to their disadvantage and were

"Victory is not won in miles but in inches. Win a little now, hold your ground, and later win a little more."
—Louis L'Amour, writer (1908–1988)

"Quitters never win and winners never quit."
—Norman Vincent Peale, writer (1898–1993)

repelled. They were attacking frontally against the regiment from Maine and, despite repeated attempts, the results were the same. However, with each attack they moved further around to the left trying to outflank the defenders. Lieutenant Colonel Chamberlain could see this tactic developing and repositioned his men so that the Confederates always met a frontal defense. In this way he was able to hold, but as the day ground on he took casualties, and ammunition was running low. They wouldn't be able to hold for very much longer.

With no indication that they would receive reinforcements or resupply, he decided a desperate situation called for desperate measures. On the next Confederate attack, Lieutenant Colonel Chamberlain ordered, "Fix bayonets." With the ground in his favor and the element of surprise on his side, he attacked the attackers. The Confederates, having suffered tremendous casualties throughout the day, couldn't withstand the bayonet charge, and many surrendered while others withdrew to fight another day.

The fight for the left flank was over. Lieutenant Colonel Chamberlain and his regiment from Maine had held and saved the day for the Union. Although all his men fought bravely, it was the courage and determination of their leader to fight this fight to the end that inspired this victory.

Law-Enforcement Story—Bill and the Bear

A very good friend of MilCun and one of our favorite people is a neighbor of ours. Bill is a decorated retired police officer who saw his fair share of on-the-job unpleasantries and now lives with his wife in the peace and quiet of a small rural community. Well . . . it's mostly peace and quiet.

One day Bill was splitting wood in his backyard. While focusing on his job, he was attacked and taken down by a black bear. The bear clawed and bit him on his face and shoulders and tried to drag him away.

It's often said that police officers never retire; they just go off and do something different someplace else. Bill had spent a career being in control of the situation, knowing there is no second place winner. Winning is the only option. This bear thought he had an easy meal but didn't realize that he had yet to convince Bill.

Bill fought back in the only way he knew. Bloody and torn, he eventually killed the bear with the axe he was using to split the wood. He then drove himself into town, where he received medical attention. Bill lived, although with the physical scars of his confrontation, while the bear did not.

Whenever we run one of our police marksmanship courses, we make sure this story is told every time. Sooner or later Bill will show up to rub elbows with the blue fellowship, and we're proud that he does. We always ask Bill to tell the young officers the motto they can all take away from this story. Bill smiles shyly, never one to honk his own horn, and then looks seriously at the class. "Always stay in the fight until one of you is dead," he says. "Winning is the only option."

"Great works are performed not by speed or strength but perseverance."
—Samuel Johnson, writer (1709–1784)

"Masters of one art have mastered all because they have mastered themselves . . . The experts shine in the competitive arena; the masters shine everywhere."
—Dan Millman in *Body Mind Mastery*

"Nobody hands you excellence on a silver platter. You earn it through planning, preparing, and persisting."
—Terry Orlick in *In Pursuit of Excellence*

Secrets of Mental Marksmanship

HUNTING

Hunter Story—Jesse's Deer

Keith had grown up in an era when it was a very normal thing to take a week off from school to go deer hunting. It was common to see the classrooms shrink to half their normal size for the opening day and gradually come back to normal as the week progressed. It was a right of passage that he fondly remembers still.

But when his own sons came to this age, he also remembered the difficulty of trying to catch up on the missed schoolwork and decided to not push the issue (at times, now, regretting this decision).

Now with busy lives of their own, the boys try hard to make it home for the deer hunt, and their dad cherishes every moment he gets to spend with them. And this past year he got to watch his favorite youngest son show what he is made of.

Jesse wanted to hunt on the west side of the property, and Keith had established a hide overlooking a good area. There were lots of sign that deer were using the area, and it looked very likely that one would be taken from there.

Keith was some distance away in his own blind when he heard a shot, which seemed to come from the direction Jesse was hunting. He waited as long as he could stand it and then sent a text message to Jesse asking if he had fired. A message soon came back saying he had and was on a blood trail but had followed it a long way and was concerned about the shot he had made. Keith replied that he would be there soon and to meet him at the hide.

Keith arrived about 30 minutes later. He and Jesse discussed the situation and decided that with the heavy blood trail, the deer had to be down. Jesse said that the deer had bolted as he fired, and he may have hit it in the rear quarters. It was clear his self-image was taking a hit for having fired such a shot and now having a badly wounded deer to deal with.

They followed the wounded deer for about 300 meters until they came to a muskeg[1] that was about 100 meters wide. By this time Keith was thinking they should wait for about an hour to give the deer a chance to bleed out. This is always a hard decision to make with such a heavy blood trail.

Just then, Keith spotted the deer on a small wooded ridge almost at the other side of the muskeg. Just its head was silhouetted through a small hole in the tree line. By the time he got Jesse onto the target, it had disappeared. Clearly it was hurt badly, and they decided they would give it some time once they got over the muskeg. It would take awhile to cross the dangerous muskeg, and then they would wait a bit longer on the other side.

It took several minutes to get to where they had spotted the deer. Looking in the direction that the sign indicated the deer had taken, Keith again spotted it trying to get up the ridge. It was struggling with the steep incline and needed the final shot to end this. He instructed Jesse to hit the deer in the head and to do it very quickly before it had a chance to escape again.

It was here that Jesse took control of the situation. He had a quick look through his optic sight and very quickly analyzed that he couldn't hold well enough to guarantee a hit in the deer's head. He dropped to kneeling and came to the same conclusion. Keith was urging him to make a shot quickly, but Jesse had the situational awareness and conscious thought to recognize that he needed a prone supported position to guarantee the head shot.

He settled in to make the shot. The deer struggled to get to its feet, moving its head about, and then it paused in its efforts for just a moment. Jesse fired and the deer collapsed and laid still.

Jesse had overcome his initial confidence-shaking experience and was determined to make it right. He had turned his self-image around and back to the good shot we all knew he was. He allowed his conscious mind the opportunity to analyze his position selection and had come up with the correct option. And finally, he overcame the urgency of the situation and let his subconscious mind take over to fire a perfect shot.

And Dad was very proud.

Although this was a very difficult shot, as with most good hunts, the shot actually turned out to be the easiest part. Keith and Jesse were well over half a kilometer from the nearest bush road, and getting back to the road meant crossing the dangerous muskeg again, this time with an extra 200 pounds of deadweight. The other option involved dragging the deer to the nearest waterway, where the tippiest canoe in North America waited with malicious intent.

Conclusion: The Final Power—The Power of Perseverance

They chose the canoe route, and after roping the deer into a man-harness, they took turns slogging through the bush, choosing a path wide enough for the deer, and not necessarily the straightest or easiest route. The deer was an uneasy passenger in the canoe, and Jesse had to play the role of ballast to keep the boat upright and the three of them from "swimming with the fishes."

It was dark by the time they arrived at the cabin, just about the same time that the rest of the hunters came in for the night.

"How was your day?" the others asked, not having any idea that they were about to hear a story that would eventually be used in this book.

COMPETITION

Competition Story—"Don't Quit on Me Now"
When we do our mental marksmanship seminar, the last part of it has to do with the attitude of "staying in the fight." There are lots of stories about this, and the one Keith likes to tell is the one we call the "Don't quit on me now" speech by Sandy Peden.

Sandy is one of Canada's top fullbore Target Rifle shooters and coaches. He has always been the pivotal point on Canada's international teams and has been hired by other countries to get their Target Rifle program started.

In 1987, Keith was a shooting member of a Canadian team to Bisley, England, the Mecca of Target Rifle shooters from around the world. The matches there, especially the team matches, are always hard fought, and victories are taken away with great pride.

The MacKinnon is just one of these matches. It's shot from 900 and 1,000 yards. The shooters are there only to fire shots, while the wind coaches decide the windage and elevation settings. The shooter often has the easier job, as the wind conditions on Stickledown range can be a torment to deal with. Keith picks up the story . . .

We had just finished the 900-yard phase of the match and it was dismal. The winds were the worst that anyone had experienced, and although the wind coaches had worked hard to get every wind call just right, we were, in fact, 13 points behind the Brits. Now in fairness to the wind coaches, five of those 13 points were the result of one of the shooters cross-firing, which scored the team a zero for that shot. But the fact is that no one gives the Brits a 13-point advantage going into the 1,000-yard phase, on their home range, and realistically expects to win. I mean, the odds, the math, and the reality of it is that you're now in an impossible place, and winning is no longer an option. I and several other shooters had given up on this one. Nice try, but the Brits were too good on their home range in tricky winds. Let's get this over with quickly, get out of the heat, and have a cold one back at the quarters.

As I think back on it, I am embarrassed to recall how completely I had given up. I was an infantry officer, in the game where there are no second place winners, where I was expected to lead by example, and I was well aware of the many heroic stories of victory being snatched from the jaws of defeat. But it was Sandy who put the fight back into all of us.

He called us into a circle and began his now famous "Don't quit on me now" speech . . .

"The miracle, or the power, that elevates the few is to be found in their industry, application, and perseverance under the prompting of a brave, determined spirit."
—Mark Twain, writer (1835–1910)

"Perseverance is the hard work you do after you get tired of doing the hard work you already did."
—Newt Gingrich, politician (1943~)

"Life is not easy for any of us, but what of that? We must have perseverance and, above all, confidence in ourselves."
—Marie Curie, physicist (1867–1934)

"It would seem that we're now in a bit of an impossible situation," he began. "But you know what? It's not over yet. Can you imagine the victory this would be if we came back and beat the Brits on their home range, under these conditions? There would be no greater victory, no greater honor. Each and every one of you has it in you to do this. All you have to do is your job. All you have to do is fire each and every shot as good as it can be. All the wind coaches have to do is call the wind just a little bit better. All each of you have to do is want it . . . is go get it and . . . and don't quit on yourself, don't quit on your teammates, and . . . don't quit on me now."

I still get chills running up my spine when I think of the situation we were in and how Sandy was going to keep trying until it was over. None of us wanted to let our teammates down, and if Sandy was going to keep trying, then so would we. I remember thinking, "Just tell me what you want on these sights for windage, and then get out of my way!"

When we started the 1,000-yard phase, the winds were the same—very high velocity and continuously changing direction. Our first four shooters to the firing line came off with respectable scores for the conditions—in the high 30s and low 40s out of a possible 50 points. The Brits were shooting quickly and processing their shooters through as fast as they could. They would accept the odd less-than-perfect shot delivery in order to save the wide and near-miss shots. They, too, were scoring as we had.

But we needed more. We had to make up points, not just stay with them, if we were going to win. Sandy decided to call a halt and wait for the conditions to settle. He told us he had never seen the wind changing directions in such an exaggerated fashion. This was unusual for even Stickledown, and perhaps if we waited a few minutes it might settle to a more constant direction.

And so we waited. The Brits shot on, staying with their tactic of shooting fast. But we waited.

We waited until the Brits were finished. Their whole team had scored as they had started. We waited to the point where the team captain went up to Sandy to remind him of the time we had left to finish the match. Sandy said he was aware of the time, and we waited some more.

Finally, Sandy called our second of three relays to the firing line. He told us that the wind was now the steadiest it had been all day. Other teams, as well as the Brits, who were by now finished with their shoots, were gathering behind us to watch.

The second relay came off the firing line with scores in the low and mid 40s. We had gained ground. As we moved up onto the firing point, a good friend of mine, Jim Bullock, was shooting on the target next to me. He caught my eye and said, "You know we can do this." Now, being one who pays no attention to the scoreboard while shooting, I thought he meant that we had the mental discipline to shoot well on the last relay. I am so glad I didn't know that he had been doing the math on the scores and meant that if we just shot well, we could win this match. Ignorance is such bliss sometimes.

The winds held steady. The wind coaches worked their magic, the shooters fired perfect shot after perfect shot, and Sandy held steady at the helm. The four of us on this last relay came off with scores in the mid to high 40s.

The Brits, always gentlemen to the end, had been keeping a running tally of the score and, as soon as our last shot was scored, knew that we had beat them by four points. They were the first to congratulate us all, and we all basked in this victory because this victory was won over our attitudes. And in the end, our attitude was one that said, "This ain't over till I say it's over!"

CHAPTER SUMMARY

The final power is completely yours to control. It's the most extraordinary of all the powers you have. It is the power to persevere. The only unforgivable sin is to quit. Whatever is happening to you on the firing point, in life, or on operations, always stay in the fight. The match, the hunt, or the mission is over only when the last shot is fired.

Conclusion: The Final Power—The Power of Perseverance

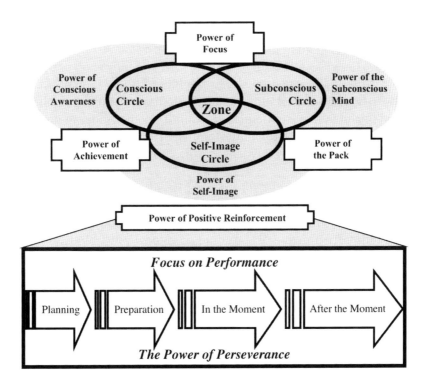

Always stay focused on your performance. Don't let your aching muscles or a throbbing heart distract you from your cause. Keep your mind on what you need to do now, and keep doing it.

Always keep your attitude positive. Keep thinking that you will be able to put one foot ahead of the other until you have reached your destination. Keep thinking that you will come out of this situation. Keep thinking that you will come out of this situation victorious.

NOTE

1. Muskeg is a quaking bog or swamp, where the peat moss floats on the water, providing a sometimes passable, and sometimes dangerous, walkway.

— Bibliography —

BOOKS, ARTICLES, AND FILMS

Anderson, Gary. *Marksmanship*. New York: Simon & Schuster, 1972.

Bahmanyar, Mir. *Shadow Warriors*. Oxford: Osprey Publishing, 2005.

Bartlett, Derrick D. *Snipercraft: The Art of the Police Sniper*. Manchester, CT: Precision Shooting, Inc., 1999.

Bassham, Lanny. *With Winning in Mind: The Mental Management System*. Book Partners, 1996

Benson, Herbert. *The Relaxation Response*. New York: Avon Books, 1976.

Berton, Pierre. *Vimy*. Toronto: McClelland & Stewart Limited, 1986.

Bompa, Tudor. *Theory and Methodology of Training: The Key to Athletic Performance*. Dubuque, IA: Kendall Hunt Publishing Co., 1997.

Boyden, Joseph. *Three Day Road*. Toronto: Penguin Group, 2006.

Branden, Nathaniel. *The Six Pillars of Self-Esteem*. New York: Bantam Books, 1995.

Brown, Barbara B. *Stress and the Art of Biofeedback*. New York: Bantam Books, 1978.

Bühlmann, Gaby, Heinz Reinkemeier, Maik Eckhardt, and Bill Murray. *Ways of the Rifle*. Dortmund, Germany: MEC, 2002.

Burke, Lt. Col. Desmond T. *Canadian Bisley Shooting*. Oakville, Ontario, Canada: self-published, 1970.

Butler, Pamela E. *Talking to Yourself*. New York: HarperSanFrancisco, 1991.

Byrne, Rhonda. *The Secret*. New York: Atria Books, 2006.

Caldwell, Taylor. *On Growing Up Tough*. Greenwich, CT: Fawcett Publications, 1973.

Capstick, Peter Hathaway. *Death in the Long Grass*. New York: St. Martin's Press, 1977.

Carron, Albert V. *Motivation (Implications for Coaching & Teaching)*. London: Ontario, Canada: Sports Dynamics, 1984.

Chandler, Roy F., and Norman A. Chandler. *White Feather*. Jacksonville, NC: Iron Brigade Armory Publishing, 1977.

Chapel, Charles Edward. *The Art of Shooting*. New York: A. S. Barnes & Company, 1960.

Coughlin, GSgt. Jack, and Capt. Casey Kuhlman, with Donald A. Davis. *Shooter*. New York: St. Martin's Press, 2006.

Crews, Jim. *Some of the Answer: Urban Carbine*. Avondale, AZ: self-published, 2000.

Dallaire, Lt. Gen. Roméo, with Maj. Brent Beardsley. *Shake Hands with the Devil*. Toronto: Vintage Canada, 2004.

Dalloway, Marie. *Visualization: The Master Skill in Mental Training*. Sunnyvale, CA: Optimal Performance Institute, 1994.

———. *Concentration: Focus Your Mind, Power Your Game*. Sunnyvale, CA: Optimal Performance Institute, 1993.

———. *Drive and Determination: Developing Your Inner Motivation*. Sunnyvale, CA: Optimal Performance Institute, 1993.

———. *Reflections on the Mental Side of Sports*. Sunnyvale, CA: Optimal Performance Institute, 1994.

———. *Risk Taking: Performing Your Best During Critical Times*. Sunnyvale, CA: Optimal Performance Institute, 1993.

De Bono, Edward. *Lateral Thinking*. Markham, Ontario, Canada: Penguin Books, 1982.

———. *Six Thinking Hats*. Markham, Ontario, Canada: Penguin Books, 1987.

Domey, Richard L. *Mental Training for Shooting Success*. College Hill Communications, 1989.

Downs, Frederick. *The Killing Zone*. New York: The Berkley Publishing Group, 1983.

Ebon, Martin (editor). *TM: How to Find Peace of Mind Through Meditation*. Signet Books, 1976.

Estés, Clarissa Pinkola. *Women Who Run With the Wolves*. New York: Ballantine Books, 1997.

Bibliography

Etzel, Edward F. "Validation of a Conceptual Model Characterizing Attention among International Rifle Shooters." *Journal of Sport Psychology* (1979): 1(4), 281–290.

Evans, Nicholas. *The Horse Whisperer*. New York: Dell Publishing, 1996.

Fast, Julius. *Body Language*. Markham, Ontario, Canada: Pocket Books, 1975.

Fawcett, Bill. *How to Lose a Battle*. New York: HarperCollins Publishers, 2006.

Folkman, Joe. *Turning Feedback into Change*. Provo, UT: Novations Group Inc., 1996.

Fuoss, Donald, and Robert Troppmann. *Effective Coaching (A Psychological Approach)*. John Wiley & Sons, 1981.

Gaffen, Fred. *Unknown Warriors*. Toronto: Dundum Press, 1990.

Gallwey, W. Timothy. *The Inner Game of Tennis*. New York: Random House, 1974.

———. *Inner Tennis*. New York: Random House, 1976.

Garfield, Charles A. *Peak Performance*. New York: Warner Books, 1985.

George, Lt. Col. John. *Shots Fired in Anger*. Washington, DC: National Rifle Association of America, 1981.

Gilbert, Adrian. *Sniper*. New York: St. Martin's Press, 1994.

Goleman, Daniel. *Emotional Intelligence*. New York: Bantam Books, 1995.

Grossman, Lt. Col. Dave. *On Killing*. New York: Back Bay Books/Little, Brown & Company, New York, 1996.

Grossman, Lt. Col. Dave, with Loren W. Christensen. *On Combat*. PPCT Research Publications, 2007.

Haas, Robert. *Eat to Win*. Scarborough, Ontario, Canada: The New American Library of Canada, 1985.

Hargrove, Robert. *Masterful Coaching*. San Francisco: Pfeiffer, 1995.

Harris, Dorothy V., and Bette L. Harris. *The Athlete's Guide to Sports Psychology: Mental Skills for Physical People*. New York: Leisure Press, 1984.

Headquarters, Department of the Army. *Sniper Training and Employment, TC 23-14*. Washington, DC: Headquarters, Department of the Army, 1989.

Helmstetter, Shad. *The Self-Talk Solution*. Pocket Books, 1990.

Helmstetter, Shad, with Bob Schwartz. *Self-Talk for Weight Loss*. New York: St. Martin's Press, 1996.

Henderson, Charles. *Marine Sniper*. Briarcliff Manor, NY: Stein & Day Publishers, 1986.

Herrigel, Eugen. *Zen in the Art of Archery* (Vintage Books Edition). New York and Toronto: Random House, 1989.

Hesketh-Prichard, Maj. H. *Sniping in France*. Livonia, NY: R&R Books, and Mt. Ida, AR: Lancer Militaria, 1993.

Hicks, Esther, et al. *The Secret*. Prime Time Productions, 2006 (DVD film based on the book).

Hittleman, Richard. *Yoga*. New York: Bantam Books, 1982.

Hofstadter, Douglas R. *Gödel, Escher, Bach: An Eternal Golden Braid*. New York: Vintage Books, 1980.

Hooper, Judith, and Dick Teresi. *The 3-Pound Universe*. New York: Dell Publishing Co., 1987.

Horneber, Ralf, translated by Bill Murray, with assistance from Hans Heidermann. *Olympic Target Rifle Shooting*. Munich, Germany: F.C. Mayer Verlag, 1993.

Howe, MSG Paul R. *Leadership and Training for the Fight*. Bloomington, Indiana: AuthorHouse, 2006.

Jordan, William H. *No Second Place Winner*. Shreveport. LA: self-published, 1984.

Karas, Lester W. *Competitive Shooting Excellence with the High Power Target Rifle*. Newmarket, Ontario, Canada: self-published, 1995.

Kingsley-Heath, John. *Hunting the Dangerous Game of Africa*. Boulder, CO: Sycamore Island Books, 1998.

Klavora, Peter, and Juri V. Daniel. *Coach, Athlete, and the Sport Psychologist*. Human Kinetics, 1979.

Klein, Chuck. *Instinct Combat Shooting: Defensive Handgunning for Police*. Flushing, NY: Looseleaf Law Publications, Inc., 2004.

Klinger, Bernd. *Rifle Shooting as a Sport* (two volumes). London: Butler & Tanner Ltd., 1981.

Krilling, William. *Shooting for Gold*. Self-published, 1992.

Lauck, Dave M. *The Tactical Marksman*. Boulder, CO: Paladin Press, 1996.

Le Shan, Lawrence. *How to Meditate*. Bantam Books, 1975.

Lewis, David, and James Greene. *Thinking Better*. New York: Rawson, Wade Publishers, 1982.

Loehr, James E., and Peter J. McLaughlin. *Mentally Tough*. Totem Books, 1987.

Lösel, Dr. Heinz. *Competitive Sport Shooting—Practical Sport Psychology*. Munich, Germany: International Shooting Union [now International Shooting Sports Federation], 1998.

Bibliography

Maltz, Dr. Maxwell. *Psycho-Cybernetics: A New Technique for Using Your Subconscious Powers*. Simon & Schuster, 1969.

Matunas, Edward A. *Modern African Adventures*. Manchester, CT: Precision Shooting, Inc., 1998.

McBride, Capt. Herbert W. *A Rifleman Went to War*. Mt. Ida, AR: Lancer Militaria, 1987.

McIntyre, Dr. Ray G. *Bowhunting Whitetails*. Lakeland, FL: Larsen's Outdoor Publishing, 1996.

McPherson, James M. *Battle Cry of Freedom*. New York: Ballantine Books, 1989.

Meyers, Stuart A. *A Guide to Police Sniping*. Gaithersburg, MD: Operational Tactics, Inc., 1996.

Miller, Linda K., and Keith A. Cunningham. *Favorite Stories for the Competition Coach*. Burnt River, Ontario, Canada: MilCun Marksmanship Complex, 2003.

———. *Favorite Stories from a Professional Perspective*. Burnt River, Ontario, Canada: MilCun Marksmanship Complex, 2004.

———. *Favorite Stories on Attitude*. Burnt River, Ontario, Canada: MilCun Marksmanship Complex, 2002.

———. *Favorite Stories on Winning*. Burnt River, Ontario, Canada: MilCun Marksmanship Complex, 2003.

———. *The Dream Team*. Burnt River, Ontario, Canada: MilCun Marksmanship Complex, 2003.

Millman, Dan. *Body Mind Mastery*. Novato, CA: New World Library, 1994.

———. *The Inner Athlete*. Walpole, NH: Stillpoint Publishing, 1994.

Nideffer, R. M. *The Inner Athlete*. New York: Cromwell, 1976.

North, Oliver. *War Stories*. Washington, DC: Regnery Publishing, 2003.

Orlick, Terry. *In Pursuit of Excellence*. Champaign, IL: Leisure Press, 1990.

Orlick, Terry, and John Partington. *Psyched*. Ottawa, Ontario, Canada: Coaching Association of Canada, 1986.

Ostrander, Sheila, and Lynn Schroeder. *Super-Learning*. New York: Dell Publishing, 1997.

Patton, Gen. George S., Jr. *War As I Knew It*. New York: Bantam Books, 1980.

Peale, Norman Vincent. *The Power of Positive Thinking*. New York: Prentice-Hall, 1956.

———. *You Can If You Think You Can*. New York: Fireside, 1987.

Pearson, Carol S. *The Hero Within*. New York: HarperCollins Publishers, 1989.

Pegler, Martin. *Out of Nowhere*. Oxford: Osprey Publishing, 2006.

Pincus, Rob. *Combat Focus Shooting: Intuitive Shooting Fundamentals*. Telluride, Colorado: ICE Publishing Company, 2007.

Pirsig, Robert M. *Zen and the Art of Motorcycle Maintenance*. New York: Bantam Books, 1975.

Pullum, Bill, and Frank T. Hanenkrat. *Successful Shooting*. Washington, DC: The National Rifle Association of America, 1981.
———. *Position Rifle Shooting*. South Hackensack, NJ: Stoeger Publishing Company, 1975.

Reinkemeier, Heinz. *On The Training of Shooters* (two volumes). Translated by Stan Greer with assistance from Bill Murray, Bisley, England: National Smallbore Rifle Association, 1992.

Reynolds, E. G. B., and Robin Fulton. *Target Rifle Shooting*. London: Barrie & Jenkins, 1972.

Rivers, Gayle. *The War Against the Terrorists*. Briarcliff Manor, NY: Stein & Day, 1986.

Robbins, Anthony. *Unlimited Power*. New York: Free Press, 2003.

Roosevelt, Theodore. *African Game Trails*. New York: St. Martin's Press, 1988.

Rushall, Brent S. *Psyching in Sport*. London: Pelham, 1979.

Scahill, Jeremy. *Blackwater: The Rise of the World's Most Powerful Mercenary Army*. New York: Nation Books, 2008.

Schubert, Dr. Frank. *Psychology from Start to Finish*. Sport Books Publishers, 1986.

Scott, Harriet Fast, and William F. Scott. *The Armed Forces of the USSR*. Boulder, CO: Westview Press, 1979.

Scott-Donelan, David. *Tactical Tracking Operations*. Boulder, CO: Paladin Press, 1998.

Selye, Hans. *Stress Without Distress*. Philadelphia: J. B. Lippincott, 1974.

Shaw, John, with Bill Currie. *Shoot to Win*. Memphis: Mid-South Institute of Self-Defense, 1985.

Shore, Capt. Clifford. *With British Snipers to the Reich*. Georgetown: Small-Arms Technical Publishing Co., 1948 (reprinted by Lancer Militaria, Mt. Ida, AR, 1988).

Skinner, B. F. *Beyond Freedom and Dignity*. New York: Alfred A. Knopf, 1971.

Stanford, Andy. *Surgical Speed Shooting: How to Achieve High-Speed Marksmanship in a Gunfight*. Boulder, Colorado: Paladin Press, 2001.

The Sunday Times of London Insight Team. *War in the Falklands*. New York: Harper & Row, 1982.

Bibliography

Sweet, James. *Competitive Rifle Shooting*. Maroubra, NSW, Australia: Shooting Book Publisher, 1973.

Tubb, G. David. *High Power Rifle*. Clifton, CO: Zediker Publishing, 1993.

Tutko, Tom, and Umberto Tosi. *Sports Psyching*. 1976.

USAMU. *United States Army Marksmanship Unit International Rifle Marksmanship Guide*. U.S. Government Printing Office, 1984-746-005/10006.

Wacker, Albrecht. *Sniper on the Eastern Front*. Barnsley, South Yorkshire, United Kingdom: Pen & Sword Books, 2005.

Waitley, Denis. *The Psychology of Winning*. New York: Berkley Publishing Group, 1984.

———. *Seeds of Greatness*. Pocket Books, 1988.

Ward, Joseph, T. *Dear Mom*. New York: Ballantine Books, 1991.

Whiting, Charles. *Patton*. New York: Ballantine Books, 1976.

Yur'Yev, A.A. *Competitive Shooting*. English translation edited by Gary L. Anderson. Washington, DC: The National Rifle Association of America, 1985.

PERIODICALS

Accurate Rifle. Precision Shooting, Inc., Manchester, CT.

American Rifleman. National Rifle Association of America, Washington, DC.

CoachNet newsletter. MilCun Marksmanship Complex, Burnt River, Ontario, Canada.

Precision Shooting. Precision Shooting, Inc., Manchester, CT.

Rifle: The Sporting Firearms Journal. Mark Harris Publishing Associates, Inc., dba Wolfe Publishing Company, Prescott, AZ.

Sniper, a publication of Snipercraft, American Sniper Association, Fort Lauderdale, FL.

SniperNet newsletter. MilCun Marksmanship Complex, Burnt River, Ontario, Canada (circulated by e-mail to police and military snipers).

Tactical Edge. National Tactical Officers Association, Doylestown, PA.

Tactical Rifle. Precision Shooting, Inc., Manchester, CT.

— About the Authors —

Linda K. Miller

Linda has more than 25 years of business experience, including business planning, management, marketing, and information systems. She has considerable experience in international smallbore target shooting as a member of Canada's National Shooting Team, winning medals at the 1993 Mexico World Cup, 1994 Commonwealth Games, and 1995 Cuba World Cup. In 1999, Linda became the first woman to win the Ontario Lieutenant Governor's Medal for fullbore shooting, a competition with a proud and honored history of over 125 years. In 2002 she shot F-Class and became the top female provincially, nationally, and at the world championships. In 2008, Linda became the National Sniper/Precision Rifle Champion, again the first female to win this honor. Linda is an accomplished and internationally certified marksmanship coach. She also has volunteered as a director, manager, administrator, and consultant in provincial and national shooting sports organizations. She was the editor of a periodical for coaches (*CoachNet*) for more than 10 years. She is a designer of courses for competitive and professional marksmen and an author of numerous articles on shooting skills.

Linda K. Miller accepts the National Sniper/Precision Rifle Champion trophy from Col. P. J. Ward (Director of Army Training), with Lt. Col. Bill Molnar (Ret.) officiating.

Secrets of Mental Marksmanship

Capt. Keith A. Cunningham (Ret.)

Keith is a career military officer with more than 25 years' experience with the Canadian Forces and U.S. Army. He has considerable practical experience, including a combat tour in Vietnam, peacekeeping and countersniper operations in Cyprus, and annual unit- and command-level military exercises in North America and Europe. Keith has taught marksmanship courses at the Canadian Forces Infantry School and to many police services in Canada. He was a certified instructor/examiner for the Firearms Safety Education Service of Ontario and a Hunter Safety Instructor/Examiner. Keith is an internationally certified shooting coach and has successfully coached numerous teams to national and international excellence. As an internationally renowned gunsmith with more than 25 years' experience, specializing in long-range practical rifles, he has built and regulated rifles for competitors around the world. Keith is a prize-winning international rifle and pistol competitor, having won honors at Bisley, the World Long Range Championships, and the Commonwealth Games. He is a member of the Canadian Forces Sports Hall of Fame and the Dominion of Canada Rifle Association Sports Hall of Fame (in both the Target Rifle and Service Rifle categories).

Keith and Linda hold many provincial and national titles and records and have been members of several Canadian teams to international championships throughout the world. Linda is the current national sniper marksmanship champion and Keith is the current national service rifle and three-gun champion. In 2007, 2008, and 2009, they coached the Canadian Forces Combat Shooting Team to many honors at Bisley,

Keith A. Cunningham, having won the 2008 National Service Rifle championship, is chaired from the range by past students. Queen's Medalists WO Gary Desroches (QM 2007) and Capt. Sean Gagnon (QM 2003 and 2008) lead the carriers.

England. They have coached 12 members of the military to a Queen's Medal, the top award for marksmanship within the Canadian Forces. They're the only couple to have both won the Ontario Provincial Championship (Keith in 1990, 1995, 2003, and 2004; Linda in 1999). They're also one of the few couples who have been members of Canadian national fullbore teams, having been members of the Palma team competing in South Africa in 1999, the team shooting at the Millennium Target Rifle World Championships at Bisley in 2000, and the Canadian national team to the Palma World Championships in Canada in 2007. They're the only couple to have ever coached the Canadian Forces Combat Shooting Team (2007, 2008, and 2009). They are popular guest lecturers and speakers, providing seminars and courses to police, military, and civilian marksmen in Canada and internationally. Their articles on marksmanship have been published in such shooting magazines as *Precision Shooting*, *The Accurate Rifle*, *Tactical Shooter*, *The Canadian Marksman*, *The Canadian Forces Infantry Journal*, and *Aim*. They are the authors of *The Wind Book for Rifle Shooters*, published by Paladin Press.

About the Authors

Linda and Keith with some of their 2008 prizes won at the Canadian
National Sniper/Precision Rifle Championship.

Linda and Keith with some of their 2008 prizes won at the Canadian
National Service Conditions Championship.

Secrets of Mental Marksmanship

About MilCun Marksmanship Complex

MilCun Marksmanship Complex is a registered Ontario company, founded in 1996. Its purpose is to promote competitive marksmanship and educate and train both recreational and professional marksmen. Services offered include:

- Gunsmithing—Complete line of gunsmithing services, specializing in long-range rifles for the competitive marksman as well as the police sniper. We offer a line of custom-made rifles for competitive and professional use.
- Marksmanship training—Competitive marksmanship courses, including technical and mental skills. We also offer a complete line of police sniper, police tactical marksmanship, and custom "train the trainer" courses.
- Consulting—We provide consulting services to coaches, trainers, program developers, range developers, and marksmanship businesses of all types.
- Range facilities—We have a range facility in Haliburton County, Ontario, Canada, approximately two hours from metropolitan Toronto.

Keith is the chief operations officer, chief instructor, and head gunsmith. Linda is the chief executive officer and coaching specialist. You can contact Keith or Linda through MilCun at www.milcun.com.

About the Operational Shooting Association (OSA)

OSA is a not-for-profit shooting association of civilians, law-enforcement (including police, security, and conservation officers), and military personnel. The purpose of OSA is to provide training, practice, and competition that is operationally oriented. We currently focus on:

- Duty/service pistol
- Tactical/service rifle
- Sniper/precision rifle

We provide both entry-level and advanced training clinics in these firearms. For each type of firearm, we have designed a progressive course of fire that will develop operational skills for those on active duty as well as extend marksmanship skills leading to national and international competition.

All OSA events are organized and run by fully trained range personnel. Dates are scheduled yearly in advance. We offer structured practice days, training clinics (basic and advanced), and competitions in a friendly atmosphere.

OSA was incorporated in 2006. Keith is the president and Linda is the secretary-treasurer. To contact OSA or for more information (including our courses of fire), visit www.osacanada.ca.